HOSTILITY
COPING
& HEALTH

HOSTILITY

COPING

& HEALTH

Edited By Howard S. Friedman

American Psychological Association

Washington, DC

Published by
American Psychological Association
Washington, DC

Copies may be ordered from
APA Order Department
P.O. Box 2710
Hyattsville, MD 20784

Designed by Grafik Communications Ltd.
Typeset by Harper Graphics, Waldorf, MD
Printed by Braun-Brumfield, Inc., Ann Arbor, MI
Technical editing and production coordinated by Deborah Segal

Library of Congress Cataloging-in-Publication Data

Hostility, coping, and health / edited by Howard S. Friedman.
   p. cm.
   Includes bibliographical references and index.
   ISBN 1-55798-138-8: (acid-free paper) $40.00 ($32.00 to members)
   1. Hostility (Psychology) 2. Adjustment (Psychology) 3. Stress (Physiology) 4. Cardiovascular system—Diseases—Psychological aspects. 5. Medicine, Psychosomatic. I. Friedman, Howard S.
   [DNLM: 1. Adaptation, Psychological. 2. Health Status.
3. Hostility. 4. Stress, Psychological. BF 575.H6 H831]
BF575.H6H67 1991
155.9—dc20
DNLM/DLC
for Library of Congress
91–31602
CIP

Printed in the United States of America
First edition

To Margaret Chesney
for her
ideas and support
on this project

Contents

Part Three: The Coping Perspective

Part Four: Conclusion

Contributors

Michael R. Adams, Bowman Gray School of Medicine
John C. Barefoot, Duke University Medical Center
John W. Burns, State University of New York at Stony Brook
Charles S. Carver, University of Miami
Alan J. Christensen, University of Utah
Thomas B. Clarkson, Bowman Gray School of Medicine
Robert A. Emmons, University of California, Davis
Susan Folkman, University of California, San Francisco
Howard S. Friedman, University of California, Riverside (editor)
Vicki Gluhoski, State University of New York at Stony Brook
Jay R. Kaplan, Bowman Gray School of Medicine
Robert M. Kaplan, University of California, San Diego
Edward S. Katkin, State University of New York at Stony Brook
Eileen Kennedy-Moore, State University of New York at Stony Brook
Ron Kessler, University of Michigan
Stephen B. Manuck, University of Pittsburgh
James W. Pennebaker, Southern Methodist University
Christina Pozo, University of Miami
Rena L. Repetti, University of California, Los Angeles
Reiner Rugulies, University of Bielefeld, Germany
Michael F. Scheier, Carnegie Mellon University
Larry Scherwitz, University of California, San Francisco
Collette Sheedy, State University of New York at Stony Brook
Carol A. Shively, Bowman Gray School of Medicine
Sally Shumaker, Bowman Gray School of Medicine
Judith M. Siegel, University of California, Los Angeles
Timothy W. Smith, University of Utah
Daniel Stokols, University of California, Irvine
Arthur A. Stone, State University of New York at Stony Brook
Barbara J. Tinsley, University of California, Riverside
Camille B. Wortman, State University of New York at Stony Brook

Foreword

R ecent research advances that demonstrate how behavior influences the health status of humans have captured the attention not only of the media but of an expanding corps of psychological scientists. In recent years, there has been a proliferation of data on smoking, exercise, drinking, diet, drug use, and a host of other life-style factors and how they impinge on susceptibility to disease or incapacity due to injury, death, and other adverse outcomes.

With so much new and vital research appearing in this important area, it is imperative that time and financial resources be invested in collaborative deliberation over the data from different laboratories and diverse study methods. Conferences, and rapid publication of the written documents resulting from these, often provide the most appropriate medium for collation of research advances and dissemination of the work of experts. We believe that a felicitous union of these objectives was achieved in the present instance, and the American Psychological Association (APA) is pleased to have contributed to this important endeavor.

A conference entitled "Hostility, Coping, and Health" was held in November 1990. The meeting, which was the basis for this volume, was cosponsored by the Science Directorate of APA and the University of California. The organizers provided for a fruitful exchange among researchers, in a pleasant setting, of the psychological processes that connect the disposition and behaviors known as *hostility*, as well as the coping mechanisms associated with hostility, to health conditions. Among the topics considered at the conference were anger and cardiovascular health, life-style and hostility, the repressive personality and social support, and the related phenomena of stress, coping, and social support.

Federal research agencies closed down most support of investigator-initiated state-of-the-art research conferences in scientific psychology over a decade ago. Moreover, the resources from these agencies for basic and fundamental psychological research have been significantly diminished in the past decade because of governmental austerity measures. During this period, however, the field has continued to grow, and scientific psychologists have adapted their talents to an ever-expanding variety of behavioral domains. Experimental psychologists, psychophysicists, and experts in animal and human learning are finding that their special expertise can be transported into the field of health psychology or behavioral medicine. Their methods lead to better understanding of the behavioral causes of disease and debility and illumination of the psychological consequences of acquiring a disability. Yet there have been few opportunities for investigators in such new and promising research areas to convene in special settings to discuss their findings.

As part of its continuing and expanding effort to enhance the dissemination of scientific psychological knowledge, a Scientific Conferences Program was established by the Science Directorate of APA, which, in concert with the publications office of APA, now produces a series of volumes resulting from these conferences. An annual call for proposals is issued by the APA Science Directorate, which, collaboratively with the APA Board of Scientific Affairs, evaluates the proposals and subsidizes several conferences each year. Proposals from all areas of psychological research are welcome.

Lewis P. Lipsitt, PhD
Executive Director for Science

Virginia E. Holt
Manager, Scientific
Conferences Program

T he APA Science Directorate's conferences funding program, from its inception in 1988 through mid-1991, has supported 19 conferences. To date, 11 volumes resulting from conferences have been published:

> *Best Methods for the Analysis of Change: Recent Advances, Unanswered Questions, Future Directions*
>
> *Cognitive Bases of Musical Communication*
>
> *Conceptualization and Measurement of Organization–Environment Interactions*
>
> *Hostility, Coping, and Health*
>
> *Organ Donation and Transplantation: Psychological and Behavioral Factors*
>
> *Perspectives on Socially Shared Cognition*
>
> *Researching Community Psychology: Issues of Theory and Methods*
>
> *Sleep and Cognition*
>
> *Taste, Experience, and Feeding*
>
> *The Perception of Structure*
>
> *The Suggestibility of Children's Recollections: Implications for Eyewitness Testimony*
>
> *Through the Looking Glass: Issues of Psychological Well-Being in Captive Nonhuman Primates*

APA expects to publish volumes on the following conference topics:

> Cardiovascular Reactivity to Psychological Stress and Cardiovascular Disease
>
> Developmental Psychoacoustics
>
> Lives Through Time: Assessment and Theory in Personality Psychology From a Longitudinal Perspective
>
> Maintaining and Promoting Integrity in Behavioral Science Research
>
> Psychological Testing of Hispanics
>
> Study of Cognition: Conceptual and Methodological Issues
>
> The Contributions of Psychology to Mathematics and Science Education

Preface

S ubstantial progress is being made in understanding the links between psychosocial
factors and physical health. As the field of health psychology has taken formal
shape during the past decade, significant areas of focus have emerged. In particular, there
is a great deal of attention to the role played by hostility and to the processes of coping
with stress and illness. It is important for researchers in this field to stay abreast of rapidly improving concepts and methods. Furthermore, as this book demonstrates, it is important for researchers to stay in touch with developments in neighboring fields—coping
researchers should know something about hostility, and hostility researchers should follow developments in coping research.

This book was based on a conference, but this is not a book of conference pro-
ceedings. A group of 80 outstanding faculty and graduate students in health psychology
converged at a mountain retreat in Lake Arrowhead, California, in November 1990, in order to discuss cutting-edge developments in hostility and coping research. The discussions were broad enough to encourage wide-ranging thoughts and new ideas, but focused
enough to proceed at a sophisticated level. In the past, we have found that the ideas generated in such high-level conference discussions carry on in many ways for many years.
So I asked a number of the distinguished participants to explain what they see as important new developments and challenges. This book is the result.

The idea for this project grew out of an ongoing cooperative effort in health psychology among the various campuses of the University of California (UC). Starting back
in the late 1970s, several of us at University of California campuses found ourselves
working in this new field called health psychology. Before long, we had a health psychology steering committee and began a series of meetings and conferences—at Riverside,
Irvine, San Francisco, Berkeley, and several at the UCLA conference center at Lake Arrowhead. Many, many people have taken time from their busy schedules to promote educational efforts and close ties in this new discipline. These efforts are now paying off in

the rapid advancement of knowledge. The University of California has continued its support of our efforts by providing matching funds for the conference on which this book is based.

Once we had decided that it would be important to bring together researchers on hostility and coping, we faced the problem of funding. Fortunately, the American Psychological Association (APA), through its Science Directorate, came to the rescue with generous support of a conference that would bring leading researchers and some top graduate students from around the country together with those from the University of California. At APA, Virginia Holt was always helpful and supportive.

Roxanne Cohen Silver was my co-chair for the conference and deserves a lot of credit for the successful results. Many others have also played special roles: Jim Kulik, who handled the national graduate student competition; the faculty liaisons (including Christina Maslach, Nancy Adler, Fran Cohen, Dan Stokols, Chris Dunkel-Schetter, and Bob Kaplan), who went begging to their deans for matching funds; Bob Emmons, who set up the poster session and more; Tim Smith, who helped organize an excellent symposium; Margaret Chesney, who . . . well, I promised Margaret I wouldn't give her any credit, but if you know Margaret . . . ; and of course all the conference participants. Dianne Fewkes did a great job handling many administrative details. And Joan Tucker did most of the conference legwork; she made it all come together. My own research efforts in this area are being supported in part by grant #R01 AG08825 from the National Institute on Aging.

Howard S. Friedman

PART ONE

Introduction

CHAPTER 1

Understanding Hostility, Coping, and Health

Howard S. Friedman

I t is healthy to cope well, and it is healthy to avoid chronic anger and hostility. These assertions are almost broad and vague enough to be meaningless, but not quite. As a convergence of recent reviews make clear, the pressures of major external challenge, chronic negative emotions, and poor coping can upset internal bodily equilibrium and increase the likelihood that illness will develop or progress (Antonovsky, 1990; Cohen & Williamson, 1991; Friedman, 1991; Kamarck & Jennings, 1991; Williams & Barefoot, 1988). The problem comes in articulating precisely what is meant by these broad assertions and in explaining the mechanisms that account for the links between psychosocial factors and disease.

It is a tremendous and misleading oversimplification to say that adopting a positive attitude will help one overcome cancer or that an easygoing person will most likely avoid cardiovascular disease. The falsity of such simple prescriptions has led to a certain unease in the health care system, which therefore often disregards psychosocial factors altogether. Fortunately or unfortunately, recent conceptual and theoretical developments

My research is supported in part by Grant R01# AG08825 from the National Institute on Aging, Howard S. Friedman, principal investigator. The opinions expressed here are those of the author and do not necessarily reflect the views of the National Institutes of Health.

make it clear that the relations among psychosocial factors and health are complex. This book presents some of the latest thinking on what this complexity is all about and how to deal with it.

The central concept in health psychology is *stress*, vaguely defined as the process of adapting to challenge (Friedman & DiMatteo, 1989). There is some dysregulation or disequilibrium that must be redressed. Roughly speaking, stress researchers have divided into two camps. The first focuses on the *emotional* and *motivational* aspects of stress, including hostility, Type A personality, physiological reactivity, and anxiety and depression. The second camp tends to be more concerned with *coping*, including appraisal processes, cognitive style, social support, social environment, hassles, and self-disclosure (for example, there are books on coping and social support, and different sorts of books on hostility and reactivity). Although the two perspectives overlap and have obvious implications for each other, there is often insufficient communication between them. This book brings together researchers from both perspectives, who were asked to think broadly about their work.

Great progress in studying stress has been made in recent years, and a number of important issues have been uncovered. Some of the issues have been resolved, but others remain challenging. In particular, significant attention has been drawn to the depth of our concepts and to the generality of our empirical methods.

The Search for the Holy Grail

For many years now, researchers in behavioral medicine have been devotedly searching for the true pathogenic factor in cardiovascular disease. The empirical quest began in earnest with the Type A behavior pattern, a competitive, impatient, hurrying behavioral–emotional style. The Type A pattern, if measured by a structured interview, does predict heart disease, but key questions remain unanswered (Booth-Kewley & Friedman, 1987; Friedman & Booth-Kewley, 1988; Matthews, 1988; Siegel, this volume). Many scientists are galloping off in National Institutes of Health (NIH) armor endeavoring to discover the truly harmful element in the Type A pattern. As this book makes clear, some aspect of hostility seems to be a likely candidate. Perhaps if we could find the right questionnaire or measure, the relations between hostility and cardiovascular illness would become clear.

We should be careful. Anger and hostility are defined in different ways by different investigators, are not simple to measure, are affected by other individual differences, and occur in different personal and social contexts (Barefoot, this volume; Smith & Christensen, this volume). Depression, anxiety, and related states may also be relevant (Ahern et al., 1990; Carney et al., 1988; Friedman & Booth-Kewley, 1987b; Talbott, Kuller, Perper, & Murphy, 1981). This complexity must (and can) be taken into account. Regularities are being discovered, but not simple answers.

Researchers of coping also initially set out to find the best ways to cope, but quickly learned to rephrase the questions. Now coping is viewed as an ongoing process that must be understood in terms of the sundry pressures on the individual.

In this volume, we have subsumed the topic of social support under the coping label. This merger is meant only as a means of encouraging reflection about the larger picture. Although socially integrated and involved people generally are healthier than those who are isolated and aloof, it is an oversimplification to assert that social support is good (Emmons, this volume; Repetti, this volume; Wortman et al., this volume). The differing impacts of social relations on health are discussed in this book.

Multiple Links

How are hostility and coping related to health? For current purposes, we can isolate three basic kinds of causal links, one basic reverse causal link, and artifactual links (Friedman, 1990, 1991; Friedman & Booth-Kewley, 1987a). Each of these in turn has several common realizations or variations.

First, psychosocial disturbances can promote disease through psychophysiological effects: alterations in the nervous system, the immune system, and the endocrine system. Second, hostility and poor coping can lead to disease through health-related behaviors: smoking, overeating, abusing drugs, failing to take prophylactic measures, and so on (Scherwitz & Rugulies, this volume). Third, underlying third variables, such as CNS-based temperament or strong socialization pressures, can be causally related to both coping/hostility and health. In terms of reverse causation, it is often the case that illness itself affects one's emotions, relationships, and coping efforts (Carver, Scheier, & Pozo, this volume; Taylor & Aspinwall, 1990). Finally, various artifacts, especially subject selection biases and self-report biases, can produce meaningless but observable associations between hostility/coping and health.

It may often be the case that all sorts of these links are operating simultaneously. For example, consider the hypothetical case of a temperamentally aggressive boy who grows up in frustrating circumstances to become an insecure, socially aloof, cigarette-smoking, and aggressive man, who shuns self-disclosure and drowns his troubles and angina pains in alcohol. Any single-variable or single-path approach to understanding such a person would prove hopelessly inadequate. The different problems are correlated, and it would be a mistake to try to "control away" any one of them. As the contributors to this volume make clear, this complexity does not mean that the links cannot be studied. Rather, we should not expect any simple-minded prescriptions for good health to emerge.

Naturalistic Studies

Hostility and coping efforts may be viewed as transactional, meaning that they arise from an interaction between the person and the environment. Furthermore, they may be closely tied to important demographic variables, such as socioeconomic status, sex, age, and ethnicity (Barefoot et al., 1991). Thus, attempts to study the intrapsychic workings of the individual or attempts to study the social causes of illness are doomed to be incomplete. This book illustrates how the person–situation interaction can be taken into account.

At the moment, there is an urgent need for more naturalistic studies. More studies of women, ethnic minorities, children, and the elderly are needed in a variety of settings: rural and urban environments, work environments, and institutional settings (Revenson, 1990; Stokols, this volume; Tinsley, this volume). This is not only a call to see if existing findings are generalizable, but it is also a call to improve the scientific validity of our theories.

Behavior Sampling

For a host of reasons, retrospective self-reports have proved to be totally inadequate in studying hostility, coping, and health. Simple prospective designs are also often inadequate. Rather, it now appears that we need to sample behavior and feelings at random times and develop a detailed description of common patterns. That is, we need rich, longitudinal data. Diaries and random telephone polling are useful here, as are long-term studies. What is the hostile, repressive Mr. Z actually doing and thinking at 6:00 p.m. on Monday? Is he quarreling with his wife, having another beer with friends, jogging while worrying about his heart, munching chips and watching TV, or cursing his fellow drivers on the jammed highway? Do these have implications for his feelings and behaviors and physiological reactions 5 hours later at 11:00 p.m.? Do they have implications for his health in the following months? We know terribly little about the natural history of coping, emotions, and health.

Perhaps surprising to some, it is also true that assessments of illness have often depended heavily on self-reports and, thus, are problematic. Illness diagnoses range from those that depend wholly on patient report (e.g., nonspecific, "idiopathic" fatigue or aches and pains) to those that depend heavily on self-report (e.g., migraines and angina) to those illnesses that have a clear organic component but have a marked variation in the degree to which they are noted by and cause distress in patients (e.g., gallstones, anemia, hypertension, ulcers, and many viral infections). In other words, it is often not simple to define a clear organic endpoint that can be predicted from truly independent precursors (see also Kaplan, Manuck, & Shumaker, this volume). This is a sticky issue that will most likely remain with us and one that should be addressed study by study.

Time, Change, and Feedback

As one delves deeper into the study of hostility, coping, and health, the temporal dimension looms larger. How is mood on one day related to mood one week later? Can self-disclosure, repression, or social interaction that is adaptive this month given present circumstances turn maladaptive next month given different circumstances? How does coping change across the life span and vary for different people? What are the reverberations of each development on all the other elements of the person's world (Pennebaker, this volume)?

To address such issues, various authors have suggested systems approaches, feedback processes, and equilibrium models. Structural equation modeling sometimes seems a promising statistical technique. Unfortunately, such complex models are notoriously difficult to develop, test, and understand. Researchers generally want to know whether cancer support groups promote health, not whether self-disclosing group members sleep better for several months, feel more in control, score lower on the Cook-Medley hostility scale, and so on. Many researchers would rather have test statistics and relative risks rather than a table of partial correlations. We need a balance of studies, concepts, and methods that avoid compilations of narrow, sterile associations, but still allow sensible health recommendations to be made.

In sum, exciting progress is being made in health psychology, with quick quantum leaps in research sophistication. This book provides a good sampling of where the action is in the field of hostility, coping, and health. The contributors have expertly explained what they see to be the challenging research issues of the near term and the most promising ways to address these issues. They have done so while keeping their hostility level down and while coping well with complexity.

References

Ahern, D., Gorkin, L., Anderson, J., Tierney, C., Hallstrom, A., Ewart, C., Capone, R., Schron, E., Kornfeld, D., Herd, J., Richardson, D., & Follick, M. (1990). Biobehavioral variables and mortality or cardiac arrest in the cardiac arrhythmia pilot study (CAPS). *American Journal of Cardiology, 66*, 59–62.

Antonovsky, A. (1990). Personality and health: Testing the sense of coherence model. In H. S. Friedman (Ed.), *Personality and disease* (pp. 155–177). New York: Wiley.

Barefoot, J. C., Peterson, B., Dahlstrom, W. G., Siegler, I., Anderson, N., & Williams, R. B., Jr. (1991). Hostility patterns and health implications: Correlates of Cook-Medley hostility scale scores in a national survey. *Health Psychology, 10*, 18–24.

Booth-Kewley, S., & Friedman, H. S. (1987). Psychological predictors of heart disease: A quantitative review. *Psychological Bulletin, 101*, 343–362.

Carney, R. M., Rich, M. W., Freedland, K. E., Saini, J., teVelde, A., Simeone, C., & Clark, K. (1988). Major depressive disorder predicts cardiac events in patients with coronary artery disease. *Psychosomatic Medicine, 50*, 627–633.

Cohen, S., & Williamson, G. M. (1991). Stress and infectious disease in humans. *Psychological Bulletin, 109*, 5–24.

Friedman, H. S. (Ed.). (1990). *Personality and disease.* New York: Wiley.

Friedman, H. S. (1991). *Self-healing personality: Why some people achieve health and others succumb to illness.* New York: Henry Holt.

Friedman, H. S., & Booth-Kewley, S. (1987a). The "disease-prone personality": A meta-analytic view of the construct. *American Psychologist, 42*, 539–555.

Friedman, H. S., & Booth-Kewley, S. (1987b). Personality, Type A behavior, and coronary heart disease: The role of emotional expression. *Journal of Personality and Social Psychology, 53*, 783–792.

Friedman, H. S., & Booth-Kewley, S. (1988). The validity of the Type A construct: A reprise. *Psychological Bulletin, 104*, 381–384.

Friedman, H. S., & DiMatteo, M. R. (1989). *Health psychology.* Englewood Cliffs, NJ: Prentice Hall.

Kamarck, T., & Jennings, J. R. (1991). Biobehavioral factors in sudden cardiac death. *Psychological Bulletin, 109*, 42–75.

Matthews, K. A. (1988). Coronary heart disease and Type A behaviors. *Psychological Bulletin, 104*, 373–380.

Revenson, T. A. (1990). All things are not equal: An ecological approach to personality and disease. In H. S. Friedman (Ed.), *Personality and Disease* (pp. 65–94). New York: Wiley.

Talbott, E., Kuller, L., Perper, J., & Murphy, P. (1981). Sudden unexpected death in women. *American Journal of Epidemiology, 114,* 671–682.

Taylor, S. E., & Aspinwall, L. G. (1990). Psychological aspects of chronic illness. In G. R. VandenBos & P. T. Costa, Jr. (Eds.), *Psychological aspects of serious illness: Chronic conditions, fatal diseases, and clinical care* (pp. 7–60). Washington DC: American Psychological Association.

Williams, R. B., Jr., & Barefoot, J. C. (1988). Coronary-prone behavior: The emerging role of the hostility complex. In B. K. Houston & C. R. Snyder (Eds.), *Type A behavior pattern* (pp. 189–211). New York: Wiley.

PART TWO

The Hostility Perspective

CHAPTER 2

Developments in the Measurement of Hostility

John C. Barefoot

T here are many ways to assess hostility in psychological research (Matthews, Jamison, & Cottington, 1985). These measures have been derived for many different purposes and are based on a variety of theoretical notions about the nature of hostility. This chapter will review some of these measures, highlight measurement issues that are important for research in this area, and outline some developments that could improve the quality of hostility assessment in the future.

The plethora of instruments to measure hostility creates the potential for miscommunication and confusion if it is incorrectly assumed that all hostility measures reflect the same psychological construct. In fact, measures of hostility are often only moderately intercorrelated (e.g., Musante, MacDougall, Dembroski, & Costa, 1989). The problem this can cause is illustrated in the Type A behavior-pattern literature. There are a number of measures of Type A behavior, but their intercorrelations are low (Byrne, Rosenman, Schiller, & Chesney, 1985), probably because they are measuring different aspects of the complex Type A construct. Despite this, there has been the understandable tendency to assume that Type A measures are assessing the same set of tendencies. Obviously, the

This work was supported by National Institutes of Health Grant HL-3687 and National Institute on Aging Grant AG-09276.

tendency to treat noncomparable measures as equivalent is counterproductive if we wish to develop a coherent research literature. Hostility is also a complex concept that can be measured with moderately related instruments that tap different aspects of the construct. We must be aware of the differences between measures if we are to avoid the mistakes of the Type A literature. A comprehensive definition of hostility might be helpful in avoiding such confusion by providing an organizing framework to view the interrelationships of the various hostility measures.

Defining Hostility

Most concepts in psychology are identified by terms adopted from the common parlance. Such terms are often vague because they were not originally derived for scientific purposes. This is the case for the concept of *hostility*, for it is associated with a host of phenomena (anger, aggression, disgust, suspicion, cynicism, etc.), and those researchers who specify their interpretation of the term (e.g., Buss & Durkee, 1957; Izard, 1977; Zillman, 1979) offer very different definitions.

The definition of hostility to be presented here grew out of efforts to understand the item content of the Cook-Medley hostility scale and to identify those item subsets that best predict health outcomes (Barefoot, Dodge, Peterson, Dahlstrom, & Williams, 1989). The definition has been influenced by previous theories of anger and aggression (Bandura, 1973; Berkowitz, 1963; Novaco, 1985) and social information processing (Dodge, Petit, McClaskey, & Brown, 1986) and is based on the widely recognized division of experience into three components: cognitive, affective, and behavioral (Hilgard, 1980).

The cognitive component of hostility consists of negative beliefs about others. The hostile person endorses statements that others are untrustworthy, undeserving, and immoral. These beliefs produce attributional biases that make it more likely that the behavior of others will be interpreted as antagonistic or threatening. They can also serve to justify the hostile person's own antagonistic behavior toward others. A distinction can be made between *cynicism*, negative beliefs about human nature in general, and *hostile attributions*, beliefs that the antagonistic behavior of others is directed specifically at the self (Barefoot et al., 1989). Hostile-attribution bias leads to the perception of others as threatening and tends to produce *reactive* aggression, rather than the less-defensive *proactive* form of aggression (Dodge & Coie, 1987).

Several emotional states, including anger, annoyance, resentment, disgust, and contempt, may be included in the affective component (Buss & Durkee, 1957; Izard, 1977).

Some researchers (e.g. Costa, McCrae, & Dembroski, 1989; Siegman, Dembroski, & Ringel, 1987) contend that, by itself, the affective component of hostility is unrelated to disease outcomes. However, affective arousal is clearly accompanied by cardiovascular reactivity that, in turn, is thought to play a role in the pathogenesis of coronary heart disease (CHD) (e.g., Suarez & Williams, 1989).

Aggression is certainly one aspect of the behavioral component of hostility. There are strong societal sanctions against overt physical aggression, so it is a relatively rare phenomenon in everyday life and is usually directed against children when it does occur (Averill, 1982). Verbal aggression and other forms of antagonistic behavior are more frequent and can be expressed in very subtle ways that do not violate social norms. These subtle forms of antagonism appear to be as strongly related to health outcomes as more overtly aggressive acts (see discussion of interview-based measures later).

A final aspect of this definition of hostility concerns the interrelationships among the three components. Although the three components undoubtedly covary, it is not necessary for them always to occur together. Cynicism, anger, or antagonistic behavior can be present in the absence of the other two. Thus, it should not be surprising if hostility measures that assess different components have only moderate correlations with each other.

This definition has been presented here to facilitate communication about the different aspects of hostility that are being measured with various instruments. To illustrate, some of the more prominent hostility measures will be considered in light of this definition. Only those measures found to predict health outcomes in prospective data or angiographic patient samples will be considered in this review. This decision was made to maximize the relevance of the discussion to health psychology, even though it leads to the omission of some hostility measures that are more desirable on theoretical and psychometric grounds.

Self-Report Measures

Cook-Medley Ho Scale

The most widely used hostility questionnaire in health psychology is the Cook and Medley Hostility (Ho) scale (Cook & Medley, 1954), which is taken from the Minnesota Multiphasic Personality Inventory (MMPI) and was originally devised as an instrument to identify teachers who had difficulty getting along with their students. The scale was rarely used until Williams and his associates (Williams et al., 1980) found it to be related to coronary artery disease (CAD) severity in cardiac patients. The popularity of the Ho scale is partially attributable to the existence of large archives of MMPI data that make it possible to retrieve Ho scores on cohorts studied in the past. This makes it relatively easy to follow up those who took the MMPI several decades ago, ascertain their current health status, and test the ability of the Ho scale to predict health outcomes in prospective data (Barefoot, Dahlstrom, & Williams, 1983; Barefoot et al., 1989; Hearn, Murray, & Luepker, 1989; Leon, Finn, Murray, & Bailey, 1988; McCranie, Watkins, Brandsma, & Sisson, 1986; Shekelle, Gale, Ostfeld, & Paul, 1983; Siegler, Peterson, Barefoot, & Williams, 1991).

Although a good deal of interesting and important research has been done using the Ho scale, there have also been questions about its construct validity (e.g., Matthews, 1985; Megargee, 1985), which probably stem from its origin as an empirically derived scale to identify teachers with poor student rapport. Studies examining the construct validity of the Ho scale (e.g., Barefoot et al., 1989; Costa, Zonderman, McCrae, & Williams, 1986; Greenglass & Julkunen, 1989; Smith & Frohm, 1985) agree that cynicism is most clearly represented in the Ho items. There are also a number of items dealing with hostile attributions, some reflecting paranoid content. One study (Barefoot et al., 1989) suggested that there are smaller numbers of items dealing with hostile affects as well as aggressive responding—a tendency to admit to aggressive acts or endorse aggression as a legitimate problem-solving strategy. Several items in the Ho scale do not appear to measure hostility at all, but this should not be surprising because the scale was not constructed to measure hostility specifically. In sum, although there is some diversity in item content, the Ho scale primarily measures the cognitive component of hostility.

In prospective data, Ho scores have successfully predicted CHD events (Barefoot et al., 1983; Shekelle et al., 1983) and total mortality (Barefoot et al., 1983; Barefoot et al., 1989; Shekelle et al., 1983). However, three studies (Hearn et al., 1989; Leon et al., 1988; McCranie et al., 1986) found that Ho scores failed to predict either of these outcomes.

Recently, Ho scores have been shown to predict overall risk profiles over a 22-year follow-up period in a sample of over 4,700 men and women (Siegler et al., 1991). Persons with higher Ho scores in college were more likely at follow up to be smokers and to have a larger body mass index, a higher lipid ratio, and higher caffeine consumption. Cross-sectional analyses using Ho scores obtained at follow up confirmed these findings and also showed that Ho scores were correlated with alcohol consumption and a history of hypertension. This cross-sectional association of high Ho scores with a poor health risk profile has also been found in the data of the CARDIA (Coronary Artery Risk Development in Young Adults) study (Scherwitz, Perkins, Chesney, & Hughes, 1991), and in a sample of healthy adults screened at a preventive cardiology clinic (Cornell, Slater, Norvell, Grissett, & Limacher, 1990).

In other cross-sectional studies, Joesoef, Wetterhall, DeStefano, Stroup, and Fronek (1989) found that U.S. Army veterans with higher Ho scores were more likely to have peripheral artery disease, and Williams et al. (1980) observed a relationship between Ho scores and CAD severity in cardiac patients. Other cross-sectional studies in patient samples (e.g., Dembroski, MacDougall, Williams, Haney, & Blumenthal, 1985; Friedman & Booth-Kewley, 1987; Seeman & Syme, 1987) have failed to find relations between Ho scores and disease status, raising methodological issues that will be discussed in more detail later.

Factor L

Factor L is a subscale of Cattell's Sixteen Personality Factor Questionnaire (16PF) inventory (Cattell, Eber, & Tatsuoka, 1970) and is defined as a measure of suspiciousness versus trust. Like the cynical tendencies measured by the Ho scale, the suspiciousness dimension is part of the cognitive component of hostility. As one would expect, Factor L scores are highly correlated with Ho scores (Barefoot et al., 1987).

Factor L has been shown to be a significant predictor of health outcomes in two prospective studies. Ostfeld, Lebovitz, Shekelle, and Paul (1964) found Factor L scores to predict CHD events (myocardial infarction or angina pectoris) over a 4½-year follow up in a sample of nearly 1,900 men. Barefoot et al. (1987) found that Factor L scores predicted total mortality in a sample of 500 older men and women over a follow-up period of approximately 15 years. This finding remained significant after adjusting for sex, age, cholesterol, smoking, alcohol use, and physician's ratings of functional health at intake. The same study also found that high suspiciousness scores were associated with relatively poor functional health at the time of intake.

Buss-Durkee Hostility Inventory (BDHI)

The BDHI is one of the most comprehensive self-report hostility instruments in that it contains seven subscales designed to tap different manifestations of hostility. The cognitive component is represented by the Suspicion subscale, and the Irritability and Resentment subscales measure aspects of the affective component. The behavioral component is assessed by four subscales that represent different modes of hostility expression (Assault, Indirect, Verbal, and Negativism). Factor analyses yielded two factors. Factor 1 was defined primarily by the Resentment and Suspicion subscales and probably represents neurotic aspects of hostility as conceptualized by Siegman et al. (1987). Factor 2 appears to measure the expressive aspects of hostility with high loadings from the behavioral subscales: Assault, Indirect, Verbal, and Negativism (women's data only); and one affective subscale: Irritability.

Siegman et al. (1987) administered the BDHI to 72 coronary angiography patients using the Resentment and Suspicion subscale scores to represent Factor 1 and the Assault, Verbal, and Indirect subscales to represent Factor 2. The Factor 2 (expressive) scores were positively correlated with an index of CAD severity in patients 60 years or younger, but not in older patients. The absence of an effect in older patients is in keeping with previous research that has observed that the strength of the relations between risk factors and CAD is age dependent (Williams et al., 1988). There was also a tendency for Factor 1 (neurotic) scores of younger patients to be negatively correlated with CAD. This is probably a reflection of the association between neuroticism and somatic complaints, which leads neurotic individuals to be referred for angiography in the absence of significant coronary disease (Costa, 1986).

Finnish Twin Study Scale

Perhaps the simplest hostility measure to be used in health research is a three-item scale administered to 3,750 men in the Finnish Twin Cohort (Koskenvuo et al., 1988). The items are self-ratings of anger-proneness, irritability, and argumentativeness, apparently tapping the affective and behavioral components. Cross-sectional analyses at baseline found these ratings to be associated with the prevalence of angina pectoris, as well as with several CHD risk factors (hypertension, smoking, heavy alcohol use, and snoring). Prospectively, the high self-ratings of hostility were associated with increased all-cause mortality and cardiovascular mortality over a 3-year follow-up period. However, this prospective association was not present when those with hypertension or coronary disease at baseline were omitted from the analysis.

Problems With the Use of Self-Report Measures

Questionnaire measures of hostility are easy to administer and have been the basis of very valuable research, but there are problems with self-report that can threaten the validity of the measures.

Self-Presentation Biases

Foremost among these problems is the pressure on the respondent to give socially desirable responses. Because hostility is negatively valued by society, the self-presentation bias probably has more of an impact on the measurement of hostility than on the measurement of most other psychological characteristics. Furthermore, self-presentation pressures may result in more than simply lowering the hostility scores of everyone in the sample: It has been suggested that those who are most hostile and suspicious may be more likely to distort their responses than their more trusting counterparts (Rotter, 1971).

Self-presentation biases are likely to have a special impact in settings where the respondents feel they are being evaluated. The importance of evaluative testing conditions can be illustrated by comparing mean levels of Cook-Medley Ho scores across studies. Studies conducted in evaluative settings have found much lower Ho scores than those studies conducted under less threatening conditions. Barefoot et al. (1983) observed a mean Ho level of 13.3 ($SD = 6.6$) in a sample of medical students taking the MMPI as part of a class exercise. In contrast, McCranie et al. (1986) obtained a mean Ho level of 10.6 ($SD = 5.6$) in a study of medical students who took the MMPI as part of their application for admission to medical school. The average Ho score for a man in his late 20s was found in a national survey to be approximately 18 (SD approximately 7.75), although this varied with race, education, and socioeconomic status (Barefoot, Peterson, et al., 1991). By comparison, a recent study of Ho scores of job applicants observed a mean Ho score of only 8.6 ($SD = 5.0$) (Carmody, Crossen, & Wiens, 1989), far below what would be expected on the basis of the national-survey data.

What can be done about the problem of self-presentation biases? One solution is to develop new questionnaires that pose questions in a way that makes it more socially acceptable to admit to hostility. Novaco's Anger Inventory (Novaco, 1975), which asks for the respondent's feelings in reaction to a hypothetical provocation, is an example of one way to accomplish this. Second, the social acceptability of a hostile response can also be increased through the use of subtle wording that makes the hostile content less blatant. For example, it is easier to respond positively to the question "I strongly defend my own opinions as a rule" (taken from Cook & Medley, 1954) than to the question "People who continually pester you are asking for a punch in the nose" (taken from Buss & Durkee, 1957). Finally, it is desirable to intersperse hostility items with carefully chosen filler items that give the respondents an opportunity to say positive things about themselves. This strategy may make it more acceptable for respondents to admit hostility because they are not presenting a totally negative picture of themselves.

Question Difficulty

A second set of problems with questionnaire measures stems from the tendency of psychologists to develop their instruments on college students or other highly educated populations. The complexity and hypothetical nature of the resulting questions may make the questions difficult for respondents in less-educated samples to understand. This problem has been very apparent in our studies of cardiac patients at Duke Medical Center, where we have been unable to administer several promising questionnaires because a large number of the patients had difficulty completing them. In the same vein, many of the patients did not appear to be very introspective, perhaps a result of their ongoing health problems. Consequently, they appeared to report factual matters accurately, but they had more difficulty responding to hypothetical questions. It is also possible that the less introspective patients may not be adequately aware of their hostility to report it accurately.

Special Issues in Clinical Settings

Our experience with cardiac patients also illustrates a set of special problems with self-report data obtained in some health-care settings. The cardiac patients that we study are being asked to respond to questionnaires while in the midst of a significant health crisis, undoubtedly influencing many of the feelings that we are interested in and probably distracting the patient from providing full cooperation. In addition, most patients appear to be aware of the dangers of anger and hostility for those with coronary disease (perhaps reflecting the successful dissemination of psychological research findings to the public) and, therefore, may be motivated to deny the presence of the very characteristic that we are trying to assess. Furthermore, the hospital setting is unstandardized, with many interruptions and the presence of family and friends who sometimes influence the patient's responses.

Over the past 5 years, we have administered batteries of questionnaires to over 3,000 cardiac patients undergoing diagnostic coronary angiography. They have included several measures of hostility, such as the Ho scale, the NEO Personality Inventory (Costa & McCrae, 1985), the Anger Expression scale (Spielberger et al., 1985), the Buss-Durkee Hostility Inventory, and Factor L from the 16PF. In addition, we administered questionnaires that measured related constructs, such as optimism (Scheier & Carver, 1985), emotional expressivity (Friedman, Prince, Riggio, & DiMatteo, 1980), leadership style (Fielder & Chemers, 1984), and social support (Cohen & Hoberman, 1983). Despite large sample sizes (over 1,500 for some questionnaires), we found no replicable significant correlations between self-report hostility measures and CAD severity.

Does this set of null findings lead me to question my belief in the relationship between hostility and the development of coronary disease? Not at all, for there are two strong arguments against such a conclusion. First, self-report measures of hostility continue to predict a variety of health-related outcomes outside of patient populations (described earlier). Second, behavioral measures of hostility that do not rely on self-report correlate very strongly with disease severity in the cardiac patients we have studied (described later). Thus, it appears that there are special problems of self-report in patients facing serious illness, and these difficulties appear to have a serious impact on the validity of some types of questionnaire responses obtained in those settings. We will now explore an alternative approach to hostility measurement that avoids many of these problems.

Interview-Based Measures of Hostility

The second general approach to the measurement of hostility relies on clinical judgments of the respondent's behavior. Although there are procedures for rating hostile behavior in a variety of settings (e.g., Dodge & Coie, 1987; Smith, Sanders, & Alexander, 1990), most studies involving health outcomes have relied on judgments of behavior during the structured interview (SI), which was originally devised for the assessment of Type A behavior in the Western Collaborative Group Study (WCGS; Rosenman, 1978). Trained auditors make ratings of hostility (and other dimensions of behavior) that are based on detailed examination of recordings of the interview. There are several coding schemes to guide the auditors in making these judgments (e.g., Dembroski et al., 1985; Friedman & Powell, 1984; Matthews, Glass, Rosenman, & Bortner, 1977). Two recently proposed systems are of special interest because of findings produced by their use and because they have significantly influenced our own coding system, which will be discussed in detail later.

HFSS

Dembroski, MacDougall, Costa, & Grandits (1989) introduced a new scoring system, referred to here as the Hostility Facet Scoring System (HFSS), which measures Total Potential for Hostility and three hostility facets: Content, Intensity, and Style. Ratings of Hostile Content are based on the manifest content of the respondent's speech, Intensity of Hostility is scored on both content and speech stylistics, and ratings of Hostile Style are based on the tenor of the respondent's interaction with the interviewer. The ability of HFSS ratings to predict CHD events was evaluated in a sample of 576 interviews (192 cases and

384 controls) obtained from participants in the Multiple Risk Factor Intervention Trial (MRFIT) Behavior Pattern study. Only Total Potential for Hostility and Hostile Style were related to CHD in any of the analyses and, as would be predicted from previous research (Williams, et al., 1988), the effects were stronger among the younger (<48 years) participants. Because the Hostile Style component predicted disease and the Hostile Content component did not, the study clearly demonstrated the advantage of treating the respondent's behavior during the interview as an indicator of hostility that is independent of the manifest content of the respondent's self-reports.

HFSS ratings of Hostile Style have also been shown to correlate ($r = .46$, $p < .001$) with a six-level index of coronary artery disease severity (CADSEV) in a sample of 100 young (<50 years) men undergoing diagnostic angiography (Barefoot, Haney, Harper, Dembroski, & Williams, 1990). In agreement with the Dembroski et al. (1989) Multiple Risk Factor Intervention Trial data, the correlation between Hostile Style and CADSEV was not present in the data of older (>60 years) patients. Hostile Content and Hostile Intensity were not related to CADSEV in either age group.

CSS

The second important predecessor of our system is the Component Scoring System (CSS) (Chesney, Hecker, & Black, 1989; Hecker, Chesney, Black, & Frautschi, 1988), designed to rate 14 dimensions of the Type A behavior pattern, including hostility. On a theoretical level, the psychological dimension underlying the hostility rating of the CSS is very similar to that measured by the Total Potential for Hostility rating in the HFSS, but the mechanics of the assessment are quite different. One important difference is that respondent's hostility is rated on a question-by-question basis in the CSS, whereas the HFSS uses only one rating that is based on a gestalt of the entire interview. Because a much smaller unit of behavior is being judged in the CSS, the judgment is easier because the rater does not have to recall behaviors across the course of the interview. The CSS also improves on previous scoring systems by providing more explicit operational definitions of the behaviors to be judged as indicative of hostility.

Chesney et al. (1989) evaluated the predictive ability of the CSS in a reanalysis of the WCGS interviews (250 CHD cases and 500 matched controls). Although univariate analyses showed that five of the dimensions rated in the CSS (Hostility, Speaking Rate, Immediateness, Competitiveness, and Type A Content) were significantly related to CHD incidence, only the Hostility component remained significant in multiple logistic analyses.

Other recent analyses of the WCGS data have shown that the hostility component of the CSS also predicts total mortality over a 22-year follow-up period (Carmelli, Swan, Rosenman, Hecker, & Ragland, 1989).

IHAT

The HFSS and the CSS have heavily influenced the development of the most recent scoring procedure for judging hostility from interview behavior, the Interpersonal Hostility Assessment Technique (IHAT), which has been developed in our laboratories during the last 5 years. The IHAT combines the theoretical distinction between speech content and interviewee behavior that is central to the HFSS, the basic operational definitions and scoring mechanics of the CSS, and our experience with the behavior of coronary patients gained over the last 2 decades. The IHAT permits more detailed coding of hostile behaviors than previous systems, thus providing a richer set of data that can be used to address a number of new research issues involving more fine-grained analyses of the various forms of hostility expression. Therefore, we see the IHAT as a blend and extension of previous systems.

Table 1 presents brief definitions of the four types of behaviors coded as indicative of hostility. Hostile Evasions, Indirect Challenges, and Direct Challenges are geared toward the measurement of the behavioral component of hostility, whereas Irritation is designed to be an index of the affective component. As in the CSS, each question is scored separately and the four categories are added to yield a Hostile Behavior index. A summary Hostile Behavior index is obtained by averaging across questions. Unlike the CSS, the four categories are not weighted differentially, and there is no upper limit on the number of points that a respondent can receive on any one question (see Haney et al., 1991, for further details and rationales for the scoring mechanics).

Thus far, the predictive validity of IHAT ratings has been evaluated in three independent samples of patients undergoing diagnostic coronary angiography at Duke University Medical Center. Both men and women with a wide range of ages have been represented in these samples. All four studies have shown the same pattern of findings with approximately equal effect sizes. We will illustrate these findings with data from one of these samples, a study of 98 young (<50 years) men (Haney et al., 1991). Patients were administered the SI on the day following their catheterization, recordings of the interviews were coded according to the IHAT, and Hostile Behavior scores were correlated with a six-level ordinal index of coronary artery disease severity, CADSEV.

TABLE 1
IHAT Hostile Behavior Categories

Hostile withhold/evade

Failure to answer the question with an uncooperative or evasive response emitted in a manner that suggests hostility rather than lack of knowledge.

Indirect challenge

Indirectly challenging or deprecating the interview or the interviewer (e.g., answering in a fashion that suggests that the question was pointless). Such challenges are not overtly confrontational and are often judged to be present through a consideration of the response's implications.

Direct challenge

Openly confronting or contradicting the interviewer. In so doing, the respondent overtly expresses antagonism toward the interviewer or interview situation.

Irritation

Evidence of arousal in the respondent's voice stylistics indicative of the experience of hostile affect. The irritation could be directed toward the interview or interviewer, but it could also occur while reliving a previous angry episode or imagining a hypothetical situation.

Table 2 presents Spearman correlations between IHAT ratings and CADSEV. The summary Hostile Behavior index had a very strong relation to disease severity. This finding remained unchanged in logistic models controlling for age, smoking, hyperlipidemia, and history of hypertension. It should be noted that these traditional risk factors were correlated with CADSEV in analyses involving the entire population of Duke patients (Williams et al., 1988), but the correlations were not significant in sample sizes as small as the one in this study. This further underscores the magnitude of the hostility–CADSEV relations.

All of the components of Hostile Behavior were significantly correlated with disease, but Indirect Challenge was strongest, with a correlation essentially equal to the one involving the summary index. This pattern of findings was replicated in other IHAT studies. Indirect Challenge is by far the most subtle of the components and the most difficult for the untrained observer to recognize. Direct Challenges were infrequent. In settings such as the SI, people appear to avoid open confrontation and express their hostility in more indirect ways, yet careful analysis of their behaviors can detect it. The form of hostility expression may be very different in other social settings, and our future research will investigate this possibility through the manipulation of the social parameters of the interview setting.

The correlations between Hostile Behavior and CADSEV in the four studies of Duke patients were so large as to raise concern that we may have been rating a behavior that was a consequence, rather than a precursor, of disease. For example, the presence of significant heart disease and its symptoms might make the patients more irritable, which might produce hostile behavior toward the interviewer. However, there are two strong arguments against this position. The first is that CSS and HFSS ratings, which are related to IHAT ratings, successfully discriminated between CHD cases and controls in prospective data (Chesney et al., 1989; Dembroski et al., 1989).

The second argument comes from a unique study of IHAT ratings and early-stage CAD that we conducted on Air Force pilots who underwent angiography at the U.S. Air Force School of Aerospace Medicine (Barefoot, Patterson, Haney, & Williams, 1991). All of these pilots were asymptomatic, but were suspected of having CAD on the basis of noninvasive tests (EKG, treadmill, and thallium). We tested the ability of IHAT ratings to discriminate between cases ($n = 24$) and controls ($n = 25$) and found the summary Hostile Behavior index to be a significant predictor of disease status ($p = .03$, two-tailed). The most important implication of this result stems from the fact that the participants were asymptomatic and cases had early-stage coronary disease. Only 4 of the 24 cases had clinically significant levels of disease (75% occlusion of a coronary artery). Therefore, it is most unlikely that the hostility observed in the cases was the result of chest pain or other symptoms of advanced disease.

TABLE 2

Hostile Behavior Ratings and CAD Severity

Rating	Correlation with CADSEV	p
Withhold/evade	.31	<.002
Indirect challenge	.63	<.001
Direct challenge	.24	<.02
Irritation	.25	<.02
Total hostile behavior	.59	<.001

In addition to the index of Hostile Behavior, we have also scored an interview-based index of Self-Report Hostility, which is based on the number of times the respondent admits to anger or aggression. We have found that Self-Report Hostility does not correlate significantly with CADSEV. There are several possible explanations for this result. First, Dembroski et al. (1989) found that Hostile Style predicted disease, whereas Hostile Content did not and argued that Hostile Style reflects the expression of anger, which is related to disease, whereas Hostile Content reflects the experience of anger, which is not related to disease. Second, we have already discussed (earlier in chapter) a number of barriers to valid self-reports that could also influence the correlation between Self-Report Hostility and CADSEV. Finally, we should note that the SI was devised to measure Type A behavior rather than hostility, so perhaps it is not surprising that the responses to the questions are poor indicators of hostility.

Problems With the Use of Interview Measures

The most significant barriers to the use of interview-based hostility measures are the difficulties of their administration and scoring. Interviewers must be trained, the interview is time consuming to administer, and logistic problems often make it impractical to introduce interviews into large-scale epidemiologic studies. The task of training assessors to make reliable and valid assessments is even more difficult. For example, the subtlety of the hostile behaviors coded with the IHAT presents a special challenge for the training of assessors and the exporting of the rating system to other laboratories. Although we have achieved acceptable interrater reliabilities (e.g., .85, in the study presented in Table 2), we have found that a period of training is necessary to learn the technique and that some individuals cannot learn to recognize the critical behaviors, despite training. In collaboration with Larry Scherwitz, we are now in the process of devising a training program to make it easier for researchers to learn the IHAT. I cannot overemphasize that researchers should not attempt to make IHAT ratings (or those of any other interview-based assessment procedure) simply on the basis of the published descriptions of the procedures.

Although interview-based assessment techniques, such as the IHAT, avoid most of the problems of self-reports, they are not immune to the special problems of data collection in clinical settings. For example, patients with serious illnesses, such as coronary disease, have a high prevalence of reactive depression. This depression can mask affective expression and thereby suppress the intensity with which hostility is expressed (Barefoot, Haney, Simpson, Blumenthal, & Williams, 1990).

Conclusions

Comparing the current status of hostility assessment with the state of affairs that existed just a few years ago (Matthews, 1985), it is apparent that researchers have made considerable progress. In particular, we know more about the construct validity of many of our measures, additional measures of hostility have been related to health outcomes, and significant advances have been made in interview-based assessment procedures. However, many of the problems, especially those affecting the validity of self-reports, remain unsolved.

One way to achieve a more coherent assessment strategy would be to develop instruments that are more comprehensive in the aspects of hostility that they measure. Interview-based assessment techniques, such as IHAT, pay little attention to the cognitive component of hostility, but questions designed to elicit cynicism and hostile attributions could be easily added to the protocol. Likewise, it would be useful to develop questionnaire instruments that assess all three hostility components while minimizing some of the problems of self-report discussed earlier. Even so, the nature of self-report data makes it unlikely that questionnaire responses can ever reflect all of the features of hostile behavior that can be measured with interview methods (Friedman & Powell, 1984).

A more comprehensive measurement strategy would allow us to pay increased attention to the diverse forms of hostility expression. The interview-assessment strategy is useful in that it does not constrain the respondent's behavior to a few predefined responses, and one of the most salient impressions that comes from listening to a large number of interviews is the variety of ways that the disposition of hostility can be manifested in behavior. The processes that translate the underlying trait of hostility to observable behaviors constitute variables in the middle level of personality description (Cantor, 1990). The middle-level units of analysis involve acknowledgment of the importance of the reciprocal interactions between personality variables, such as hostility, and the social environment. The middle-level unit of analysis holds great promise, not only because of the many interesting research questions it can address, but because research at this level is more likely than trait-level research to produce interventions for the alleviation of the negative health consequences of hostility.

References

Averill, J. R. (1982). *Anger and aggression: An essay on emotion.* New York: Springer-Verlag.

Bandura, A. (1973). *Aggression: A social learning analysis.* Prentice-Hall: Englewood Cliffs, NJ.

Barefoot, J. C., Dahlstrom, W. G., & Williams, R. B., Jr. (1983). Hostility, CHD incidence, and total mortality: A 25-year follow-up study of 255 physicians. *Psychosomatic Medicine, 45,* 59–63.

Barefoot, J. C., Dodge, K. A., Peterson, B. L., Dahlstrom, W. G., & Williams, R. B., Jr. (1989). The Cook-Medley hostility scale: Item content and ability to predict survival. *Psychosomatic Medicine, 51,* 46–57.

Barefoot, J. C., Haney, T. L., Harper, R. R., Dembroski, T. M., & Williams, R. B., Jr. (1990, August). *Interview-assessed hostility and the severity of coronary artery disease.* Paper presented at the 98th Annual Convention of the American Psychological Association, Boston, MA.

Barefoot, J. C., Haney, T. L., Simpson, S., Blumenthal, J. A., & Williams, R. B., Jr. (1990). Depression and the assessment of Type A behavior in a clinical population. *Psychological Assessment: A Journal of Consulting and Clinical Psychology, 2,* 483–485.

Barefoot, J. C., Patterson, J., Haney, T. L. & Williams, R. B., Jr. (1991, March). *Hostility and early-stage coronary artery disease: An angiographic study of asymptomatic men.* Paper presented at the meeting of the American Psychosomatic Society, Santa Fe, NM.

Barefoot, J. C., Peterson, B. L., Dahlstrom, W. G., Siegler, I. C., Anderson, N. B., & Williams, R. B., Jr. (1991). Hostility patterns and health implications: Correlates of Cook-Medley hostility scale scores in a national survey. *Health Psychology, 10,* 18–24.

Barefoot, J. C., Siegler, I. C., Nowlin, J. B., Peterson, B. L., Haney, T. L., & Williams, R. B., Jr. (1987). Suspiciousness, health, and mortality: A follow-up study of 500 older adults. *Psychosomatic Medicine, 49,* 450–457.

Berkowitz, L. (1963). *Aggression: A social psychological analysis.* New York: McGraw-Hill.

Buss, A. H., & Durkee, A. (1957). An inventory for assessing different kinds of hostility. *Journal of Consulting Psychology, 42,* 155–162.

Byrne, D. G., Rosenman, R. H., Schiller, E., & Chesney, M. A. (1985). Consistency and variation among instruments purporting to measure the Type A behavior pattern. *Psychosomatic Medicine, 46,* 242–261.

Cantor, N. (1990). From thought to behavior: "Having" and "doing" in the study of personality and cognition. *American Psychologist, 45,* 735–750.

Carmelli, D., Swan, G. E., Rosenman, R. H., Hecker, M. H., & Ragland, D. R. (1989, March). *Behavioral components and total mortality in the WCGS.* Paper presented at the meeting of the Society of Behavioral Medicine, San Francisco, CA.

Carmody, T. P., Crossen, J. R., & Wiens, A. N. (1989). Hostility as a health risk factor: Relationships with neuroticism, Type A behavior, attentional focus, and interpersonal style. *Journal of Clinical Psychology, 45,* 754–762.

Cattell, R. B., Eber, H. W., & Tatsuoka, M. M. (1970). *Handbook for the Sixteen Personality Factor Questionnaire (16PF).* Champaign, IL: Institute for Personality and Ability Testing.

Chesney, M. A., Hecker, M., & Black, G. W. (1989). Coronary-prone components of Type A behavior in the WCGS: A new methodology. In B. K. Houston & C. R. Snyder (Eds.), *Type A behavior pattern: Research, theory and intervention,* (pp. 168–188). New York: Wiley.

Cohen, S., & Hoberman, H. M. (1983). Positive events and social supports as buffers of life change stress. *Journal of Applied Social Psychology, 13,* 99–125.

Cook, W. W., & Medley, D. M. (1954). Proposed hostility and pharasaic-virtue scales for the MMPI. *Journal of Applied Psychology, 38,* 414–418.

Cornell, C. E., Slater, S. J., Norvell, N. K., Grissett, N. I., & Limacher, M. C. (1990, August). *Variables related to risk for coronary heart disease in healthy adults.* Paper presented at the 98th Annual Convention of the American Psychological Association, Boston, MA.

Costa, P. T., Jr. (1986). Is Neuroticism a risk factor for CAD? Is Type A a measure of Neuroticism? In T. Schmidt, T. Dembroski, & G. Blumchen (Eds.), *Biological and psychological factors in cardiovascular disease* (pp. 85–95). New York: Springer-Verlag.

Costa, P. T., Jr., & McCrae, R. R. (1985). *The NEO Personality Inventory manual.* Odessa, FL: Psychological Assessment Resources.

Costa, P. T., Jr., McCrae, R. R., & Dembroski, T. M. (1989). Agreeableness versus antagonism: Explication of a potential risk factor for CHD. In A. W. Siegman & T. M. Dembroski (Eds.), *In search of coronary-prone behavior: Beyond Type A* (pp. 41–63). Hillsdale, NJ: Erlbaum.

Costa, P. T., Jr., Zonderman, A. B., McCrae, R. R., & Williams R. B., Jr. (1986). Cynicism and paranoid alienation in the Cook and Medley hostility scale. *Psychosomatic Medicine, 48,* 283–285.

Dembroski, T. M., MacDougall, J. M., Costa, P. T., Jr., & Grandits, G. A. (1989). Components of hostility as predictors of sudden death and myocardial infarction in the Multiple Risk Factor Intervention Trial. *Psychosomatic Medicine, 51,* 514–522.

Dembroski, T. M., MacDougall, J. M., Williams, R. B., Jr., Haney, T. L., & Blumenthal, J. A. (1985). Components of Type A, hostility, and anger-in: Relationship to angiographic findings. *Psychosomatic Medicine, 47,* 219–233.

Dodge, K. A., & Coie, J. D. (1987). Social-information processing factors in reactive and proactive aggression in children's peer groups. *Journal of Personality and Social Psychology, 53,* 1146–1158.

Dodge, K. A., Petit, G. S., McClaskey, C. L., & Brown, M. (1986). Social competence in children. *Monographs of the Society for Research in Child Development, 51*(2, Serial No. 213).

Fiedler, F., & Chemers, M. M. (1984). *Improving leadership effectiveness: The leader match concept.* (2nd ed.). New York: Wiley.

Friedman, H. S., & Booth-Kewley, S. (1987). Personality, Type A behavior, and coronary heart disease: The role of emotional expression. *Journal of Personality and Social Psychology, 53,* 783–792.

Friedman, H. S., Prince, L. M., Riggio, R. E., & DiMatteo, M. R., (1980). Understanding and assessing nonverbal expressiveness: The affective communication test. *Journal of Personality and Social Psychology, 39,* 333–351.

Friedman, M., & Powell, L. H. (1984). The diagnosis and quantitative assessment of Type A behavior: Introduction and description of the videotaped structured interview. *Integrative Psychiatry, 2,* 123–131.

Greenglass, E. R., & Julkunen, J. (1989). Construct validity and sex differences in Cook-Medley hostility. *Personality and Individual Differences, 10,* 209–218.

Haney, T. L., Barefoot, J. C., Houseworth, S., Scherwitz, L., Herskowitz-Hall, B., Saunders, W. B., & Williams, R. B., Jr. (1991). *The Interpersonal Hostility Assessment Technique.* Manuscript submitted for publication.

Hearn, M. D., Murray, D. M., & Luepker, R. V. (1989). Hostility, coronary heart disease, and total mortality: A 33-year follow-up study of university students. *Journal of Behavioral Medicine, 12,* 105–121.

Hecker, M., Chesney, M. A., Black, G. W., & Frautschi N. (1988). Coronary-prone behaviors in the Western Collaborative Group Study. *Psychosomatic Medicine, 50,* 153–164.

Hilgard, E. R. (1980). The trilogy of mind: Cognition, affection and conation. *Journal of the History of the Behavioral Sciences, 16,* 107–117.

Izard, C. E. (1977). *Human emotions.* New York: Plenum.

Joesoef, M. R., Wetterhall, S. F., DeStefano, F., Stroup, N. E., & Fronek, A. (1989). The association of peripheral arterial disease with hostility in a young, healthy population. *Psychosomatic Medicine, 51,* 285–289.

Koskenvuo, M., Kaprio, J., Rose, R. J., Kesaniemi, A. Heikkila, K., Langinvainio, H. (1988). Hostility as a risk factor for mortality and ischemic heart disease in men. *Psychosomatic Medicine, 50,* 330–340.

Leon, G. R., Finn, S. E., Murray, D., & Bailey, J. M. (1988). The inability to predict cardiovascular disease from hostility scores or MMPI items related to Type A behavior. *Journal of Consulting and Clinical Psychology, 56,* 597–600.

Matthews, K. A. (1985). Assessment of Type A behavior, anger, and hostility in epidemiological studies of cardiovascular disease. In A. M. Ostfeld & E. D. Eaker (Eds.), *Measuring psychosocial variables in epidemiologic studies of cardiovascular disease* (NIH Publication No. 85-2270, pp. 153–184). Washington, DC: U.S. Department of Health and Human Services.

Matthews, K. A., Glass, D. C., Rosenman, R. H., & Bortner, R. W. (1977). Competitive drive, Pattern A, and coronary heart disease: A further analysis of some data from the Western Collaborative Group Study. *Journal of Chronic Diseases, 30,* 489–498.

Matthews, K. A., Jamison, J. W., & Cottington, E. M. (1985). Assessment of Type A, anger, and hostility: A review of scales through 1982. In A. M. Ostfeld & E. D. Eaker (Eds.), *Measuring psychosocial variables in epidemiologic studies of cardiovascular disease* (NIH Publication No. 85-2270, pp. 207–312). Washington, DC: U.S. Department of Health and Human Services.

McCranie, E. W., Watkins, L. O., Brandsma, J. M., & Sisson, B. D. (1986). Hostility, coronary heart disease (CHD) incidence and total mortality: Lack of association in a 25-year follow-up study of 478 physicians. *Journal of Behavioral Medicine, 9,* 119–125.

Megargee, E. I. (1985). The dynamics of aggression and their application to cardiovascular disorders. In M. A. Chesney & R. H. Rosenman (Eds.), *Anger and hostility in cardiovascular and behavioral disorders* (pp. 31–57). New York: McGraw-Hill and Hemisphere.

Musante, L., MacDougall, J. M., Dembroski, T. M., & Costa, P. T., Jr. (1989). Potential for hostility and dimensions of anger. *Health Psychology, 8,* 343–354.

Novaco, R. W. (1985). Anger and its therapeutic regulation. In M. A. Chesney & R. H. Rosenman (Eds.), *Anger and hostility in cardiovascular and behavioral disorders* (pp. 203–226). New York: McGraw-Hill and Hemisphere.

Novaco, R. W. (1975). *Anger control: The development and evaluation of an experimental treatment.* Lexington, MA: Lexington Books.

Ostfeld, A. M., Lebovitz, B. L., Shekelle, R. B., & Paul, O. (1964). A prospective study of the relationship between personality and coronary heart disease. *Journal of Chronic Disease, 17,* 265–276.

Rosenman, R. H. (1978). The interview method of assessment of the coronary-prone behavior pattern. In T. M. Dembroski, S. M. Weiss, J. L. Shields, S. G. Haynes, & M. Feinleib (Eds.), *Coronary-prone behavior* (pp. 55–69). New York: Springer-Verlag.

Rotter, J. (1971). Generalized expectancies for interpersonal trust. *American Psychologist, 26,* 443–452.

Scheier, M. F., & Carver, C. S. (1985). Optimism, coping and health: Assessment and implications of generalized outcome expectancies. *Health Psychology, 4,* 219–247.

Scherwitz, L., Perkins, L., Chesney, M., & Hughes, G. (1991). Cook-Medley hostility scale and subscales: Relationship to demographic and psychosocial characteristics in CARDIA. *Psychosomatic Medicine, 53,* 36–49.

Seeman, T. E., & Syme, S. L. (1987). Social networks and coronary artery disease: A comparison of the structure and function of social relations as predictors of disease. *Psychosomatic Medicine, 49,* 341–354.

Shekelle R. B., Gale, M., Ostfeld, A. M., & Paul, O. (1983). Hostility, risk of coronary heart disease, and mortality. *Psychosomatic Medicine, 45,* 109–14.

Siegler, I. C., Peterson, B. L., Barefoot, J. C., & Williams, R. B., Jr. (1991). *Hostility during late adolescence predicts coronary risk factors at midlife.* Manuscript submitted for publication.

Siegman, A. W., Dembroski, T. M., & Ringel, N. (1987). Components of hostility and the severity of coronary artery disease. *Psychosomatic Medicine, 49,* 127–135.

Smith, T. W., & Frohm, K. D. (1985). What's so unhealthy about hostility? Construct validity and psychological correlates of the Cook and Medley Ho scale. *Health Psychology, 4,* 503–520.

Smith, T. W., Sanders, J. D., & Alexander, J. F. (1990). What does the Cook and Medley hostility scale measure? Affect, behavior and attributions in the marital context. *Journal of Personality and Social Psychology, 58,* 699–708.

Spielberger, C. D., Johnson, E. H., Russell, S. F., Crane, R. J., Jacobs, G. A., & Worden, T. J. (1985). The experience and expression of anger: Construction and validation of an anger expression scale. In M. A. Chesney & R. H. Rosenman (Eds.), *Anger and hostility in cardiovascular and behavioral disorders* (pp. 5–30). New York: McGraw-Hill and Hemisphere.

Suarez, E. C., & Williams, R. B., Jr. (1989). Situational determinants of cardiovascular and emotional reactivity in high and low hostile men. *Psychosomatic Medicine, 51,* 404–418.

Williams, R. B., Jr., Haney, T. L., Lee, K. L., Kong, Y., Blumenthal, J. A., & Whalen, R. (1980). Type A behavior, hostility, and coronary atherosclerosis. *Psychosomatic Medicine, 42,* 539–549.

Williams, R. B., Jr., Barefoot, J. C., Haney, T. L., Harrell, F. E., Blumenthal, J. A., Pryor, D. B., Peterson, B. L. (1988). Type A behavior and angiographically documented coronary atherosclerosis in a sample of 2289 patients. *Psychosomatic Medicine, 50,* 139–152.

Zillman, D. (1979). *Hostility and aggression.* New York: Wiley.

CHAPTER 3

Hostility, Health, and Social Contexts

Timothy W. Smith and Alan J. Christensen

T he assumption that chronic anger and hostility contribute to the development of disease has been endorsed by a variety of biomedical and psychological scholars for centuries. It is only within the past decade, however, that a sufficient number of so-phisticated, large-scale studies have appeared to allow a thorough evaluation of this psy-chosomatic hypothesis. Although the results are not entirely consistent, meta-analytic reviews of the available research suggest that hostile persons are at significantly greater risk of cardiovascular and other life-threatening illnesses (Booth-Kewley & Friedman, 1987; Matthews, 1988).

This tentative evidence of the adverse consequences of hostility has fueled a con-siderable amount of research on a variety of related topics. Several issues have emerged from this activity as potential impediments to continued progress in the area. Although the balance of relevant prospective studies support the basic psychosomatic view, trou-bling inconsistencies exist in the literature. Interpretation of the available studies as re-flecting the effects of the construct of hostility on health has been hampered by questions surrounding the personality measures they use. Several plausible mechanisms underlying the statistical association between hostility and health have been suggested, but evalua-tions of these models are preliminary and the results are often mixed. As a result, the activity and progress witnessed in recent years has prompted relatively equal amounts of enthusiasm, caution, and skepticism.

The present discussion is not intended as a comprehensive review of the evolving literature on hostility and health and the associated controversies. Rather, our purpose is to illustrate the value of a basic proposition in the much-needed future research in this area. Simply put, our view is that the potential influence of hostility on health is best understood through consideration of social contexts. Although traditionally seen as a characteristic of individuals, hostility and any health risks it confers are inherently social in nature. This rather obvious assertion may prove useful in empirical efforts to address current limitations in the field.

To illustrate this argument, we will discuss two central issues in the recent literature on hostility and health: the evaluation of available assessment procedures and the nature of mechanisms underlying the statistical association between these measures and health. Consideration of social contexts is likely to be of equal value in research on the development and therapeutic reduction of hostility, as well as in tests of the basic association between hostility and health. Detailed consideration of these latter applications is beyond our present scope, however. Furthermore, this discussion will primarily focus on our work with one approach to the assessment of hostility, but it is equally relevant to others.

Assessment of Hostility

Negative studies notwithstanding, the bulk of the available evidence indicates that several measures of hostility may have predictive utility in efforts to identify persons at risk for cardiovascular and other diseases. However, interpretation of such studies as reflecting the association between the personality trait of hostility and subsequent health requires independent evidence of the construct validity of these measurement procedures. If the only goals of epidemiological studies of psychosocial risk factors were the improvement of predictive equations and refinements in assessment of individuals' risk of disease, strictly speaking, it would not matter what constructs were reflected in scores on the psychosocial measures they use. Although these goals are clearly important, most work in this area is more ambitious. It is directed toward testing the importance of various psychosocial dimensions or constructs as influences on health. Thus, the distinction between predictive utility and conceptual hypothesis testing underscores the importance of construct validity in this area of research.

One of the more commonly used measures in this context is the Cook and Medley (1954) Hostility (Ho) scale. Three prospective studies have found significant associations between Ho scores and subsequent health (Barefoot, Dahlstrom, & Williams, 1983; Barefoot, Dodge, Peterson, Dahlstrom, & Williams, 1989; Shekelle, Gale, Ostfeld, & Paul, 1983), and three similar studies have failed to replicate this effect (Hearn, Murray, & Luepker, 1989; Leon, Finn, Murray, & Bailey, 1988; McCranie, Watkins, Brandsma, & Sisson, 1986). Until recently, interpretation of these mixed results as reflecting possible effects of hostility on health was hindered by a lack of compelling evidence of the construct validity of the Ho scale (Megargee, 1985). The small number of studies available suggested that the scale was not a good predictor of aggressive behavior in criminal and psychiatric populations. These results are not directly relevant to the question of the scale's validity in normal populations, which is a more traditional reference group in the study of health and behavior.

Subsequent studies indicated that the Ho scale displayed large, expected correlations with self-reports of anger proneness and aspects of hostility, such as resentment, suspicion, and irritability (Barefoot et al., 1989; Smith & Frohm, 1985; Smith, Pope, Sanders, Allred, & O'Keeffe, 1988). Furthermore, although the Ho scale was also significantly correlated with measures of other negative affects, such as anxiety and depression, it was more closely correlated with measures of anger and hostility (Barefoot et al., 1989; Pope, Smith, & Rhodewalt, 1990; Smith & Frohm, 1985). Thus, correlations with other self-report inventories provide at least some support of the convergent and discriminant validity of the Ho scale.

However, convergence among self-report measures is a relatively weak and potentially misleading source of information regarding construct validity. Such correlations could be interpreted as simply reflecting the consistent endorsement of similarly worded items on separate questionnaires (Nicholls, Licht, & Pearl, 1982). That is, common method variance could inflate estimates of construct validity in studies using only self-report inventories. Furthermore, conceptual definitions of hostility include references to both cognitive processes and overt interpersonal behavior (Barefoot et al., 1989; Megargee, 1985; Spielberger et al., 1985). Individual differences in hostility are typically seen as directly involving—or at least closely associated with—specific ways of thinking about and behaving toward other people. Therefore, more complete evaluation of the construct validity should include cognitive and behavioral correlates of the Ho scale in social contexts.

Hostility is often described as an attitudinal variable, reflecting the tendency to view others as motivated by selfish concerns, likely sources of provocation and mistreatment, untrustworthy, and generally unworthy. This view suggests that individual differences in hostility involve consistent tendencies in social cognition. Hostile persons apparently maintain a "hostile other" schema, potentially influencing their perception of others and their processing of related social information.

Several studies of self-reported cognitive processes provide evidence of this hypothesized hostile cognitive style. High scores on the Ho scale have been found to be associated with a greater reported frequency of angry and suspicious thoughts during daily activities and with the tendency to interpret the behavior of others as intentionally provocative (Pope et al., 1990; Smith, Sanders, & Alexander, 1990). However, self-report assessments of cognitive processes have several potential limitations, not the least of which is the inclusion of items similar to those on the Ho scale itself. Thus, as described earlier, these results could also reflect consistent endorsement of similarly worded items, rather than an association between the related yet distinct constructs of hostility and negativistic social cognition.

To evaluate the cognitive aspect of the conceptual definition of hostility without the potential limitations of common method variance, Allred and Smith (in press) used an incidental recall measure of information-processing tendencies. High- and low-scoring subjects on the Ho scale were randomly assigned to experimental conditions involving high or low levels of interpersonal conflict. After interacting with a confederate behaving in either a neutral or antagonistic manner, subjects rated the confederate using a series of trait adjectives. Some of the adjectives reflected hostile content (e.g., rude, unfriendly, etc.), and the remainder reflected generally negative and positive content. Not surprisingly, high-scoring Ho subjects rated their interaction partners as more hostile than did low-scoring Ho subjects. More importantly, however, the subsequent incidental recall measure indicated that following the antagonistic interaction, hostile subjects recalled more hostile-trait adjectives than did nonhostile subjects in this condition and more than either hostile or nonhostile subjects following the neutral interaction. Hostility and the tone of the interaction did not facilitate recall of generally negative- or positive-trait adjectives. This pattern is consistent with the hypothesis that hostile persons maintain a hostile schema concerning others, which once activated or primed by related events facilitates the processing of schema-consistent information. As such, the results provide strong evidence for the construct validity of the Ho scale.

Conceptual definitions of hostility are not limited to cognitive processes. Although it is certainly not synonymous with overt aggressive behavior, most views of hostility suggest that hostile persons are more likely to display aggressive behavior (Megargee, 1985;

Spielberger et al., 1985). Without evidence of expected behavioral correlates of the Ho scale, our interpretation of this scale as reflecting individual differences in hostility would be constrained or altered (cf. Kagan, 1988). As noted earlier, until recently, the limited evidence available concerning the behavioral correlates of the Ho scale indicated that it was unrelated to aggressive behavior in psychiatric and criminal populations (Megargee, 1985). Such results could raise concerns about the construct validity of the Ho scale, but are also not necessarily relevant to variations in aggressive behavior in normal populations.

A recent study of overt behaviors during marital interactions provides some evidence of the validity of the Ho scale. Smith, Sanders, and Alexander (1990) asked married couples to discuss a sequence of three topics: a low-conflict topic, a high-conflict topic, and a second low-conflict topic. The frequency of hostile and dominant behaviors was assessed through the use of videotapes of the three discussions, and subjects reported their levels of anger as well. Among the husbands, high Ho scores were associated with more frequent hostile behaviors across all three discussions, but particularly during the high-conflict discussion. Ho scores were unrelated to dominant behavior. Ho scores were also associated with parallel increases in reported anger. Interestingly, Ho scores were only weakly related to overt behaviors and reported affect among wives. Thus, at least for men in this study, assessment of interactional behaviors provided additional evidence of the construct validity of the Ho scale.

The results of these two studies support the interpretation of studies using the Ho scale as reflecting individual differences in hostility. We do not mean to imply that the Ho scale is without potential limitations. Indeed, its uncertain internal structure (Contrada, Jussim, Posluszny, & Bender, 1990) and considerable overlap with measures of neuroticism (Barefoot et al., 1989; Blumenthal, Barefoot, Burg, & Williams, 1987; Carmody, Crossen, & Wiens, 1989) may undermine its usefulness in this area of research. Rather, these two studies are intended to illustrate the value of evaluating the construct validity of scales used in this area of research in social contexts relevant to the conceptual definitions of hostility. Such evaluations provide more complete and compelling evidence than that obtained through the use of self-report methods alone. Perhaps even more important, this more thorough explication of the construct can also shed light on related issues, such as possible mechanisms linking hostility and health or relevant targets for interventions. It could be argued that these comprehensive evaluations are less necessary in the case of the potentially more objective measures of hostility that are based on careful observation and ratings of behavior in the interpersonal context of the Type A structured interview (e.g. Dembroski, MacDougall, Costa, & Grandits, 1989; Hecker, Chesney, Black, & Frautschi, 1988). However, correlations with behavior in other contexts and with cognitive processes would strengthen the interpretation of these interview-based measures as reflecting hostility.

Mechanisms Linking Hostility and Health

If individual differences in hostility are related to the risk of disease, an obvious avenue of investigation is the evaluation of possible mechanisms underlying this association. To date, four models have been proposed. They are by no means mutually exclusive, and in some instances, are closely related. In all cases, however, consideration of social contexts is potentially helpful in explaining the effects of hostility on health.

The Psychophysiological Reactivity Model

Williams, Barefoot, and Shekelle (1985) proposed that hostility contributes to disease by way of increased physiological responses to potential stressors. Briefly, this model suggests that hostile persons experience more frequent and more extreme episodes of anger and are more frequently in a state of vigilant observation of their social environments. Anger and vigilance, in turn, are associated with elevated levels of cardiovascular and neuroendocrine responses, possibly contributing to the development of disease.

Initial tests of the hypothesized association between individual differences in hostility and physiological reactivity using the Ho scale were not consistent with the model. Ho scores were unrelated to cardiovascular responses to traditional laboratory stressors such as mental arithmetic and the Stroop color–word task (Sallis, Johnson, Trevorrow, Kaplan, & Melbourne, 1987; Smith & Houston, 1987). A recent study confirmed this lack of an association with reactivity to cognitive stressors (Kamark, Manuck, & Jennings, 1990).

Given the conceptual and empirical descriptions of hostility presented earlier, it is perhaps not surprising that the Ho scale is not related to physiological responses to traditional, nonsocial tasks. This individual difference would appear to be more relevant to interpersonal stressors. Several recent studies have tested this view, and the results are generally consistent. Hardy and Smith (1988) measured systolic and diastolic blood pressure (SBP, DBP) before and during role-played interactions involving high or low levels of interpersonal conflict. Subjects with high Ho scores displayed larger increases in DBP than did subjects with low Ho scores during the high-conflict interactions. Hostility was unrelated to reactivity during the low-conflict interactions, however.

In a similar study, Suarez and Williams (1989) measured cardiovascular responses of men with high and low Ho scores working on a stressful word-identification task. In one condition, subjects were harassed while working on the task, and in the other, they received neutral comments from the experimenter. Hostility was associated with heightened cardiovascular reactivity during the word-identification task if subjects were harassed by the laboratory assistant. The word-identification task alone did not elicit increased reactivity among subjects with high Ho scores. Hostility as measured by the Ho scale has also been found to be associated with larger increases in blood pressure during a current-events debate task. Smith and Allred (1989) asked pairs of subjects to discuss a series of current events. Subjects were assigned to opposite sides of the issues (e.g., "Should abortion be outlawed?", etc.) and engaged in a structured debate. Compared with subjects with low Ho scores, hostile subjects displayed larger increases in SBP and DBP during the debate.

These studies suggest that hostility is associated with more pronounced cardiovascular reactivity to interpersonal conflict and provocation. Other social aspects of hostility suggest that additional interpersonal stressors might elicit enhanced reactivity as well. For example, Averill (1982) argued that anger and hostility often represent attempts to regulate or control the actions of others. Effortful attempts to influence others have been found to produce increases in cardiovascular reactivity (Smith, Allred, Morrison, & Carlson, 1989; Smith, Baldwin, & Christensen, 1990). If hostile people are particularly concerned with controlling others, then situations requiring the assertion of social control might elicit heightened reactivity, especially among hostile subjects. To test this hypothesis, Smith and Brown (in press) asked married couples to solve a hypothetical problem through discussion. One half of the subjects were given an incentive to influence their spouse's behavior in the problem-solving task, while the other subjects were asked simply to discuss the problem. Among husbands, hostility was associated with larger increases in SBP and DBP when they were attempting to influence their spouses, but was associated with smaller increases during simple discussions. Ho scores of the wives were unrelated to blood pressure reactivity in either condition. Thus, at least for men, social situations involving attempts to exert interpersonal control or influence may elicit heightened reactivity. Interestingly, wives' blood pressure reactivity was positively related to their husbands' Ho scores, suggesting that interactions with hostile people may be stressful.

Previous research has indicated that hostility as measured by the Ho scale is associated with mistrust of others (Smith & Frohm, 1985). Therefore, social situations involving trust or self-disclosure represent another class of stimuli that are likely to elicit heightened reactivity among hostile persons. Christensen and Smith (1991) randomly assigned men with high and low Ho scores to one of two discussions with a stranger, actually a confederate. Subjects were asked to discuss either a hypothetical stressful event that happened to someone else or the most stressful personal event they were willing to discuss in this situation. A standard series of prompts led the subjects to describe the event, its impact, and outcome, as well as to explain their responses. Compared with the group with low Ho scores, hostile subjects displayed heightened blood pressure reactivity during the interaction task requiring self-disclosure of personally stressful events. In the parallel interaction task without self-disclosure, hostility was not related to cardiovascular reactivity. These results confirm the importance of social contexts in evaluations of the psychophysiological model and seem to add situations involving trust and self-disclosure of stressful experiences to the list of relevant interpersonal settings. This pattern may also indicate that the otherwise beneficial effects of social support and disclosure of stressful events (Pennebaker, Colder, & Sharp, 1990; Pennebaker, Kiecolt-Glaser, & Glaser, 1988) may be undermined for hostile persons.

Overall, these studies indicate that consideration of social contexts conceptually related to hostility provides an informative evaluation of the psychophysiological reactivity model. Curiously, when hostility is quantified through interview methods rather than with the Ho scale, hostility is not associated with increased reactivity to social stressors (Suls & Wan, 1990). Obviously, additional work is needed to address this inconsistency. Contextual variables also appear to be useful in clarifying the association between anger coping styles or modes of anger expression and cardiovascular reactivity (Engebretson, Matthews, & Scheier, 1989). Reactivity is greatest when individuals' typical style is inconsistent with social constraints, such as when people who usually express anger are required to avoid doing so.

The Psychosocial Vulnerability Model

A second potential link between hostility and health involves the interpersonal correlates of hostility. In light of the conceptual and empirical descriptions of this trait, it is not surprising that high scores on the Ho scale are associated with reports of fewer and less satisfactory social supports (Barefoot et al., 1983; Blumenthal et al., 1987; Hardy & Smith, 1988; Houston & Kelley, 1989; Smith & Frohm, 1985; Smith et al., 1988). Hostile persons also report interpersonal conflict at work, in their families of origin, and in their marriages, although the latter effect has been found for men but not women (Houston &

Kelley, 1989; Smith et al., 1988). This increased psychosocial vulnerability across domains could contribute to the development of disease among hostile individuals.

One possible limitation of these studies is their reliance on self-reports of hostility and psychosocial factors. As noted earlier, consistent endorsement of similar items on separate inventories could contribute to the apparent correlations between distinct constructs. Common method variance does not account for the previously described association between Ho scores and frequency of hostile behaviors in the context of marital interactions. Thus, the apparent psychosocial vulnerability of hostile individuals may not be readily interpreted as simple method artifacts, but caution is appropriate.

This qualification notwithstanding, hostile persons apparently do not simply respond to interpersonal stressors with increased physiological reactivity. Their typical social environments may include a larger number of such stressors than environments of more agreeable individuals. Even if interpersonal stressors elicited equivalent physiological reactions in people with high and low Ho scores, the preponderance of stressful events could increase the risk of disease for hostile persons. This more taxing social environment associated with hostility suggests a possibly fruitful integration of models of hostility and health with the relatively separate literature on social relations and health (House, Landis, & Umberson, 1988). The independent studies on the health effects of hostility and social relations may reflect two sides of a single psychosocial process influencing disease.

The Transactional Model

The increased levels of interpersonal conflict and decreased levels of social support experienced by hostile individuals are probably not accidental. Given their typical beliefs and expectations about the intentions and behavior of others, it is understandable that hostile people are likely to behave in a disagreeable, antagonistic, or oppositional manner toward others. Such behaviors, in turn, are likely to elicit similar behaviors from the people they encounter and may also undermine potential sources of support. Once created, such a social environment is likely to confirm the hostile individual's cynical world view and increase the associated antagonistic tendencies. This reciprocal relationship between the cognitive and behavioral correlates of hostility and the social environment forms the basis of the transactional model of hostility and health (Smith, 1989; Smith & Pope, 1990).

The transactional model is an integration of the psychophysiological and psychosocial vulnerability models. From this perspective, the greater physiological arousal associated with hostility reflects the impact of two distinct classes of events: larger physiological responses to the ubiquitous and unavoidable interpersonal hassles experienced by both hostile and nonhostile people, as well as responses to the more frequent, prolonged, and severe interpersonal stresses and strains engendered by the social and cognitive correlates of hostility. Heightened physiological activity could also reflect the lower levels of otherwise ameliorative social support. Thus, hostile persons do not simply respond to the presence of interpersonal conflict and the absence of social support with physiological arousal. They create these unfavorable circumstances through their thoughts and actions. Once created, this social environment hypothetically has the dual maladaptive effects of exacerbating the psychophysiological correlates of hostility and maintaining—if not strengthening—the stress-engendering process.

To date, no direct tests of the transactional model have been reported. Although a variety of psychophysiological and psychosocial observations are consistent with this view, translating the model into research operations is a formidable challenge. The most valuable contribution to this approach may be its description of the active psychosomatic process, through which interacting features of individuals and social environments combine to hasten disease. Empirical tests of this approach are not impossible; however, and the emerging cognitive–social approach to personality (Bandura, 1986; Cantor, 1990) provides general models and specific techniques (e.g., Emmons, Diener, & Larsen, 1986) that are potentially useful in explicating these transactional aspects of hostile lives.

The Health-Behavior Model
A common assumption of the models described thus far is that stress physiology is the final common pathway linking hostility and health. Leiker and Hailey (1988) recently proposed a different model. They argued that hostile persons may be at increased risk of illness, at least in part, because of their daily habits. For example, these investigators found that high scores on the Ho scale were associated with reports of less physical activity, less self-care (e.g., dental hygiene and adequate sleep), and more frequent episodes of drinking and driving. Similar health-behavior correlates of the Ho scale have been reported by other investigators (Houston & Vavak, 1991), and other studies indicated that various measures of hostility are also associated with smoking and heavy alcohol consumption (Koskenvuo et al., 1988; Shekelle et al., 1983). Obviously, unhealthy habits such as these could contribute to the greater risk of disease among hostile persons.

The health behaviors examined in this area of research to date are not obviously interpersonal in nature. However, this view could easily incorporate more social health behaviors. For example, distrust of health professionals or a generally oppositional and cynical orientation might lead hostile persons to avoid or delay seeking medical treatment. Such behavior could be life threatening (e.g., failing to respond to early warning signs of cancer or the symptoms of an impending heart attack). Similar characteristics might contribute to poor adherence to prescribed treatments among hostile patients. An overtly antagonistic interpersonal style during interactions in medical settings could undermine the quality of health care received by hostile individuals. Thus, although it has not encompassed social processes to date, the health-behavior model might be fruitfully extended in this regard.

General Issues in Social Aspects of Hostility and Health

Our discussion thus far has illustrated the potential value of consideration of social contexts in two areas of research on hostility and health. An interpersonal perspective in construct validation provides a more complete empirical evaluation of measures intended to assess what is clearly a social construct. Although appropriately described as an individual-difference dimension, the prevailing nomological net surrounding hostility includes explicit ties to social cognition and interpersonal behavior. As a result, comprehensive validation research must include assessments in social contexts. Consideration of social contexts might also contribute to our understanding of mechanisms linking hostility and health. Results from the small number of studies available using the Ho scale are consistent with the psychophysiological reactivity model when relevant social stressors are used. Clarification of the hostile cognitive and behavioral style also highlights the likely health-relevant psychosocial correlates of this trait and suggests possible dynamic relationships between hostile persons and taxing social environments. A social perspective is similarly useful in heuristic extensions of the health-behavior model.

Some evidence indicates that the interpersonal approach may have further applications. Most obviously, correlations between hostility and aspects of the early family context could provide valuable information concerning the development of this risk factor (Houston & Vavak, 1991; Woodall & Matthews, 1989). If hostility proves to be a robust risk factor, then therapeutic interventions to reduce hostility could become an important addition to prevention efforts. Some studies indicate that interventions designed to alter maladaptive interpersonal behaviors and foster less combative social skills can reduce hostility and associated cardiovascular reactivity during taxing interactions (Ewart, Taylor, Kraemer, & Agras, 1984; Moon & Eisler, 1983).

The addition of social variables to epidemiological studies may increase the predictive utility of individual differences in hostility. Most descriptions of the effect of hostility on health use a person-by-person situation interactional framework (Endler & Magnusson, 1976). In response to certain classes of social situations, hostile people display responses that ultimately contribute to disease. By implication, hostility may be related to health outcomes in some contexts but not others. That is, social factors may moderate the impact of hostility on health. In contrast to the usual procedure in which only the effects of hostility are considered, the statistical interaction of hostility and aspects of the social environment may provide additional explanatory power (Matthews, 1983; Smith, 1989; Suarez & Williams, 1989).

Consideration of social contexts also provides interesting parallels between the hostility and health literature and recent developments in related animal research. For example, among male cynomolgus monkeys, dominant animals subjected to the chronic stress of repeated reorganization of their social groups develop coronary atherosclerosis more rapidly and extensively than do their subordinate counterparts. Furthermore, the individual–difference dimension of dominance–submission is unrelated to atherosclerosis in animals housed in stable social groups (Kaplan, Manuck, Adams, Weingard, & Clarkson, 1987; Kaplan, Manuck, Clarkson, Lusso, & Taub, 1982). Thus, a socially defined, stable individual-difference dimension interacts with features of the social environment to influence the initial development of cardiovascular disease. Furthermore, induction of an anger-like state in dogs through competition with other dogs for access to food has been found to precipitate myocardial ischemia among animals with partially occluded coronary arteries (Verrier, Hagestad, & Lown, 1986). Therefore, consideration of anger, hostility, and related social situations may help to explicate the potential influence of psychological factors on acute coronary events (Kamark & Jennings, 1991).

It is unfair to suggest that previous research on hostility and health has ignored interpersonal factors. That is clearly not the case, as many investigators have made important contributions by explicitly incorporating social variables. However, it is true that this area of research is heavily influenced by the strong individual-difference tradition in the study of personality and health. This particular personality characteristic requires a broader perspective. By increasing our attention to the social context of hostility, we may acquire a more complete understanding of the biopsycho*social* processes linking hostility and health.

References

Allred, K. D., & Smith, T. W. (in press). Social cognition in cynical hostility. *Cognitive Therapy and Research.*

Averill, J. R. (1982). *Anger and aggression: An essay on emotion.* New York: Springer-Verlag.

Bandura, A. (1986). *Social foundations of thought and action: A social cognitive theory.* Englewood Cliffs, NJ: Prentice-Hall.

Barefoot, J. C., Dahlstrom, W. G., & Williams, R. B., Jr. (1983). Hostility, CHD incidence, and total mortality: A 25-year follow-up study of 255 physicians. *Psychosomatic Medicine, 45,* 59–63.

Barefoot, J. C., Dodge, K. A., Peterson, B. L., Dahlstrom, W. G., & Williams, R. B., Jr. (1989). The Cook-Medley Hostility scale: Item content and ability to predict survival. *Psychosomatic Medicine, 51,* 46–57.

Blumenthal, J. A., Barefoot, J., Burg, M. M., & Williams, R. B., Jr. (1987). Psychological correlates of hostility among patients undergoing coronary angiography. *British Journal of Medical Psychology, 60,* 349–355.

Booth-Kewley, S., & Friedman, H. S. (1987). Psychological predictors of heart disease: A quantitative review. *Psychological Bulletin, 101,* 343–362.

Cantor, N. (1990). From thought to behavior: "Having" and "doing" in the study of personality and cognition. *American Psychologist, 45,* 735–750.

Carmody, T. P., Crossen, J. R., & Wiens, A. N. (1989). Hostility as a health risk factor: Relationships with neuroticism, Type A behavior, attentional focus, and interpersonal style. *Journal of Clinical Psychology, 45,* 754–762.

Christensen, A. J., & Smith, T. W. (1991). *Cynical hostility and cardiovascular reactivity during self-disclosure.* Manuscript submitted for publication.

Contrada, R. J., Jussim, L., Posluszny, D., & Bender, D. (1990, August). Comparison of three measurement models for the Cook-Medley Hostility scale. Paper presented at the annual convention of the American Psychological Association, Boston, MA.

Cook, W. W., & Medley, D. M. (1954). Proposed hostility and pharisaic-virtue scales for the MMPI. *Journal of Applied Psychology, 38,* 414–418.

Dembroski, T. M., MacDougall, J. M., Costa, P. T., Jr., & Grandits, G. A. (1989). Components of hostility as predictors of sudden death and myocardial infarction in the Multiple Risk Factor Intervention Trial. *Psychosomatic Medicine, 51,* 514–522.

Emmons, R. A., Diener, E., & Larsen, R. J. (1986). Choice and avoidance of everyday situations and affect congruence: Two models of reciprocal interactionism. *Journal of Personality and Social Psychology, 51,* 815–826.

Endler, N. S., & Magnusson, D. (Eds.). (1976). *Interactional psychology and personality.* New York: Wiley.

Engebretson, T. O., Matthews, K. A., & Scheier, M. F. (1989). Relations between anger expression and cardiovascular reactivity: Reconciling inconsistent findings through a matching hypothesis. *Journal of Personality and Social Psychology, 57,* 513–521.

Ewart, C. K., Taylor, C. B., Kraemer, H. C., & Agras, W. S. (1984). Reducing blood pressure reactivity during interpersonal conflict: Effects of marital communication training. *Behavior Therapy, 15,* 473–484.

Hardy, J. D., & Smith, T. W. (1988). Cynical hostility and vulnerability to disease: Social support, life stress, and physiological response to conflict. *Health Psychology, 7,* 447–459.

Hearn, M. D., Murray, D. M., & Luepker, R. V. (1989). Hostility, coronary heart disease, and total mortality: A 33-year follow-up study of university students. *Journal of Behavioral Medicine, 12,* 105–121.

Hecker, M. H. L., Chesney, M. A., Black, G. W., & Frautschi, N. (1988). Coronary-prone behaviors in the Western Collaborative Group Study. *Psychosomatic Medicine, 50,* 153–164.

House, J. S., Landis, K. R., & Umberson, D. (1988). Social relationships and health. *Science, 241,* 540–545.

Houston, B. K., & Kelley, K. E. (1989). Hostility in employed women: Relation to work and marital experiences, social support, stress, and anger expression. *Personality and Social Psychology Bulletin, 15,* 175–182.

Houston, B. K., & Vavak, C. R. (1991). Hostility: Developmental factors, psychosocial correlates, and health behaviors. *Health Psychology, 10,* 9–17.

Kagan, J. (1988). The meanings of personality predicates. *American Psychologist, 43,* 614–620.

Kamark, T. W., & Jennings, R. (1991). Biobehavioral factors in sudden cardiac death. *Psychosomatic Bulletin, 109,* 42–75.

Kamark, T. W., Manuck, S. B., & Jennings, J. R. (1980). Social support reduces cardiovascular reactivity to psychological challenge: A laboratory model. *Psychosomatic Medicine, 52,* 42–58.

Kaplan, J. R., Manuck, S. B., Clarkson, T. B., Lusso, F. M., & Taub, D. M. (1982). Social status, environment, and atherosclerosis in cynomolgus monkeys. *Arteriosclerosis, 2,* 359–368.

Kaplan, J. R., Manuck, S. B., Adams, M. R., Weingard, K. W., & Clarkson, T. B. (1987). Propramolol inhibits coronary atherosclerosis in behaviorally predisposed monkeys fed an atherogenic diet. *Circulation, 26,* 1364–1373.

Koskenvuo, M., Kapiro, J., Rose, R. J., Kesnaiemi, A., Sarnaa, S., Heikkila, K., & Langivanio, H. (1988). Hostility as a risk factor for mortality and ischemic heart disease in men. *Psychosomatic Medicine, 50,* 330–340.

Leiker, M., & Hailey, B. J. (1988). A link between hostility and disease: Poor health habits? *Behavioral Medicine,* 129–133.

Leon, G. R., Finn, S. E., Murray, D., & Bailey, J. M. (1988). The inability to predict cardiovascular disease from hostility scores of MMPI items related to Type A behavior. *Journal of Consulting and Clinical Psychology, 56,* 597–600.

Matthews, K. A. (1983). Assessment issues in coronary-prone behavior. In T. M. Dembroski, T. H. Schmidt, & G. Blumchen (Eds.), *Biobehavioral bases of coronary heart disease* (pp. 62–78). Basel, Switzerland: Karger.

Matthews, K. A. (1988). CHD and Type A behaviors: Update on and alternative to the Booth-Kewley and Friedmann quantitative review. *Psychological Bulletin, 104,* 373–380.

McCranie, E. W., Watkins, L. O., Brandsma, J. M., & Sisson, B. D. (1986). Hostility, coronary heart disease (CHD), incidence, and total mortality: Lack of association in a 25-year follow-up study of 478 physicians. *Journal of Behavioral Medicine, 9,* 119–125.

Megargee, E. I. (1985). The dynamics of aggression and their application to cardiovascular disorders. In M. A. Chesney & R. H. Rosenman (Eds.), *Anger and hostility in cardiovascular and behavioral disorders* (pp. 31–57). Washington, DC: Hemisphere.

Moon, J. R., & Eisler, R. M. (1983). Anger control: An experimental comparison of three behavioral treatments. *Behavior Therapy, 14,* 493–505.

Nicholls, J. G., Licht, B. G., & Pearl, R. A. (1982). Some dangers of using personality questionnaires to study personality. *Psychological Bulletin, 92,* 572–580.

Pennebaker, J. W., Colder, M., & Sharp, L. K. (1990). Accelerating the coping process. *Journal of Personality and Social Psychology, 58,* 528–537.

Pennebaker, J. W., Kiecolt-Glaser, J., & Glaser, R. (1988). Disclosure of traumas and immune function: Health implications for psychotherapy. *Journal of Consulting and Clinical Psychology, 56,* 239–245.

Pope, M. K., Smith, T. W., & Rhodewalt, F. (1990). Cognitive, behavioral, and affective correlates of the Cook and Medley Hostility scale. *Journal of Personality Assessment, 54,* 501–514.

Sallis, J. F., Johnson, C. C., Trevorrow, T. R., Kaplan, R. M., & Melbourne, F. H. (1987). The relationship between cynical hostility and blood pressure reactivity. *Journal of Psychosomatic Research, 31,* 111–116.

Shekelle, R. B., Gale, M., Ostfeld, A. M., & Paul, O. (1983). Hostility, risk of coronary heart disease, and mortality. *Psychosomatic Medicine, 45,* 109–114.

Smith, M. A., & Houston, B. K. (1987). Hostility, anger, expression, cardiovascular responsivity, and social support. *Biological Psychology, 24,* 39–48.

Smith, T. W. (1989). Interactions, transactions, and the Type A pattern: Additional avenues in the search for coronary-prone behavior. In A. W. Siegman & T. M. Dembroski (Eds.), *In search of coronary-prone behavior* (pp. 91–116). Hillsdale, NJ: Erlbaum.

Smith, T. W., & Allred, K. D. (1989). Blood pressure responses during social interaction in high and low cynically hostile males. *Journal of Behavioral Medicine, 12,* 135–143.

Smith, T. W., Allred, K. D., Morrison, C., & Carlson, S. (1989). Cardiovascular reactivity and interpersonal influence: Active coping in a social context. *Journal of Personality and Social Psychology, 56,* 209–218.

Smith, T. W., Baldwin, M., & Christensen, A. J. (1990). Interpersonal influence as active coping: Effects of task difficulty on cardiovascular reactivity. *Psychophysiology, 27,* 429–437.

Smith, T. W., & Brown, P. W. (in press). Cynical hostility, attempts to exert social control, and cardiovascular reactivity in married couples. *Journal of Behavioral Medicine.*

Smith, T. W., & Frohm, K. D. (1985). What's so unhealthy about hostility? Construct validity and psychosocial correlates of the Cook and Medley Ho scale. *Health Psychology, 4,* 503–520.

Smith, T. W., & Pope, M. K. (1990). Cynical hostility as a health risk. Current status and future directions. *Journal of Social Behavior and Personality, 5,* 77–88.

Smith, T. W., Pope, M. K., Sanders, J. D., Allred, K. D., & O'Keeffe, J. L. (1988). Cynical hostility at home and work: Psychosocial vulnerability across domains. *Journal of Research in Personality, 22,* 525–548.

Smith, T. W., Sanders, J. D., & Alexander, J. F. (1990). What does the Cook and Medley Hostility scale measure? Affect, behavior and attributions in the marital context. *Journal of Personality and Social Psychology, 58,* 699–708.

Spielberger, C. D., Johnson, E. H., Russel, S. F., Crane, R. J., Jacobs, G. A., & Worden, T. J. (1985). The experience and expression of anger. Construction and validation of an anger expression scale. In

M. A. Chesney & R. H. Rosenman (Eds.), *Anger and hostility in cardiovascular and behavioral disorders* (pp. 5–30). Washington, DC: Hemisphere.

Suarez, E. C., & Williams, R. B., Jr. (1989). Situational determinants of cardiovascular and emotional reactivity in high and low hostile men. *Psychosomatic Medicine, 51*, 404–418.

Suls, J., & Wan, C. K. (1990, April). *Hostility and cardiovascular reactivity: A meta-analytic progress report.* Paper presented at the annual meeting of the Society for Behavioral Medicine, Chicago, IL.

Verrier, R. L., Hagestad, E. L., & Lown, B. (1986). Delayed myocardial ischemia induced by anger. *Circulation, 75,* 249–254.

Williams, R. B., Jr., Barefoot, J. C., & Shekelle, R. B. (1985). The health consequences of hostility. In M. A. Chesney & R. H. Rosenman (Eds.), *Anger and hostility in cardiovascular and behavioral disorders* (pp. 173–185). Washington, DC: Hemisphere.

Woodall, K. L., & Matthews, K. A. (1989). Familial environment associated with Type A behaviors and psychophysiological responses to stress in children. *Health Psychology, 8,* 403–426.

CHAPTER 4

Anger and Cardiovascular Health

Judith M. Siegel

T he relationship between emotions and health is central to the field of health psychology. Anger, in particular, has been studied extensively because of its potential prognostic significance for cardiovascular disease (CVD). The purposes of this chapter are to provide an overview of the literature related to anger and cardiovascular disease, describe the development of an inventory that assesses multiple dimensions of anger, discuss applications of the anger inventory in two populations, and make suggestions for future research concerned with anger and cardiovascular health.

In the inaugural issue of *Psychosomatic Medicine*, Alexander (1939) hypothesized that suppressed anger was related to elevated blood pressure (BP). According to Alexander, the person with elevated BP is caught in a psychodynamic conflict of passiveness and hostile impulses. A chronic tension results when these impulses are repressed. As acute elevations of BP are normally associated with rage, it followed that chronic inhibition of rage could lead to hypertension.

There is a body of cross-sectional data, both laboratory and community-based, which suggests that conflicts with anger are characteristic of the hypertensive (Baer, Collins, Bourianoff, & Ketchel, 1979; Barefoot, Dahlstrom, & Williams 1983; Dimsdale et al., 1986; Esler et al., 1977; Goldstein, Edelberg, Meier, & Davis, 1988; Harburg et al., 1973; Harburg, Blakelock,

The author gratefully acknowledges the contribution of Eric M. Cottington to the research on anger, anxiety, and hypertension.

& Roeper, 1979; Harris, Sokolow, Carpenter, Friedman, & Hunt, 1953; Hokanson, 1961a, 1961b; Hokanson & Burgess, 1962; Holmes, 1966; Kalis, Harris, Bennett, & Sokolow, 1961; Kalis, Harris, Sokolow, & Carpenter, 1957). These studies do not clearly show, however, that the mode of anger expression accounts for the relationship nor can they rule out the possibility that anger may be secondary to hypertension, either as an emotional response to the diagnosis or as a manifestation of changes in physiology, or both.

To date, two longitudinal studies have examined the relation between anger and BP. The Israeli Ischemic Heart Disease Study (Kahn, Medalie, Neufeld, Riss, & Goldbourt, 1972) showed that self-reports of brooding and restraining retaliation in response to being hurt by one's superior were related to incidence of hypertension among 10,000 initially normotensive male civil service workers. In a study of college men, themes of dominance and aggression in response to certain Thematic Apperception Test (TAT) protocols were predictive of elevated BP 20 years later (McClelland, 1979). The relationship persisted when controlling for college BP level.

The Type A individual, who is thought to be at elevated risk for coronary heart disease (CHD), is characterized by extremes of competitiveness–achievement-striving, aggressiveness–hostility, and speed–impatience (Rosenman, 1978). Studies that look at aspects of the behavioral pattern as predictors of CHD make evident the importance of the anger–hostility component. Jenkins (1966), reporting on data from the Western Collaborative Group Study, found that silent myocardial infarction cases scored higher on potential for hostility than did controls, as assessed by interviewers' ratings. Potential for hostility is based on voice cues and on facial and postural gestures exhibited during the interview. Further analysis of data from the Western Collaborative Group Study showed that of seven Type A interview items that were capable of discriminating cases from controls, four were related to anger–hostility (Matthews, Glass, Rosenman, & Bortner, 1977). In the prospective Multiple Risk Factor Intervention Trial (MRFIT), hostility toward the interviewer during the Type A interview was predictive of CHD incidence among younger men (age 47 or less; Dembroski, MacDougall, Costa, & Grandits, 1989). Global Type A was not predictive of CHD in this population of high-coronary-risk men.

There are data showing that anger is related to CHD independently of Type A behavior. In the Framingham population, *anger-in* (not discussing or showing anger) was related to CHD incidence in both men and women, and this association was independent of the association of Type A behavior and CHD incidence (Haynes, Feinleib, & Kannel, 1980). Williams et al. (1980) administered the Type A interview and a battery of self-report instruments, including the MMPI, to their sample of coronary angiography patients. Previous research (Cook & Medley, 1954) identified a subset of the MMPI items as a measure of hostility. Williams and colleagues reported that gender, the MMPI hostility score, and behavior-type classification (A or B), in that order, were the strongest (and independent) predictors of degree of atherosclerosis. Additional analyses showed that the MMPI items indicative of chronic hate and anger were the most significant discriminators.

In a cohort of medical students, scores on the Cook-Medley inventory were predictive of CHD incidence (myocardial infarction, angina, and CHD death), as well as mortality from all causes, after adjusting for other CHD risk factors (Barefoot, Dahlstrom, & Williams, 1983). Similarly, Shekelle, Gale, Ostfeld, and Paul (1983) found that scores on the Cook-Medley inventory were related to 20-year mortality from CHD and to total mortality among initially disease-free employees of the Western Electric Company. However, the relationship with CHD was reduced to nonsignificance when including other CHD risk factors in the multivariate analyses. Three other prospective studies failed to confirm a relation between scores on the Cook-Medley inventory and subsequent health status (Hearn, Murray, & Luepker, 1989; Leon, Finn, & Bailey, 1986; McCranie, Watkins, Brandsma, & Sisson, 1986). Although there is no readily apparent explanation for these discrepancies, analyses on subsets of items from the Cook-Medley inventory indicate that certain subsets of items are more strongly related to health outcomes than others (Barefoot, Dodge, Peterson, Dahlstrom, & Williams, 1989). Additionally, neither anger-in nor *anger-out* (derived from an interview) were related to cardiovascular disease after a 35-year follow up of a college population (Russek, King, Russek, & Russek, 1990).

Using a measure of suspiciousness, Factor L, of the Sixteen Personality Factor Questionnaire (16PF), which is conceptually similar to the Cook-Medley inventory, Barefoot et al. (1987) found that suspiciousness predicted 15-year mortality risk in a cohort of men and women. The association remained significant when controlling for age, sex, physician's rating of functional health, smoking, cholesterol, and alcohol intake. Other studies of the behavioral correlates of heart disease also support the importance of hostility. For example, in a prospective investigation of Swedish workers, self-reports of hostility when faced with delay was predictive of all deaths, myocardial infarctions, and ulcers (Theorell, Lind, & Floderus, 1975).

Taken together, the data are impressive for anger–hostility playing a role in cardiovascular diseases. Although anger has been studied in connection with other diseases less often, a meta-analytic view of the "disease-prone" personality identified depression and, secondarily, anger–hostility as central to pathogenic processes (Friedman & Booth-Kewley, 1987). Furthermore, there is suggestive evidence that anger may contribute to either the etiology or progression of cancer. An early writing on psychosocial characteristics of cancer patients identified the inability to express hostile feelings as characteristic of people with cancer (LeShan, 1959). The theme of poor emotional outlets is consistent in the cancer literature, yet not all studies have specified whether anger–hostility is the emotion being contained. A longitudinal study of survival time in metastatic breast cancer showed that short-term survivors (less than 1 year) were lower in hostility levels than long-term survivors and, in general, matched the profile of the individual who has difficulty with emotional expression (Derogatis, Abeloff, & Melisaratos, 1979).

The Multidimensional Anger Inventory

The Multidimensional Anger Inventory (MAI) (Siegel, 1986) was developed to fill a need for a psychometrically sound anger inventory that simultaneously assessed the dimensions of anger that appear relevant for CVD. This inventory was designed to assess the following dimensions of anger: frequency, duration, magnitude, mode of expression, hostile outlook, and range of anger-eliciting situations. Prior research supports the importance of both mode of expression and hostile outlook for CVD. In addition to these two dimensions, a study that used discriminant functions analyses to define a pool of items that would discriminate hypertensives from normotensives implicated magnitude of anger and duration of anger response (Baer, Collins, Bourianoff, & Ketchel, 1979). On a more conceptual level, Buss (1961) and Alexander (1939) contended that hypertensives become angry more often than their normotensive counterparts because of a greater sensitivity to anger stimuli. Thus, magnitude, duration, and frequency were also hypothesized to be relevant dimensions. Last, an inspection of existing anger or hostility inventories illustrated that almost all of the items could be classified into the dimensions previously mentioned with the exception of a group of items that seemed to assess range of anger-eliciting situations. Although no previous investigation has specifically linked range of situations to CVD, the inclusion of this dimension would provide a more comprehensive measure of anger.

Questionnaire Development

The Multidimensional Anger Inventory (MAI) (Siegel, 1986) included 38 items that were selected on the basis of face validity to measure the following dimensions of anger:

frequency, duration, magnitude, range of anger arousing situations, mode of expression, and hostile outlook. Some of the items were taken from existing anger inventories and were rephrased as necessary to provide a consistent format to the MAI. Other items were conceptually based and written specifically for the MAI.

The MAI was administered to 198 college students (74 men, 124 women) and 288 male factory workers. To determine whether the proposed dimensions of the MAI were supported by factor analysis, the items were subjected to a principal-component factor analysis with varimax rotation. All of the scale items, excluding the mode-of-expression items, were included in one factor analysis. The mode-of-expression items were examined in a separate factor analysis because it was hypothesized that mode of expression may itself include several dimensions. Factor analyses of inventory responses in these two populations yielded highly similar solutions with factors of anger arousal, hostile outlook, and range of anger-eliciting situations. The anger-arousal factor, which accounted for 64% and 71% of the variance in the two populations, respectively, included items describing the frequency, intensity, and duration of the anger response. The analyses showed that these dimensions (frequency, intensity, and duration) were most adequately described as a single anger-arousal factor. Consistent with the initial conceptualization, hostile outlook and range of anger-eliciting situations emerged as orthogonal factors to the anger-arousal factor.

The mode of anger expression was best described in two dimensions: anger-in and anger-out. Of the other three hypothesized mode-of-expression dimensions (*brood, guilt,* and *anger discuss*), only the brood items loaded greater than 0.40 on any factor when data from the two populations were combined. These data suggest that guilt may not be a valid dimension of anger, but reflects instead the consequences of anger. Alternatively, it might be argued that the duration items, the guilt items, or the anger-discuss items did not emerge as separate factors because of the few items designed to tap these dimensions. Overall, the similarity of the factor structure in two populations that differ in age, geographic location, sex composition, and life-style supports the reliability of the MAI factors. The MAI items and the factor structure for the combined population are presented in Table 1.

Detailed information concerning the reliability and validity of the MAI can be found elsewhere (Siegel, 1986). Briefly, the inventory demonstrates moderate test-retest reliability (0.75) over a 3- to 4-week interval, high internal-consistency reliability ($\alpha = 0.84$ and 0.89, for the two samples), and adequate validity. Validation was provided in two ways. First, significant correlations were found between the MAI dimensions and the

TABLE 1
Dimensions of the Multidimensional Anger Inventory

Item

Anger arousal

1	I tend to get angry more frequently than most people.
6	It is easy to make me angry.
9	Something makes me angry almost every day.
10	I often feel angrier than I think I should.
14	I am surprised at how often I feel angry.
17	At times, I feel angry for no specific reason.
22	When I get angry, I stay angry for hours.
26	I get so angry, I feel like I might lose control.

Range of anger-eliciting situations

30b	I get angry when people are unfair.
30c	I get angry when something blocks my plans.
30d	I get angry when I am delayed.
30e	I get angry when someone embarrasses me.
30f	I get angry when I have to take orders from someone less capable than I.
30h	I get angry when I do something stupid.
30i	I get angry when I am not given credit for something I have done.

Hostile outlook

13	Some of my friends have habits that annoy me very much.
21	People can bother me just by being around.
30f	I get angry when I have to take orders from someone less capable than I.
30g	I get angry when I have to work with incompetent people.

Anger-in

3	I harbor grudges that I don't tell anyone about.
4	I try to get even when I am angry with someone.
12	When I am angry with someone, I take it out on whomever is around.
19	Even after I have expressed my anger, I have trouble forgetting about it.
20	When I hide my anger from others, I think about it for a long time.

Anger-out

7	When I am angry with someone, I let that person know.
29	It's difficult for me to let people know I am angry. (Reverse scored)

Note. From Chesney and Roseman's (1985) *Anger and hostility in cardiovascular and behavioral disorders.* Copyright by Hemisphere Publ. Corp. Reprinted with permission.

scores derived from the other inventories that were selected to measure a specific dimension. Second, the correlations between the MAI scales and conceptually dissimilar dimensions derived from other inventories were lower than the correlations with conceptually similar dimensions.

Applications With the Multidimensional Anger Inventory

Empirical data concerning the MAI and its relation with other variables are reported for two dissimilar populations: middle-aged, male factory workers and adolescent girls. As noted earlier, Alexander (1939) hypothesized that hypertensives could be characterized psychodynamically by conflicting impulses of passive dependency and aggressive hostility. He observed from case studies of hypertensives that "chronic, inhibited, aggressive hostile impulses, which always occur in connection with anxiety, have a specific influence upon the fluctuations of the blood pressure" (p. 175). Almost 30 years later, data published from a 20-year prospective study showed self-reports of nervousness were predictive of hypertension (Paffenbarger, Thorne, & Wing, 1968). This application examined the direct and interactive effects of anxiety and anger on BP.

Study participants were Caucasian men between the ages of 40 and 65 years, employed at a particular worksite for at least 10 continuous years. The only information available regarding those who were randomly selected, yet did not agree to participate, was their age and years of employment. No differences between the participants and nonparticipants were found for these variables. The data collection consisted of (a) an interview assessing demographic information, occupational history, medical history, and health-related behavior; and (b) actual measurements of height and weight, hearing loss (an audiogram), and BP. Six resting BP measurements were made using the standardized procedures.

A questionnaire packet, including a battery of psychological inventories, was distributed at the end of the data-collection session. Each subject was instructed to complete the questionnaires at home and return them at work. Of the 366 men who participated in the data-collection session, 288 also completed the questionnaires. The men who returned the questionnaires and the men who did not were comparable in terms of age, alcohol consumption, body mass index (a measure of weight that takes height into account), education, family history of hypertension, and diastolic BP. However, those men who withdrew from the study were more likely to be single and not widowed, separated, or divorced, than those who did not withdraw.

The measures of anger and anxiety were included in the questionnaire packet. Anger was assessed by the 38-item MAI. Anxiety-proneness was determined by the A-trait scale of the Spielberger State-Trait Anxiety Inventory (STAI) (Spielberger, Gorsuch, & Lushene, 1970). The STAI A-trait scale consists of 20 statements that ask people to describe how they generally feel.

The main and interactive effects of anger and anxiety on diastolic BP were examined. All analyses were performed excluding men currently taking antihypertensive medications ($n = 47$), to control for potential personality changes introduced by knowledge of disease status or the drugs themselves. Stepwise multiple linear regression tested the strength of the associations between diastolic BP, the five MAI anger scales, and trait anxiety, controlling for the known risk factors for hypertension (body mass index, cigarette smoking, alcohol consumption, and family history of hypertension). The risk factors, anxiety, and the specific anger dimension were entered into the model on the first step, and the appropriate anxiety–anger dimension product term was entered on the second step.

Neither anxiety nor any of the anger dimensions were significantly related to diastolic BP, controlling for relevant risk factors. However, anxiety significantly modified the relationship between diastolic BP and both hostile outlook and anger-in. The interactions between anxiety and both anger arousal and the range of anger-producing situations approached statistical significance.

To understand the direction of the significant interactions better, regression lines predicting blood pressure from anxiety and anger were plotted, modeling a procedure

TABLE 2

Multiple Linear Regression Coefficients for the Interactive Effects of Anxiety and the Anger Dimensions on Diastolic Blood Pressure of Middle-Aged, Male Factory Workers

Interaction Term (Anxiety and . . .)	Regression Coefficient	Standard Error
Anger arousal	0.016	0.009
Range of anger-producing situations	0.021	0.011
Hostile outlook	0.034*	0.017
Anger-in	0.028*	0.013
Anger-out	0.014	0.037

Note. All coefficients were derived from models with the risk factors, anxiety, and anger terms entered on an earlier step as main effects. Those taking antihypertensive medication were excluded.
* $p < .05$

used by Roth and Holmes (1985). Values that were one standard deviation above and below the mean for the anxiety and anger variables were entered into a regression equation that included the interaction term. This produced four predicted values for diastolic BP. These values were plotted, and separate regression lines were drawn for the high- and low-anxiety groups. Among men reporting high anxiety, a more hostile outlook was associated with higher diastolic BP. However, among those with low-trait anxiety, a more hostile outlook was associated with lower diastolic BP. Suppressed anger was not associated with diastolic BP among those men with high-trait anxiety, but was associated with lower diastolic BP among men who reported low-trait anxiety. Marginally significant interactions suggest that higher anger arousal and range of situations were associated with higher BP if the men were above average in anxiety.

The data do not support the hypothesis that suppressed hostility (anger-in dimension) is related to higher BP. A consideration of the interactive effects of anger and anxiety weakly conforms with Alexander's (1939) suggestion that suppressed hostility in combination with anxiety is predictive of BP. Specifically, a significant anger-in by anxiety interaction indicates a negative relationship between anger-in and blood pressure among those low in anxiety. In other words, lower pressure was associated with anger-in if the respondent was also low in anxiety.

The lowest prevalence of hypertension in this study, 17%, was among men who were low in anxiety and high in anger-out. These data indirectly support Alexander's hypothesis in that it appears to be beneficial for BP to express anger outwardly if the anger expression is not accompanied by anxiety. In a similar vein, data from a community study concerning coping responses to hypothetical situations of arbitrary frustration showed that the pattern of anger-out and no guilt was associated with the lowest prevalence of hypertension in five of eight comparisons (Harburg et al., 1973). Although we cannot directly equate our measure of low-trait anxiety with Harburg's measure of lack of guilt in response to anger directed outward, the findings from our two studies are consistent.

The second application with the MAI was a study of factors influencing the physical and mental health of adolescents. Clinical accounts have described adolescence as a period of turmoil, identity confusion, and stress (Freud, 1958; Erikson, 1950). In contrast, empirical studies have cast doubt on the notion that adolescence is inevitably stormy and instead have emphasized the continuity of development from childhood through adulthood (Weiner, 1985). These approaches converge, however, in their recognition that adolescence is a period of great change: physical, cognitive, and social. Early adolescence, in particular, has been characterized as a developmental transition because of the significant changes that occur in several aspects of development (Petersen, 1986).

The data examine the relations of stressful life circumstances, self-esteem, and anger to physical and mental health. In other analyses of these data, we showed that circumstances rated negatively were associated with poor physical and mental health (Siegel & Brown, 1988). Prospective analyses, controlling for initial physical or mental health status, revealed that negative circumstances led to reports of greater illness symptoms or depressed mood only when positive circumstances were low. The prior analyses did not include self-esteem or anger. Although there is considerable research support for a relation between self-esteem and depression (Tennen & Herzberger, 1987), there is little known about how self-esteem might be related to physical health (in this case, reports of symptoms and illnesses).

The participants were 364 adolescent girls, ages 10 to 17 years. The sample was largely Caucasian and of middle to upper social class. Data were collected during regularly scheduled classes toward the end of the spring semester. Although the study design was prospective, anger was assessed only once. Thus, the analyses reported here are cross-sectional.

Stress was measured by the Feel Bad Scale, which consists of 20 commonly occurring, stress-provoking circumstances that were generated through interviews with preadolescents (Lewis, Siegel, & Lewis, 1984). Students indicated whether each of the 20 circumstances had occurred since school had started the previous fall. They rated the circumstances they had experienced as being either "good" or "bad," and their scale consisted of the number of negative circumstances they endorsed.

Depression was assessed by the Center for Epidemiologic Studies Depression Scale (CES-D). The CES-D is designed to measure depressive symptomatology in the general population and emphasizes the affective component of the depressed mood (Radloff, 1977). The CES-D uses 4-point scales to assess the frequency with which each of 20 symptoms was experienced during the previous week. Anger was measured with the MAI and self-esteem was assessed with the Rosenberg Self-Esteem Scale (Rosenberg, 1965). The latter included 10 self-descriptive statements to which the adolescent indicated the extent of agreement. Five were phrased positively (reflecting high self-esteem), and five were phrased negatively. The latter five were reverse scored, and the extent of agreement was added up across the 10 items. Physical health was measured by the Seriousness of Illness Rating Scale (SIRS; Wyler, Masuda, & Holmes, 1968, 1970). In the present study, 39 of the 126 SIRS items were included. Items of questionable health concern (e.g., dandruff), items irrelevant to adolescents (e.g., menopause), items extremely unlikely to occur during adolescence (e.g., heart attack), and items measuring psychosomatic conditions (e.g., anxiety reaction) were eliminated.

To avoid capitalizing on chance findings, the number of analyses was limited here by using the total MAI score as the measure of anger. The dimension scores were not computed in this sample. The relations among the variables were examined in two ways. First, simple correlations were computed between the health measures (CESD, SIRS) and anger, self-esteem, and stress. Second, partial correlations were computed such that the variance attributable to the latter two variables (e.g., self-esteem and stress) was removed from the correlations between anger and the two health measures. This procedure was then repeated for self-esteem and for stress.

The six zero-order correlations were all statistically significant, ranging from .22 for anger with illness and $-.22$ for self-esteem with illness to $-.58$ for self-esteem with depression. Thus, anger, self-esteem, and stressful life circumstances each shared some common variance with the measures of both mental health and physical health. The partial correlations showed that anger, self-concept, and stress each retained a significant relation with depression, removing the common variance with the other two indices. For physical illness, however, only the partial correlation with stress was significant (r (208) $= .24$, $p<.0001$). It appears that the relation of anger to physical health in this sample is, in part, a function of the variance that both anger and physical health share with the accumulation of stressful circumstances.

Future Research

The body of literature reviewed in this chapter suggests that anger–hostility plays a role in cardiovascular disorders. Empirical data using the MAI highlight the value of looking at anger in the context of other social-psychological variables. Similar to the argument put forward regarding the study of stress (Pearlin, 1989), anger does not occur in a vacuum, but is influenced by the personal characteristics of the individual and the situational context in which he or she operates. Thus, it is important in future research to look at the person's position in the surrounding social structures, as well as other coping resources that he or she may use. Such an approach may help clarify apparently contradictory findings regarding the role of hostility and health. Hostility may influence health

TABLE 3

Correlation Coefficients of Anger, Self-Esteem, and Stressful Circumstances With Depressed Mood and Illness Symptoms of Adolescent Girls

	Zero-Order Correlation		Partial Correlation	
	Depressed Mood	Illness Symptoms	Depressed Mood	Illness Symptoms
Anger	.41 ***	.22 ***	.16 *	.07
Self-esteem	− .58 ***	− .22 **	− .48 ***	− .10
Stressful circumstances	.37 ***	.32 ***	.20 **	.24 ***

Note. The partial correlations remove the variance attributed to the other variables in the left-hand column.
* $p < .05$
** $p < .01$
*** $p < .001$

status only when other personal resources (e.g., self-esteem and positive life circumstances) are lacking.

One coping resource that is central to much of the writing in this volume is reliance on social networks. There are limited empirical data, but abundant hypothetical notions for why and how support and anger might be related. In terms of empirical evidence, individuals scoring high on the Cook-Medley hostility inventory rated their supports as less satisfying and fewer than did low scorers (Smith & Frohm, 1985). In a study of factory workers, MAI scale scores were differentially and positively related to reports of low foreman, family, and coworker support (Cottington, 1984).

When considering how anger and social support might be related, it is useful to review findings from a community survey on anger (Averill, 1982). The target of anger was human in 89% of the instances cited by Averill's respondents, suggesting that anger is an interpersonal emotion. Certainly, anger is directed at strangers sometimes, but the majority of anger is probably targeted at people in our social networks. Therefore, being part of a social network may actually increase the odds of being the focus of anger as well. Averill's data also showed that anger is experienced as overwhelmingly negative, a finding consistent with Berkowitz's recent theorizing on the formation and regulation of anger (Berkowitz, 1990). Because the key aspect of social support is thought to be its positive emotional function, support may be uniquely effective in reducing some of the negative affect associated with anger. This may be the case even when the network member is also the target of anger. Furthermore, support providers can often aid the angered person in deciding on a course of action. The high average intensity of angry feelings (6.7 on a 10-point scale in Averill's survey) increases the probability that some action will follow anger arousal (Berkowitz, 1990).

Perhaps of greatest relevance to cardiovascular health are the implications of the supportiveness of the social network of the habitually angry person. Habitual anger is usually referred to as hostility and has alternately been conceptualized as the attitudinal parameter of anger (Buss, 1961; Siegel, 1986). The Cook-Medley hostility inventory and the hostile outlook scale of the MAI assess this dimension of anger. Hypotheses about the relation of hostility to social support include, first, that the hostile person has fewer social ties, in part because hostile people may not be viewed as attractive by others. Second, the hostile person may have less supportive social ties—his or her mistrustful attitude may keep others at a distance. Third, the hostile person may perceive others as less supportive. We know, for example, that Type A individuals tend to view the world as a competitive and unfriendly place. And last, the hostile person might actually cause others to be less supportive because interacting with a hostile person could instill negative affect in others.

In outlining these possibilities, the implied assumption is that anger influences one's ability to establish and maintain social ties. Equally plausible, however, is the notion that the quantity and quality of social ties play a role in the development of hostility. For example, there is evidence that angry and hostile children come from families with low supportiveness and little interpersonal involvement (Woodall & Matthews, 1989). Future study will benefit from the use of research designs and analytic techniques that can accommodate the potentially bidirectional relation between anger and other psychological variables.

References

Alexander, F. (1939). Emotional factors in essential hypertension: Presentation of tentative hypothesis. *Psychosomatic Medicine, 1,* 173–179.

Averill, J. R. (1982). *Anger and aggression: An essay on emotion.* New York: Springer-Verlag.

Baer, P. E., Collins, F. H., Bourianoff, G. G., & Ketchel M. F. (1979). Assessing personality factors in essential hypertension with a brief self report instrument. *Psychosomatic Medicine, 4,* 321–330.

Barefoot, J. C., Dahlstrom, W. G., & Williams, R. B., Jr. (1983). Hostility, CHD incidence and total mortality: A 25-year follow-up study of 255 physicians. *Psychosomatic Medicine, 45,* 59–63.

Barefoot, J. C., Dodge, K. A, Peterson, B. L., Dahlstron, W. G., & Williams, R. B., Jr. (1989). The Cook-Medley Hostility scale: Item content and ability to predict survival. *Psychosomatic Medicine, 51*, 46–57.

Barefoot, J. C., Stiegler, I. C., Nowlin, J. B., Peterson, B. L., Haney, T. L., & Williams, R. B., Jr. (1987). Suspiciousness, health, and mortality: A follow-up study of 500 older adults. *Psychosomatic Medicine, 49*, 450–457.

Berkowitz, L. (1990). On the formation and regulation of anger and aggression. *American Psychologist, 45*, 494–503.

Buss, A. H. (1961). *The psychology of aggression.* New York: John Wiley.

Cook, W. W., & Medley, D. M. (1954). Proposed hostility and pharisaic-virtue scales for the MMPI. *Journal of Applied Psychology, 38*, 414–418.

Cottington, E. M. (1984). Occupational stress, psychosocial modifiers, and blood pressure in a blue-collar population. *Dissertation Abstracts International, 44*, 2387B. (University MicroFilms No. 44)

Dembroski, T. M., MacDougall, J. M., Costa, P. T., Jr., & Grandits, G. A. (1989). Components of hostility as predictors of sudden death and myocardial infarction in the Multiple Risk Factor Intervention Trial. *Psychosomatic Medicine, 51*, 514–522.

Derogatis, L. R., Abeloff, M. D., & Melisaratos, N. (1979). Psychological coping mechanisms and survival time in metastatic breast cancer. *Journal of the American Medical Association, 242*, 1504–1508.

Dimsdale, J. E., Pierce, C., Schoenfeld, D., Brown, A., Zusman, R., & Graham, R. (1986). Suppressed anger and blood pressure: The effects of race, sex, social class, obesity, and age. *Psychosomatic Medicine, 48*, 430–436.

Erikson, E. H. (1950). *Childhood and society.* New York: Norton.

Esler, M., Julius, S, Zweifler, A., Randall, O., Harburg, E., Gardiner, H., & De Quattro, V. (1977). Mild high-renin essential hypertension: Neurogenic human hypertension? *New England Journal of Medicine, 296*, 405–411.

Freud, A. (1958). Adolescence. *Psychoanalytical Study of the Child, 13*, 255–278. .

Friedman, H. S., & Booth-Kewley, S. (1987). The "disease-prone personality": Meta-analytic view of the construct. *American Psychologist, 42*, 539–555.

Goldstein, H. S., Edelberg, R., Meier, C. F., & Davis, L. (1988). Relationship of resting blood pressure and heart rate to experienced anger and expressed anger. *Psychosomatic Medicine, 50*, 321–329.

Harburg, E., Erfurt, J. C., Hauenstein, L. S., Chape, C., Schull, W. J., & Schork, M. A. (1973). Socio-ecological stress, suppressed hostility, skin color, and black-white male blood pressure: Detroit. *Psychosomatic Medicine, 35*, 276–296.

Harburg, E., Blakelock, E. H., & Roeper, P. J. (1979). Resentful and reflective coping with arbitrary authority and blood pressure: Detroit. *Psychosomatic Medicine, 41*, 189–202.

Harris, R. E., Sokolow, M., Carpenter, L. G., Friedman, M., & Hunt, S. P. (1953). Response to psychologic stress in persons who are potentially hypertensive. *Circulation, 7*, 874–879.

Haynes, S. G., Feinleib, M., & Kannel, W. B. (1980). The relationship of psychosocial factors to coronary heart disease in the Framingham study. III. Eight-year incidence of coronary heart disease. *American Journal of Epidemiology, 111*, 37–58.

Hearn, M. D., Murray, D. M., & Leupker, R. V. (1989). Hostility, coronary heart disease, and total mortality: A 33-year follow-up study of university students. *Journal of Behavioral Medicine, 12,* 105–121.

Hokanson, J. E., (1961a). The effects of frustration and anxiety on overt aggression. *Journal of Abnormal Psychology, 62,* 346–351.

Hokanson, J. E., (1961b). Vascular and psychogalvanic effects of experimentally aroused anger. *Journal of Personality, 29,* 30–39.

Hokanson, J. E., & Burgess, M. (1962). The effects of status, type of frustration, and aggression on vascular processes. *Journal of Abnormal and Social Psychology, 65,* 232–237.

Holmes, D. S. (1966). Effects of overt aggression on level of physiological arousal. *Journal of Personality and Social Psychology, 4,* 189–194.

Jenkins, C. D. (1966). Components of the coronary-prone behavior pattern: Their relation to silent myocardial infarction and blood lipids. *Journal of Chronic Diseases, 19,* 599–609.

Kahn, H. A., Medalie, J. H., Neufeld, H. N., Riss, E., & Goldbourt, U. (1972). The incidence of hypertension and associated factors: The Israeli ischemic heart disease study. *American Heart Journal, 84,* 171–182.

Kalis, B. L., Harris, R. E., Bennett, L. F., & Sokolow, M. (1961). Personality and life history factors in persons who are potentially hypertensive. *Journal of Nervous and Mental Diseases, 132,* 457–468.

Kalis, B. L., Harris, R. E., Sokolow, M., & Carpenter, L. G. (1957). Response to psychological stress in patients with essential hypertension. *American Heart Journal, 53,* 572–578.

Leon, G. R., Finn, S. E., & Bailey, J. M. (1986). The inability to predict cardiovascular disease from MMPI special scales related to Type A patterns. *Psychosomatic Medicine, 49,* 205.

LeShan, L. L. (1959). Psychological states as factors in the development of malignant disease: A critical review. *Journal of the National Cancer Institute, 22,* 1–18.

Lewis, C. E., Siegel, J. M., & Lewis, M. A. (1984). Feeling bad: Exploring sources of distress among pre-adolescent children. *American Journal of Public Health, 74,* 117–122.

Matthews, K. A., Glass, D. C., Rosenman, R. H., & Bortner, R. W. (1977). Competitive drive, Pattern A, and coronary heart disease: A further analysis of some data from the Western Collaborative Group Study. *Journal of Chronic Disease, 30,* 489–498.

McClelland, D. C., (1979). Inhibited power motive and high blood pressure in men. *Journal of Abnormal Psychology, 88,* 182–190.

McCranie, E., Watkins, L., Brandsma, J., & Sisson, B. (1986). Hostility, CHD incidence, and total mortality: Lack of association in a 25-year follow-up study of 478 physicians. *Journal of Behavioral Medicine, 9,* 119–125.

Paffenbarger, R. S., Jr., Thorne, M. C., & Wing, A. L. (1968). Chronic disease in former college students. VIII. Characteristics in youth predisposing to hypertension in later years. *American Journal of Epidemiology, 88,* 25–32.

Pearlin, L. I. (1989). The sociological study of stress. *Journal of Health and Social Behavior, 30,* 241–343.

Petersen, A. C. (1986). *Early adolescence: A critical developmental transition?* Paper presented at the annual meeting of the American Educational Research Association, San Francisco, CA.

Radloff, L. S. (1977). The CES-D Scale: A self report depression scale for research in the general population. *Applied Psychological Measurement, 1,* 385–401.

Rosenberg, M. (1965). *Society and the adolescent self-image*. Princeton, NJ: Princeton University Press.

Rosenman, R. H. (1978). The interview method of assessment of the coronary-prone behavior pattern. In T. M. Dembroski et al. (Eds.), *Coronary-prone behavior*. New York: Springer-Verlag.

Roth, D. L., & Holmes, D. S. (1985). Influence of physical fitness in determining the impact of stressful life events on physical and psychologic health. *Psychosomatic Medicine, 47*, 164–173.

Russek, L. G., King, S. H., Russek, S. J., & Russek, H. I. (1990). The Harvard Mastery of Stress Study 35-year follow-up: Prognostic significance of patterns of psychophysiological arousal and adaptation. *Psychosomatic Medicine, 52*, 271–285.

Shekelle, R. B., Gale, M., Ostfeld, A. M., & Paul, O. (1983). Hostility, risk of coronary heart disease, and mortality. *Psychosomatic Medicine, 45*, 109–114.

Siegel, J. M. (1985). The measurement of anger as a multidimensional construct. In M. A. Chesney & R. H. Roseman (Eds.), *Anger and hostility in cardiovascular and behavioral disorders* (pp. 59–82). New York: Hemisphere Publ. Corp.

Siegel, J. M. (1986). The Multidimensional Anger Inventory. *Journal of Personality and Social Psychology, 51*, 191–200.

Siegel, J. M., & Brown, J. B. (1988). A prospective study of stressful circumstances, illness symptoms, and depressed mood among adolescents. *Developmental Psychology, 24*, 715–721.

Smith, T. W., & Frohm, K. D. (1985). What's so unhealthy about hostility? Construct validity and psychosocial correlates of the Cook and Medley Ho Scale. *Health Psychology, 4*, 503–520.

Speilberger, C. D., Gorsuch, R. L., & Lushene, R. E. (1970). *Manual for the State-Trait Anxiety Inventory*, Palo Alto, CA: Consulting Psychologists Press.

Tennen, H., & Herzberger, S. (1987). Depression, self-esteem, and the absence of self-protective attributional biases. *Journal of Personality and Social Psychology, 52*, 72–80.

Theorell, T., Lind, E., & Floderus, B. (1975). The relationship of disturbing life-changes and emotions to the early development of myocardial infarction and other serious illness. *International Journal of Epidemiology, 41*, 281–293.

Weiner, I. B., (1985). Clinical contributions to the developmental psychology of adolescence. *Genetic, Social and General Psychology Monographs, 111*, 195–203.

Williams, R. B., Jr., Haney, T. L., Lee, K. L., Kong, Y., Blumenthal, J. A., & Whalen, R. E. (1980). Type A behavior, hostility, and coronary atherosclerosis. *Psychosomatic Medicine, 42*, 539–550.

Woodall, K. L., & Matthews, K. A. (1989). Familial environment associated with Type A behaviors and psychophysiological responses to stress in children. *Health Psychology, 8*, 403–426.

Wyler, A R., Masuda, M., & Holmes, T. H. (1968). Seriousness of illness rating scale. *Journal of Psychosomatic Research, 11*, 363–367.

Wyler, A. R., Masuda, M., & Holmes, T. H. (1970). The seriousness of illness rating scale: Reproducibility. *Journal of Psychosomatic Research, 14*, 59–64.

CHAPTER 5

Conflict-Prone and Conflict-Resistant Organizations

Daniel Stokols

T he influence of personal dispositions on individuals' health status and their susceptibility to illness has been studied extensively within the field of health psychology
(cf. Friedman, 1990). Several programs of research have demonstrated the close relationship between personal traits such as hostility, optimism, sense of coherence, hardiness,
self-esteem, and individual well-being (cf. Antonovsky, 1979; Barefoot, Dahlstrom, & Williams, 1983; Kobasa, Maddi, & Kahn, 1982; Scheier & Carver, 1985; Taylor & Brown, 1988;
Watson & Pennebaker, 1989). Other studies have examined the interplay between psychological dispositions, interpersonal behavior, and physiological processes that influence
health status and illness outcomes. Examples of this research include recent studies of
the psychophysiological underpinnings of the coronary-prone and cancer-prone behavior
patterns (cf. Krantz, Lundberg, & Frankenhaeuser, 1987; Temoshok, 1985) and the links
between personal dispositions, psychological stress, and susceptibility to infectious disease (cf. Cohen & Williamson, 1991).

In Antonovsky's (1979) terms, personal dispositions toward optimism, hardiness,
high self-esteem, and a sense of coherence are psychological resources that enable people
to resist illness when they are exposed to social and environmental stressors. On
the other hand, dispositional tendencies toward hostility, anger, low self-esteem, and
depression are "generalized resistance deficits" that heighten individuals' susceptibility to

illness, especially when they are experiencing stressful life events. The links between chronic anger, hostile or suspicious orientations toward others, and a variety of illness outcomes have been shown to be particularly strong and pervasive in health psychology research (cf. Chesney & Rosenman, 1985).

Studies of personality and health, while focusing on psychogenic aspects of illness or resistance to disease, have given less attention to the sociophysical context of health and the ways in which personal dispositions and environmental factors jointly influence well-being. From a biopsychosocial perspective (cf. Engel, 1976; Schwartz, 1982), however, an understanding of health and illness can emerge only through cross-level analyses of psychological, biogenetic, and social processes. Certainly, the influence of social support and interpersonal conflict on disease resistance and vulnerability has been widely studied (cf. Berkman & Syme, 1979; Cohen & Syme, 1985; Rook, 1984; Sarason & Sarason, 1985). But aside from these analyses of interpersonal (dyadic) processes in health and Moos' research on the links between social climate and mental and physical well-being in family and institutional settings (Moos, 1979; Holahan & Moos, 1990), the broader sociophysical context of hostility and health has been largely neglected by health psychologists.

The influence of organizational structure (e.g., the existence of competitive coalitions within a group or unstable membership and role assignments) on the occurrence and health consequences of hostility has received little attention in earlier research. The neglect of group structure and dynamics in health research is problematic for both theoretical and practical reasons. For example, analyses that focus too narrowly on personal proclivities toward hostility and illness may lead to individually targeted, therapeutic interventions that ignore the social–structural underpinnings of conflict and health impairment. Just as Steiner (1974) asked "Whatever happened to the group in social psychology?" a similar question can be posed in relation to health psychology, considering that very little emphasis on group dynamics or organizational behavior can be found in the research literature of this field. The potential integration of social–psychological, organizational, and sociological perspectives on social conflict (cf. Coser, 1956; Dahrendorf, 1958; Heider, 1958; Kelley & Thibaut, 1978; Merton, 1938; Pfeffer & Salancik, 1978; Sherif, 1958; Simmel, 1950) with personality-oriented studies of hostility and disease suggests several avenues for future research. Some of these directions are outlined in subsequent sections of this chapter.

Social–ecological and contextually oriented analyses of health (cf. Moos, 1979; Stokols, 1987) emphasize the importance of studying the transactions between individual and group behavior, on the one hand, and the environmental resources and constraints that exist within specific settings, on the other. The temporal course of interpersonal conflict within small-group and organizational settings, however, has not been addressed in prior studies of hostility and health impairment. In health–psychological research, hostility has been viewed either as an enduring personality trait (cf. Barefoot, this volume; Pope, Smith, & Rhodewalt, 1990) or in the context of short-term dyadic encounters among strangers in laboratory settings (cf. Smith, this volume). However, the ways in which various facets of group and organizational structure promote, prevent, or moderate the intensity and health consequences of interpersonal conflict (among nonstrangers who interact with each other on a regular basis) have not been examined in earlier research.

The present chapter focuses on the organizational context and temporal course of interpersonal conflict and its impact on group members' health. Whereas some earlier studies have examined the structural characteristics of "psychosomatic families" (cf. Minuchin, Rosman, & Baker, 1978) or perceptions of interpersonal conflict within group residential settings (cf. Moos, 1990), the focus here is on conflict-promotive qualities of work groups and organizations that may play a major role in influencing members' emotional and physical well-being. Work groups and organizations are an important focus for health–psychological research in view of the substantial amount of time that people spend in work settings and their high levels of psychological investment in occupational roles and activities (cf. Moos, 1986; Repetti, 1987).

Qualities of Conflict-Prone and Conflict-Resistant Organizations

The present analysis of social–structural factors in the etiology of illness is based on a fundamental assumption: Few interpersonal conflicts occur in a socially or organizationally neutral context, especially among persons who interact with each other regularly as fellow group members. More specifically, it is hypothesized that the physical environmental arrangements and social conditions existing within some organizations predispose their members toward chronic conflict and health problems, whereas the environmental and social–structural qualities of other organizations make the occurrence of interpersonal conflict less likely and its potential health impacts (when conflict does occur) less prolonged and severe. The former are referred to in this discussion as *conflict-prone organizations*, whereas the latter are termed *conflict-resistant organizations*.

Table 1 outlines some of the distinguishing qualities of conflict-prone and conflict-resistant organizations. These characteristics of organizations are clustered within three general categories: (a) *social–psychological qualities of groups*, which include norms, common goals, and members' expectations about their own and others' roles and responsibilities; (b) *organizational structure*, which encompasses the interrelations among members' roles and the processes by which group resources are managed; and (c) *environmental conditions external to the group* that exert a stabilizing or destabilizing influence on its social structure and internal processes.

Among the social–psychological qualities of organizations that may predispose members toward conflict are the absence of shared goals among group members, incompatibilities between individuals' personal styles and their role assignments in the group, and the presence of rigid ideologies among group members resulting in low tolerance for diverse points of view. Sherif's (1958) research on intergroup conflict, for example, demonstrated the powerful influence of establishing common or *superordinate* goals among the members of different groups in reducing prior conflicts and promoting greater intergroup cooperation. Sherif's findings suggest that the existence of widely shared goals among group members decreases the likelihood that interpersonal conflicts will occur and provides a cooperative basis for resolving such conflicts when they do occur.

Compatibilities between group members' styles and role assignments also encourage cooperative and friendly interpersonal relations rather than competition and hostility. Similarly, group norms that support informal sharing or communal relationships can be expected to reduce the potential for internal competition and strife (cf. Clark & Mills, 1979). Yet even within a cooperatively structured group, the presence of competitive or suspicious individuals (especially when they occupy key decision-making roles) may create an escalating pattern of conflict (cf. Kelley & Stahelski, 1970) that predisposes members of the organization to chronic conflict and health impairment.

The availability and arrangement of physical resources within organizational settings can be viewed as environmental "affordances" (Gibson, 1977) that predispose group members to conflict or cooperation. For instance, the existence of a clear-cut territorial system for organizing the use of space and other material resources enables individuals to avoid or minimize interpersonal conflicts, whereas the lack of such systems (or their ambiguity) is associated with more frequent and persisting conflicts in group situations (cf. Altman, 1976; Altman & Haythorn, 1967; Sundstrom & Altman, 1989; Taylor, 1988).

TABLE 1

Qualities of Conflict-Prone and Conflict-Resistant Organizations

Levels of Organizational Analysis	Tendencies Toward Conflict or Cohesion	
	Organizational Profiles	
	Conflict-Prone	Conflict-Resistant
Social–psychological qualities (norms, goals, and role expectations)	Absence of shared goals among group members	Presence of and commitment to shared goals among group members
	Incompatible styles and role assignments among group members	Compatible styles and role assignments among group members
	Presence of rigid ideologies; low tolerance for diverse points of view	Absence of rigid ideologies; high tolerance for diverse points of view
Organizational structure (interrelations among roles and resources)	Existence of competitive coalitions	Absence of competitive coalitions
	Nonparticipatory organizational processes	Participatory organizational processes
	Overstaffed organization; pervasive competition among members for scarce roles and resources	Adequately staffed organization; minimal competition among members for roles and resources
	Ambiguous organization of space and territory among group members	Clear-cut territorial organization and use of space among group members
	Relatively unstable role structure and membership	Relatively stable role structure and membership
	Absence of formal and informal dispute-resolution mechanisms	Availability of formal and informal dispute-resolution mechanisms
External environmental conditions	Local and remote environmental resources for meeting organizational goals are inadequate	Ample environmental resources for meeting organizational goals are available
	Environment external to the organization is anomic and turbulent	Environment external to the organization is cohesive and nonturbulent

The social–structural features of groups and organizations also exert an important influence on group tendencies toward conflict or cooperation (cf. Kelley & Thibaut, 1978; Pfeffer & Salancik, 1978). The existence of competitive coalitions within groups, for example, may encourage the development of hostile encounters as well as the escalation and prolongation of interpersonal conflicts once they arise.

Interestingly, health–psychological research has emphasized the positive effects of supportive social relationships on personal well-being, especially during times of unusual life stress (cf. Cohen & Syme, 1985; Sarason & Sarason, 1985). One issue that has received little attention in this research is the possibility that social support networks sometimes widen and prolong interpersonal conflicts. As individuals share their experiences of conflict with friends in the organization, their friends may, in turn, discuss those experiences with others, thereby involving group members in the conflict who initially were not associated with it. Through processes of information sharing and emotional support, an initially dyadic conflict can be enlarged and prolonged, to the extent that persons indirectly associated with the conflict begin to link it to other organizational agendas (e.g., preexisting tensions among subgroups and coalitions). Thus, the provision of social support to a person who is in conflict with another may have a positive effect on his or her emotional well-being in the short run, but also a negative influence on organizational cohesion in the longer run.

Several other aspects of organizational structure may encourage the development of interpersonal conflicts, including the instability of group membership and role relations (cf. Manuck, Kaplan, Adams, & Clarkson, 1988), the restriction of opportunities for individuals to participate in group decision-making processes (cf. Becker, 1990; Kanter, 1983), and the overstaffing of organizational settings resulting in competition among group members for scarce roles and resources (cf. Barker, 1968; Wicker, 1979, 1987).

Finally, the extent to which environmental conditions external to the organization are turbulent is expected to be associated with greater tendencies toward interpersonal conflict among group members (cf. Aldrich, 1979; Emery & Trist, 1965; Katz & Kahn, 1966). For example, uncertainties about the availability of local and remote environmental resources that are essential for meeting organizational goals or the prospects of unemployment stemming from economic changes at the community level can evoke tension and conflict among group members. Similarly, political conflicts in society at large may provoke hostile encounters among group members depending on their respective opinions about the relevant societal issues. The hypothesized links between extraorganizational turbulence, interpersonal conflict, and health impairment have not been examined in previous research.

The Temporal Course of Interpersonal Conflict and Health Impairment in Organizational Settings

The qualities of organizations that encourage or discourage conflict among group members are arrayed in Table 2 across three temporal phases: (a) the *preconflict phase*, (b) the *conflict-occurrence phase*, and (c) the *postconflict phase*. The various environmental and structural features of organizations shown in Table 2 function as contextual moderators of the initial occurrence, subsequent intensity, and eventual health outcomes of conflicts among group members.

The physical–environmental conditions and social–structural qualities of groups that predispose their members to conflict are listed in the first column of Table 2. Among the physical conditions that may be closely associated with the initiation of interpersonal conflict and hostility are environmental stressors such as loud noise, high density and congestion, uncomfortable temperatures, and resource scarcity (cf. Evans, 1982). Similarly, impending environmental change (e.g., geographic relocation of the organization and its facilities) and the lack or ambiguity of group territorial systems can increase the potential for interpersonal conflict. As noted earlier, social–structural qualities such as unstable group composition, the existence of competitive coalitions, ideological rigidity, overstaffing of roles, and nonparticipatory organizational processes also are expected to heighten tendencies toward interpersonal conflict.

All of the sociophysical conditions listed in the second column of Table 2 are temporally proximal to the initial occurrence of interpersonal conflict. For instance, hostilities may be triggered by one member's infringement on another's territory, the experience of abrupt environmental change, or the annoyance created by an initially neutral stressor that becomes personalized and attributed to the inconsideration or negative intent of another individual (cf. Stokols, 1975, 1976). Interpersonal conflict also can be triggered by a variety of social–psychological processes, such as the intensification of ideological and subgroup differences within an organization and heightened competition

TABLE 2

Contextual Factors That Influence the Occurrence and Outcomes of
Interpersonal Conflict

Dimensions of Organizational Environments	Temporal Course of Conflict		
	Phases of Interpersonal Conflict		
	Preconflict Phase	Conflict Occurrence	Postconflict Phase
Physical environment	Environmental stressors that evoke negative affective states (e.g., noise, density, scarce resources) High potential for physical environmental change Ambiguous organization of space and territory among group members	Personalization of initially neutral environmental stressors Abrupt environmental change (e.g., relocation of facilities) Territorial infringements Unavoidable physical proximity among conflicted individuals	Chronic persistence of environmental stressors Limited capacity to reorganize territorial system to ameliorate earlier conflicts and avert their recurrence Stigmatization of physical environments associated with earlier conflicts
Sociocultural environment	Unstable role structure and membership Presence of competitive coalitions Rigid ideologies prevail; intolerance for diverse points of view Overstaffing and resultant competition among members for scarce roles and resources Nonparticipatory organizational process	Heightened tensions among subgroups prompted by rapid environmental and organizational change Hostile incidents resulting from ideological and subgroup differences Potential reduction or widening of interpersonal conflicts through the intercession of social network members	Low potential for establishing superordinate goals among conflicted individuals and subgroups Absence of formal and informal dispute-resolution mechanisms Perpetuation and escalation of interpersonal conflicts through the involvement of social network members

among group members for scarce resources, especially during times of rapid environmental and social change. Moreover, the immediate intensity of interpersonal hostility may increase to the degree that the participants in the conflict are unable to avoid close physical proximity with each other.

Once interpersonal conflicts have occurred, their duration and potential health consequences are likely to be influenced by the sociophysical conditions listed in the third column of Table 2. For example, the duration and health impacts of interpersonal conflicts are expected to be greater when the exposure to environmental stressors is chronic rather than temporary and the opportunities to improve dysfunctional territorial systems are restricted or unavailable. Similarly, the prospects for continued conflict and related health impairments will be greater if group members are unable to establish widely shared, superordinate goals or if they lack access to formal and informal processes for dispute resolution. Conversely, the organization will be better able to defuse prior hostilities and avoid future conflicts to the degree that common group goals and dispute-resolution mechanisms are strengthened.

Summary

The present discussion of conflict-prone and conflict-resistant organizations suggests the importance of addressing the sociophysical context of hostility and illness in future research. Several physical conditions and social–structural qualities of organizations were identified that may predispose their members to chronic conflict and health impairment. Moreover, the temporal course of conflict and health problems within small-group and organizational settings was examined along a continuum ranging from preconflict to postconflict phases.

The empirical links among the variables summarized in Tables 1 and 2, the occurrence and severity of interpersonal conflict, and the duration and health consequences of such conflict remain to be tested in future studies. By developing ecologically oriented models of health and illness, it will eventually be possible to integrate earlier dispositional and dyadic analyses with those that address the etiologic significance of environmental resources, group processes, and organizational structure. Along these lines, an intriguing topic for future study is the extent to which disease-prone personalities (Friedman, 1990) are disproportionately vulnerable to the health threats posed by conflict-prone organizations.

References

Aldrich, H. E. (1979). *Organizations and environments.* Englewood Cliffs, NJ: Prentice-Hall.

Altman, I. (1976). *Environment and social behavior: Privacy, personal space, territory, and crowding.* Monterey, CA; Brooks/Cole.

Altman, I., & Haythorn, W. W. (1967). The ecology of isolated groups. *Behavioral Science, 12,* 169–182.

Antonovsky, A. (1979). *Health, stress, and coping.* San Francisco: Jossey-Bass.

Barefoot, J. C., Dahlstrom, W. G., & Williams, R. B. Jr. (1983). Hostility, CHD incidence, and total mortality: A 25-year follow-up study of 255 physicians. *Psychosomatic Medicine, 45,* 59–63.

Barker, R. G. (1968). *Ecological psychology: Concepts and methods for studying the environment of human behavior.* Stanford, CA: Stanford University Press.

Becker, F. D. (1990). *The total workplace: Facilities management and the elastic organization.* New York: Van Nostrand Reinhold.

Berkman, L. F., & Syme, S. L. (1979). Social networks, host resistance, and mortality: A nine-year follow-up study of Alameda County residents. *American Journal of Epidemiology, 109,* 186–204.

Chesney, M. A., & Rosenman, R. H. (Eds.). (1985). *Anger and hostility in cardiovascular and behavioral disorders.* Washington, DC: Hemisphere Press.

Clark, M. S., & Mills, J. (1979). Interpersonal attractions in exchange and communal relationships. *Journal of Personality and Social Psychology, 37,* 12–24.

Cohen, S., & Syme, S. L. (Eds.). (1985). *Social support and health.* Orlando, FL: Academic Press.

Cohen, S., & Williamson, G. M. (1991). Stress and infectious disease in humans. *Psychological Bulletin, 109,* 5–24.

Coser, L. (1956). *The functions of social conflict.* New York: Free Press.

Dahrendorf, R. (1958). Toward a theory of social conflict. *Journal of Conflict Resolution, 2,* 170–183.

Emery, F. E., & Trist, E. L. (1965). The causal texture of organizational environments. *Human Relations, 18,* 21–32.

Engel, G. L. (1976). The need for a new medical model. *Science, 196,* 129–136.

Evans, G. W. (Ed.). (1982). *Environmental stress.* New York: Cambridge University Press.

Friedman, H. S. (Ed.). (1990). *Personality and disease.* New York: John Wiley.

Gibson, J. J. (1977). The theory of affordances. In R. Shaw & J. Bransford (Eds.), *Perceiving, acting, and knowing* (pp. 76–82). Hillsdale, NJ: Lawrence Erlbaum Associates.

Heider, F. (1958). *The psychology of interpersonal relations.* New York: John Wiley.

Holahan, C. J., & Moos, R. H. (1990). Life stressors, resistance factors, and improved psychological functioning. An extension of the stress-resistance paradigm. *Journal of Personality and Social Psychology, 58,* 909–917.

Kanter, R. M. (1983). *The change masters: Innovation and entrepreneurship in the American corporation.* New York: Simon and Schuster.

Katz, D., & Kahn, R. L. (1966). *The social psychology of organizations.* New York: John Wiley.

Kelley, H. H., & Stahelski, A. J. (1970). The social interaction basis of cooperators' and competitors' beliefs about others. *Journal of Personality and Social Psychology, 16,* 66–91.

Kelley, H. H., & Thibaut, J. W. (1978). *Interpersonal relations: A theory of interdependence.* New York: John Wiley.

Kobasa, S. C., Maddi, S. R., & Kahn, S. (1982). Hardiness and health: A prospective study. *Journal of Personality and Social Psychology, 42*, 168–177.

Krantz, D. S., Lundberg, U., & Frankenhaeuser, M. (1987). Stress and Type-A behavior: Environmental and biological factors. In A. Baum & J. E. Singer (Eds.), *Handbook of psychology and health, Vol. 5.* (pp. 203–228). Hillsdale, NJ: Lawrence Erlbaum Associates.

Manuck, S. B., Kaplan, J. R., Adams, M. R., & Clarkson, T. B. (1988). Studies of psychosocial influences on coronary artery atherogenesis in cynomolgus monkeys. *Health Psychology, 7*, 113–24.

Merton, R. K. (1938). Social structure and anomie. *American Sociological Review, 3*, 672–682.

Minuchin, S., Rosman, B. L., & Baker, L. (1978). *Psychosomatic families: Anorexia in context.* Cambridge, MA: Harvard University Press.

Moos, R. H. (1979). Social ecological perspectives on health. In G. C. Stone, F. Cohen, & N. E. Adler (Eds.), *Health Psychology: A Handbook* (pp. 523–547). San Francisco: Jossey Bass.

Moos, R. H. (1986). Work as a human context. In M. S. Pallak & R. Perloff (Eds.), *Psychology and work: Productivity, change, and employment* (pp. 9–52). Washington, DC: American Psychological Association.

Moos, R. H. (1990). *The social ecology laboratory: An overview.* Palo Alto, CA: Department of Psychiatry and Behavioral Sciences, Stanford University.

Pfeffer, J., & Salancik, G. R. (1978). *The external control of organizations: A resource dependence perspective.* New York: Harper and Row.

Pope, M. K., Smith, T. W., & Rhodewalt, F. (1990). Cognitive, behavioral, and affective correlates of the Cook and Medley Hostility scale. *Journal of Personality Assessment, 54*, 501–14.

Repetti, R. L. (1987). Individual and common components of the social environment at work and psychological well-being. *Journal of Personality and Social Psychology, 52*, 710–720.

Rook, K. S. (1984). The negative side of social interaction: Impact on psychological well-being. *Journal of Personality and Social Psychology, 46*, 1097–1108.

Sarason, I. G., & Sarason, B. R. (Eds.). (1985). *Social support: Theory, research, and applications.* Dordrecht, The Netherlands: Martinus Nijhoff Publishers.

Scheier, M. F., & Carver, C. S. (1985). Optimism, coping, and health: Assessment and implications of generalized outcome expectancies. *Health Psychology, 4*, 219–247.

Schwartz, G. E. (1982). Testing the biopsychosocial model: The ultimate challenge facing behavioral medicine. *Journal of Consulting and Clinical Psychology, 50*, 1041–1053.

Sherif, M. (1958). Superordinate goals in the reduction of intergroup conflicts. *American Journal of Sociology, 63*, 349–356.

Simmel, G. (1950). On the significance of numbers for social life. In K. H. Wolff (Ed. and Trans.), *The sociology of Georg Simmel* (pp. 87–104). New York: The Free Press.

Steiner, I. D. (1974). Whatever happened to the group in social psychology? *Journal of Experimental Social Psychology, 10*, 93–108.

Stokols, D. (1975). Toward a psychological theory of alienation. *Psychological Review, 82*, 26–44.

Stokols, D. (1976). The experience of crowding in primary and secondary environments. *Environment and Behavior, 8*, 49–86.

Stokols, D. (1987). Conceptual strategies of environmental psychology. In D. Stokols & I. Altman (Eds.), *Handbook of environmental psychology* (pp. 41–70). New York: Wiley.

Sundstrom, E., & Altman, I. (1989). Physical environments and work group effectiveness. *Research in Organizational Behavior, 11,* 175–209.

Taylor, R. B. (1988). *Human territorial functioning.* New York: Cambridge University Press.

Taylor, S. E., & Brown, J. D. (1988). Illusion and well-being. A social psychological perspective on mental health. *Psychological Bulletin, 103,* 193–210.

Temoshok, L. (1985). Biopyschosocial studies on cutaneous malignant melanoma: Psychosocial factors associated with prognostic indicators, progression, psychophysiology, and tumor-host response. *Social Science and Medicine, 20,* 833–840.

Watson, D., & Pennebaker, J. W. (1989). Health complaints, stress, and distress: Exploring the central role of negative affectivity. *Psychological Review, 96,* 234–254.

Wicker, A. W. (1979). *An introduction to ecological psychology.* New York: Cambridge University Press.

Wicker, A. W. (1987). Behavior settings reconsidered: Temporal stages, resources, internal dynamics, context. In D. Stokols & I. Altman (Eds.), *Handbook of Environmental Psychology, Vol. 1* (pp. 613–653). New York: John Wiley.

CHAPTER 6

Life-Style and Hostility

Larry Scherwitz and Reiner Rugulies

A lthough not always consistent or linear, there is strong prospective evidence that hostility is associated with new coronary heart disease incidence (Barefoot, Dahlstrom, & Williams, 1983; Dembroski, MacDougall, Costa, & Grandits, 1989; Shekelle, Gale, Ostfeld, & Paul, 1983) and coronary artery disease severity (Williams et al., 1980). Less well substantiated because of its lower incidence is the association of hostility with other causes of mortality, including noncardiovascular disease mortality, violent deaths (Koskenvuo et al., 1988), and cancer (Barefoot et al., 1983; Shekelle et al., 1983). If hostility is related to all-cause mortality, then the way we think of hostility as a risk factor needs to be reconsidered.

This chapter is a beginning effort to characterize what it is about hostility that could lead to all-cause mortality. After a discussion of the concept of life-style, we will

We are deeply indebted to Laura Perkins who conducted the analyses reported on hostility and health behaviors in young adults as well as commented on a prior version of this chapter. We also deeply appreciate the contribution of Dean Ornish, the principal investigator of the Life-Style Heart Trial, for making the Life-Style Heart Trial study possible and allowing use of the results reported in this chapter.

The Coronary Artery Risk Development in Young Adults (CARDIA) study was supported by the National Heart, Lung, and Blood Institute, National Institutes of Health, Contracts N01-HC-48047, N01-HC-48048, N01-HC-48049, N01-HC-48050, and N01-HC-95095 to the principal investigators of each center and by NHLBI HL-29573 to Scherwitz.

The Life-Style Heart Trial was supported by grants from Gerald D. Hines Interests, Houston Endowment, Inc. The Henry J. Kaiser Family Foundation, John E Fetzer Institute, the National Heart, Lung, and Blood Institute (RO1 HL42554-01), the Department of Health Services of the State of California (# 1256SC-01), Arthur Andersen & Co., Continental Airlines/Texas Air Corporation, Quaker Oats Company, Pritzker & Pritzker, Texas Commerce Bank, First Boston Corporation, Enron Foundation, Nathan Commings Foundation, General Growth Companies, and others.

present the findings from two major studies (Ornish et al., 1990; Scherwitz, Perkins, Chesney, & Hughes, in press; Scherwitz et al., 1991; Scherwitz, Ornish, Sparler, & Brown, 1991). The primary conceptual challenge is to integrate the findings from these two studies and to draw some sound implications for future research and therapy on hostility. The first study is a prospective epidemiological study of the evolution of coronary heart disease risk factors in 5,115 young adults. This study has a unique and large population with a wide distribution of socioeconomic status. The data have provided a basis to construct an empirical picture of how hostility may be related to socioeconomic status, psychological factors, and health-related behaviors.

The second study is a controlled clinical trial primarily designed to assess whether comprehensive changes in life-style can halt or reverse coronary artery disease severity. The results published recently provide solid evidence that coronary artery disease is reversible with major comprehensive life-style changes (Ornish et al., 1990). As a secondary purpose, we also assessed whether life-style changes altered hostility and other psychosocial risk factors. If hostility relates to all-cause mortality, then we would expect that hostility may be part of a broad health behavior pattern. If we are to proceed in an attempt to identify a comprehensive risk pattern, it would be useful to give this pattern a name. We have chosen the term *life-style* to denote a hypothetical pattern of behaviors that may confer risks for several causes of mortality. There are definitions of life-style in the literature that are useful. For example, the World Health Organization (WHO) defines life-style as a social structure that mediates the individual's interactions with groups (Wenzel, 1982). More specifically, "The life-style of a social group is defined as the entirety of 'patterns of expression' which are developed by the group collectively to cope with the requirements and contradictions of the social structure and situations common to the group" (p. 58).

According to Abel, the concept of life-style has played a major role in sociological theory (1991). Mostly, it has been used as a descriptive concept to socially stratify individuals (Veblen, 1899). Karl Marx included life-style in his writings when he said "... millions of families live under economic conditions that separate their lifestyles, their interests, and their education from those in other classes ..." (Marx, 1960, p. 376). Weber indicated that life-style is determined by a distinct, but interdependent, combination of social or structural conditions and individual choice (1972). In a classic Marxist view, people don't have much control over their life-style, because it is a product of their socioeconomic conditions (Abel, 1991). In a Weberian view, life-style consists of *life chances*, which express the influence of the society and the social–economic status of the individual, and of *life conduct*, which expresses the free choices an individual can make (Abel, 1991). In his search for a health life-style, Abel followed the Weberian view, which defines health life-style as "comprised of patterns of health-related behavior, values and attitudes adapted by groups of individuals in response to their social, cultural and economic environment" (p. 4).

Another interesting aspect of the Weberian view is that a distinct life-style, which originally belonged to a special social-status group, may well spread throughout the society (as seen in the spread of the Protestant ethic into the general culture of Western society; Abel, Cockerham, Lüschen, & Kunz, 1989). It would be very interesting to know if health behaviors form a pattern and whether they too are consistent across cultures. On the basis of 29 questions about topics such as appearance, nutrition, recovery (rest and vacations), and health concerns, Abel found strong evidence for the distinctiveness of three health-related life-style patterns that are fairly consistent between the United States and Germany. A health life-style was the most distinctive cluster in both countries, suggesting an interesting consistency of some life-style patterns across the two nations (1991).

If life-style is a set of orientations and patterns for social actions, then it is reasonable to assume that hostility lies at the center of this social structure and would directly affect the interactions between the individual and social groups. Although the WHO concept of life-style is appealing, it is still too vague and broad to help us in our search for the link between hostility and all-cause mortality. We agree with Abel (1991) who chose to narrow the focus in the identification of life-style to a set of empirically measurable health and health-risk behaviors. In what follows, we will suggest three areas one needs to consider in beginning to identify a hostility-related, health-related life-style.

On the basis of the definition and use of the life-style concept to characterize differences in social classes, it is logical that we consider socioeconomic status (SES) in our search for a hostility-related health life-style. There is yet another more important reason for including socioeconomic level, that is, its consistent relationship to morbidity and mortality. In a review, Antonovsky (1967) concluded that, since the twelfth century, individuals in the lower classes invariably have had lower life expectancies and higher death rates from all causes. Despite the durability of the findings across cultures, we still do not have a satisfactory coherent explanation for how SES factors affect all-cause mortality. In undeveloped countries, people in lower social classes succumb more readily to infectious diseases, but in Western industrialized countries, those of lower social class die more frequently from chronic diseases (Syme & Berkman, 1976). Of course, SES is strongly associated with occupation, so poor working conditions—like dealing with asbestos and dangerous chemicals—and industrial accidents explain some of the variance of the relationship of SES and life expectancy (Navarro, 1986). However, we think that causes other than environmental ones should also be considered.

In two reviews of the literature on social class, Slater and Carlton (1985) and Wiley and Comacho (1980) concluded that the relationship between social class and mortality persists even when general social conditions improve and when overall mortality decreases. This is consistent with the review by Marmot, Kogevinas, and Elston (1987). Marmot, Kogevinas, and Elston concluded that social class is not a variable like any other. They mentioned that materialist explanations and cultural–behavioral ones are not alternatives, because people's SES influences their behavior, and their behavior affects their health (Marmot et al., 1987). Marmot et al. (1987) described a pattern of the spread of coronary heart disease (CHD) within a society that could explain why CHD is more common among the lower-class people. As CHD begins to rise in a developing or industrialized country, it is more common in upper-class groups, possibly because of unhealthy life-styles that include high-fat diets, lack of exercise, smoking, and stress. Later, when these life-style patterns diffuse through society, the CHD incidence increases in lower-class groups. When the upper-class groups begin changing their life-styles in a healthier direction, it takes some time for the lower-class groups to follow, so that at least for a certain time, lower-class people are living on a higher risk level (Marmot et al., 1987).

One should not forget psychosocial factors in the search for a distinctive hostility-related life-style. There is an emerging picture showing that individuals with higher hostility may have a combination of higher degrees of stress and less social support. On the basis of research from four samples, Smith and colleagues found that undergraduates with high scores on the 50-item Cook-Medley Hostility (Ho) scale, a subscale of the Minnesota Multiphasic Personality Inventory (MMPI), reported more negative life events and more frequent and severe daily hassles (Hardy & Smith, 1988; Smith & Frohm, 1985; Smith, Pope, Sanders, Allred, & O'Keeffe, 1988). Smith and colleagues also found that high-scoring undergraduates reported less quality and quantity of social support (Smith & Frohm, 1985) and less satisfaction with social support (Smith et al., 1988) than those with low Ho scores. In looking more specifically into different areas of social support, Smith and colleagues found that subjects with high Ho scores reported greater levels of family conflict and increased levels of stress in their jobs with supervisors, coworkers, and subordinates (Smith et al., 1988).

Beyond psychosocial factors, one should also include health behaviors in the search for a distinctive hostility health life-style. Even as far back as 1979, the Surgeon General's report (Healthy people, 1979) attributed up to half of the mortality in the United States to unhealthful behaviors. Thus far, hostility has been positively correlated with smoking (Dembroski et al., Koskenvuo et al., 1988; Shekelle et al., 1983), alcohol intake (Koskenvuo et al., 1988), and marijuana use (Stoner, 1988) as well as with overall health habits, drugs, and driving habits (Leiker, & Hailey, 1988).

The CARDIA Study

As indicated in the introduction, we have begun an empirical search for a hostility health life-style using data from the Coronary Artery Risk Development in Young Adults study (CARDIA). CARDIA is a prospective epidemiological study investigating the distribution, antecedents, and progression of risk factors for the development of atherosclerotic cardiovascular disease. Four clinical centers, located in Birmingham, Alabama, Chicago, Illinois, Minneapolis, Minnesota, and Oakland, California, recruited 5,115 individuals over a 16-month period (1985–1986). In each center, participants were recruited from the total community by telephone or by going door-to-door or from selected census tracts, except in Oakland where a health plan membership roster was used. The sample was approximately balanced within each center on age (18–24 years, 25–30 years), gender, race (White, Black), and level of education (high school or less, more than high school). This sampling scheme was used to provide adequate numbers of subjects in 16 subgroups. The study design, recruitment of participants, and selected baseline descriptive findings are reported elsewhere (Friedman et al., 1988).

The instrument used to measure hostility in CARDIA was the 50-item Ho scale. Others have found this scale to be primarily a measure of cynicism and resentment rather than overt aggression (Smith & Frohm, 1985; Smith et al., 1988; Smith & Allred, 1989). In order to identify aspects of the Ho scale that are most related to health outcomes, Barefoot, Dodge, Peterson, Dahlstrom, and Williams (1989) took a rational approach to describe what the Ho scale measures. Using question content as the criterion, they divided the items into six subcategories: cynicism, hostile attribution, hostile affect, aggressive responding, social avoidance, and other. Agreement between raters on these categories was acceptable. In a study of 128 University of North Carolina law students who completed the MMPI in 1956–1957, Barefoot et al. (1989) found that the sum of cynicism, aggressive responding, and hostile affect (called the sum score) was more strongly predictive of survival than the overall Ho scale scores.

Figure 1 presents the mean Ho scale score by race, gender, age, and level of education from the CARDIA study. On the basis of a regression model using main effects and all significant interactions, the Ho scale scores were significantly higher in Blacks than in Whites (22.2 and 18.0, respectively; $p < 0.001$), higher in less-educated subjects than in more-educated subjects (21.6 and 18.5, respectively; $p < 0.001$), higher in men than in women (21.2 and 19.0, respectively; $p < 0.001$), and higher in younger subjects than in older subjects (20.7 and 19.5, respectively; $p < 0.001$). Young Black men with limited education had the highest Ho scale scores, whereas older White women with more education had the lowest levels (26.2 and 15.5, respectively).

When similar analyses were conducted using the six subcategories of the Ho scale, we found the same results, indicating that SES factors influence the different aspects of

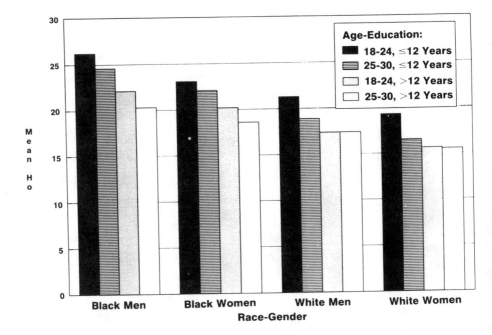

FIGURE 1   Mean Cook-Medley Hostility (Ho) score by race, gender, age, and education. From Scherwitz, Perkins, Chesney, & Hughes (in press). Copyright by the American Psychosomatic Society. Reprinted with permission.

hostility measured by the Ho scale in a similar way to the overall Ho scale. The results provide convincing evidence that SES factors have a dramatic and pervasive effect on at least the Cook-Medley measure of hostility. The results also raise the interesting possibility that the SES link with all-cause mortality may be in part mediated by differences in hostility.

Partial correlations between the Ho scale and its subcategories and the other psychosocial measures adjusting for age, race, gender, and education showed that the Ho scale was negatively correlated with social support ($r = -0.26$), positively correlated with Framingham Type A/B ($r = 0.35$) and life events ($r = 0.19$). To investigate the nature of life events further, we divided the life-event questions into groups on the basis of whether they were positive or negative and whether they were initiated by the subject or uninitiated by the subject. We found that negative life events correlated more positively with the Ho scale and the six subcategories than did the positive life events. Similarly, the uninitiated life events were correlated more strongly with the Ho scale and the six subcategories than were the initiated life events. The interview Type A/B behavior was not correlated with the Ho scale. The intercorrelations of the Ho scale with the other psychosocial factors were repeated within the four race-gender subgroups with very similar results. Thus, it appears that the relationship of the Ho scale with life events, Framingham Type A/B, and social support is stable for Blacks and Whites, as well as for men and women.

Another question we asked was how stable are the different features of hostility. On the basis of the intercorrelations of the six subcategories of the Ho scale, we replicated Barefoot et al. (1989) by showing that subcategories were moderately intercorrelated as one would expect. More interesting was how consistent these correlations were across race and gender.

The picture of hostility emerging so far suggests that the level of education, gender, age, and even race may have a strong impact on the level of hostility, and this may be a factor in the higher health risk of individuals with lower SES status. Within each of the socioeconomic levels, individuals with the highest Ho scores have more negative and uncontrollable life events happening to them, they at least perceive themselves to be Type A, and they have less social support to cope with these stressors. The next step was to assess how hostility is associated with health behaviors, measured in the 5,115 CARDIA subjects in 1985–1986.

Cigarette smoking was measured by an interviewer-administered questionnaire with current smokers defined as smoking at least five cigarettes per week, almost every week, for at least three months. Marijuana use was measured by a self-administered question-naire that asked if subjects had ever used marijuana and, if so, the frequency and quantity of use in the past 30 days. Alcohol intake was measured by an interviewer-ad-ministered questionnaire assessing consumption during the past year and the average number of drinks of beer, wine, and liquor usually consumed in a week. Dietary data were collected by a nutritionist-administered dietary history interview developed espe-cially for CARDIA (McDonald et al., in press).

Kilocalories per day and total fat, saturated fat, sucrose, and caffeine, adjusted for caloric intake (%Kcal) were used for analyses in this chapter.

Leisure-time physical activity was assessed using the questionnaire developed for CARDIA and was based on the Minnesota Leisure Time Activity (Jacobs, Hahn, Haskell, Pirie, & Sidney, 1989) and the Stanford Heart Disease Prevention Program questionnaires (Sallis et al., 1985). Physical fitness was assessed as the time taken to reach a heart rate of 130 beats per minute on a graded treadmill exercise test. Participants were considered hypertensive if either their systolic blood pressure exceeded 164 or their diastolic blood pressure exceeded 95 mmHg of the average of the last two of three readings.

Within each race–gender subgroup, linear regression analyses or logistic regression analyses were used to model the health behaviors or risk factors already described (mea-sured as continuous variables, e.g., ml of alcohol) as a function of hostility, age, number of years of education, and all two-way and three-way interactions. Hostility was catego-rized into race–gender specific quartiles for presentation.

The prevalence of cigarette smoking varied from 26% for White men to 38% for Black men. Prevalence of cigarette smoking was approximately 1.5 times higher in the high-hostility quartile compared with the low-hostility quartile; this was statistically signif-icant in all race–gender groups (See Figure 2). However, the average number of cigarettes smoked per day (18.2 for White men, 14.6 for White women, 10.9 for Black men, and 10.7 for Black women) was not associated with hostility level.

In each race–gender group except Black men, prevalence of current marijuana use within the last 30 days was positively associated with hostility, with those in the highest hostility quartile approximately 1.5 times as likely to be marijuana users than those in the lowest hostility quartile (see Figure 3). Among marijuana users, the average number of days that marijuana was used in the past month ranged from 6.9 days in White women to 11.3 days in Black men. Hostility was associated with the number of days that marijuana was used in the past month in both White men and Black women ($p = 0.005$ and 0.009, respectively).

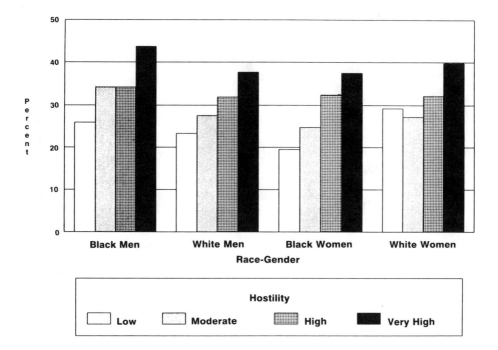

FIGURE 2   Percentage of cigarette smokers by Cook-Medley Hostility (Ho) quartile, race, and gender. Copyright by Larry Scherwitz. Reprinted by permission of Larry Scherwitz.

The percentage of subjects reporting alcohol consumption in the past year ranged from 78% in Black women to 92% in White men and was not related to hostility in any race–gender group. However, among drinkers, average weekly alcohol intake increased significantly with hostility ($p < .0001$) (See Figure 4). The increase in alcohol consumption between the lowest and highest hostility quartile was approximately 8 ml/week in both Black and White men, compared with 4.6 ml/week and 6.9 ml/week in Black and White women, respectively.

Estimated caloric intake increased significantly with hostility in each race–gender group ($p < .0001$; Table 1). Black men in the highest hostility quartile consumed an average of 628 calories per day more than Black men in the lowest hostility quartile. For Black women, this difference was 490 calories, compared with 594 calories for White men and 295 calories for White women.

Percentage of calories from fat, saturated fat, and sucrose were not associated with hostility level in any race–gender group ($p > 0.05$, data not presented). Caffeine intake

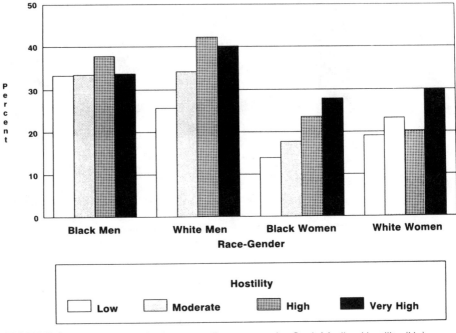

FIGURE 3   Percentage of current marijuana users by Cook-Medley Hostility (Ho) quartile, race, and gender. Copyright by Larry Scherwitz. Reprinted by permission of Larry Scherwitz.

(mg per 1,000 calories) did not differ by hostility level except in Black women, for whom caffeine intake decreased with increasing level of hostility. This decline in caffeine intake with hostility was primarily due to a negative relationship between caffeine intake and hostility in older women.

There were no significant differences by hostility quartile in reported activity level or time taken to reach a heart rate of 130 on the treadmill in men or in Black women. Only among White women was hostility positively associated with physical activity ($p = .02$), a finding consistent with the positive association in women between hostility and time taken to reach a heart rate of 130 on the treadmill ($p = .02$). There were no significant differences by hostility quartile in total cholesterol, high density lipoprotein cholesterol, or low density lipoprotein cholesterol. Although hostility did not correlate with Body Mass Index (BMI), there were consistent positive relationships for waist–hip ratio (WHR) in each of the four race–gender subgroups. Waist–hip ratio is a more specific measure of truncal or abdominal obesity than the BMI. Those with higher hostility levels

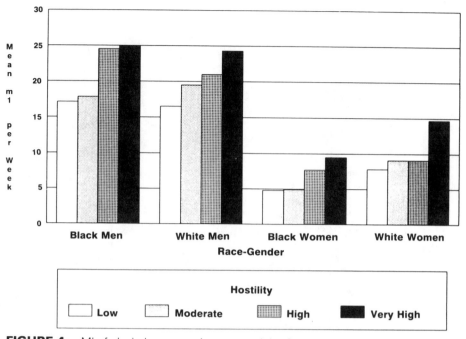

FIGURE 4   MI of alcohol consumption per week by Cook-Medley Hostility (Ho) quartile for race and gender groups. Copyright by Larry Scherwitz. Reprinted by permission of Larry Scherwitz.

had greater waist–hip ratios. However, contrary to expectations, there is a weak negative relationship between the Ho score and blood pressure, which reaches significance for systolic blood pressure in White females ($p = .01$) and diastolic blood pressure in Black females ($p = .006$). The relationship was not significant for the six remaining subgroups.

To summarize, hostility was associated with the increased prevalence of cigarette smoking, the prevalence and amount of marijuana use, alcohol consumption, total caloric intake, and waist–hip ratio. Hostility was not strongly associated with caffeine, leisure time, exercise capacity, body mass, or cholesterol.

The fact that hostility is related to cigarette smoking and alcohol intake provides a partial explanation for how hostility could be associated with all-cause mortality. It is well-known that cigarette smoking contributes to cancer and cardiovascular disease, and alcohol consumption contributes to automobile accidents and other violent deaths. The more important point of the finding is that hostility is related to a consumptive life-style, which includes, at least, food, marijuana, alcohol, and cigarettes. We do not know from

TABLE 1
Mean Total Daily Calories* and Caffeine Intake** By Cook-Medley Hostility (HO) Level, Race, and Gender

Hostility Quartile	White Men n = 1,171		White Women n = 1,306		Black Men n = 1,157		Black Women n = 1,477	
	Calories/Day (SE)	Caffeine Intake (SE)	Calories/Day (SE)	Caffeine Intake (SE)	Calories/Day (SE)	Caffeine Intake (SE)	Calories/Day (SE)	Caffeine Intake (SE)
Low	2,954 (77.6)	121.8 (11.5)	1,976 (48.9)	189.5 (16.5)	3,740 (136.4)	42.7 (4.5)	2,361 (66.9)	68.7 (6.5)
Moderate	3,292 (78.1)	129.4 (11.5)	2,165 (45.6)	188.5 (15.4)	3,897 (135.7)	33.4 (4.5)	2,576 (70.2)	71.2 (6.9)
High	3,473 (80.5)	137.9 (11.9)	2,156 (52.2)	191.9 (17.6)	4,196 (147.8)	40.8 (4.9)	2,619 (70.0)	57.3 (6.8)
Very high	3,548 (82.7)	152.1 (12.2)	2,271 (52.0)	207.6 (17.4)	4,368 (141.5)	42.2 (4.7)	2,851 (74.5)	58.1 (7.2)
TOTAL	3,292 (41.8)	133.8 (5.8)	2,136 (24.5)	194.3 (8.2)	4,040 (71.3)	39.4 (2.3)	2,590 (35.5)	63.5 (3.3)
P-Value***	.001	.154	.0001	.202	.0004	.605	.0001	.005

Note. * Mean calories are based on least square means adjusted for age, education, Body Mass Index (BMI), physical activity, and cigarette-smoking status.
**Caffeine intake is expressed as mg/day × 1,000 divided by total daily caloric intake; caffeine means are based on least square means adjusted for age and education; nonsignificant interactions dropped.
***P-values are based on regression models using Ho scale as continuous measure and adjusting for covariates in above footnote; nonsignificant interactions deleted.
Copyright by Larry Scherwitz. Reprinted by permission of Larry Scherwitz.

this cross-sectional analysis whether hostility drives individuals to consume or if consumption contributes to hostility. We suspect that the relationships between hostility and these consumptive behaviors are complex. Aspects of using the substances probably help individuals cope with negative feelings and stress, and, conversely, these substances, especially when taken together, could contribute to a lower threshold for hostile perceptions, thoughts, feelings, and behaviors.

Despite the rather ominous picture of the hostile individual as having more negative life events and less support and some questionable consumptive behaviors, there do not appear to have been deleterious effects on these young adults if we consider levels of blood pressure, body mass, exercise tolerance, and serum cholesterol. Perhaps this life-style pattern takes more time to develop before these risk factors are affected. For example, a recent prospective study of hostility and cardiovascular risk levels in middle-aged White adults found that Ho scores taken from 4,710 middle-class, primarily White college students, predicted body mass, lipid ratios (total cholesterol/high density lipoprotein cholesterol), and hypertension status measured 20 years later. We think that the effects of a hostile life-style may, like mortality itself, require the passage of time before the effects can be measured on cardiovascular risk factors.

The use of the hostility construct to begin to identify an unhealthy life-style has been fruitful. It is encouraging that the varied relationships that hostility has with socioeconomic, psychosocial, and health behaviors all make sense on the basis of other research. We know that similar measures of SES, social support, and cigarette and alcohol consumption have been linked to mortality. The next step we would like to take in CARDIA is to understand better the nature of the hostility-related life-style. For example, we would be interested to know how the psychosocial characteristics and behaviors cluster together in terms of groups of individuals. We would like to know how distinctive these groups are and how they may vary by age, gender, race, and education. Then we could see how these groups changed their cardiovascular risk status over time.

Effects of Life-Style Change on Psychosocial Status

Although it is interesting to think about life-style patterns and what these patterns may be like, another approach is to change life-styles and see what effects this has on risk factors, psychosocial status, and cardiovascular disease. We have done this in the San Francisco Life-Style Heart Trial, a study designed to assess whether comprehensive changes in life-style could halt or reverse the progression of coronary artery disease as measured by repeated quantitative coronary angiography. Accordingly, we used a random individual invitational design that assigned 48 patients to either a group receiving comprehensive life-style changes or to a control group receiving no life-style interventions, except those prescribed by their physicians.

Life-Style Change Program
Overview
To acquaint patients and their partners with the life-style program and to allow them to begin experiencing the resulting benefits, the treatment intervention began with a week-long residential retreat at a local resort hotel. Patients' spouses or partners were required to attend the retreat. During the retreat, the patient and partner were taught the life-style program, including daily lectures on the rationale for the intervention components. In addition, patients and spouses received 3 hours a day of stress-management training, 1 hour a day of aerobic exercise, and 1 hour a day of group support with a clinical psychologist.

Following the retreat, patients attended group-support meetings on Tuesday and Thursday evenings for 1 year, engaging in the following activities for 1 hour each: light aerobic exercise, stress-management, vegetarian dinner, and support-group meeting. Spouses were encouraged but not required to attend.

Diet
Experimental-group patients were asked to consume a low-fat vegetarian diet for 1 year. The diet included fruits, vegetables, grains, legumes, and soybean products without caloric restriction. No animal products were allowed except for egg whites and 1 cup a day of nonfat milk or yogurt. Salt was restricted only for those with hypertension. Alcohol was restricted to 2 oz per day or the equivalent, and caffeine was eliminated.

Stress-Management Techniques
The stress-management practices integrated stretching, relaxing, breathing, meditating, progressive relaxation, and imagery (Ornish et al., 1983; Patel et al., 1985). Each technique was presented as having the common purpose of increasing a patient's sense of relaxation, concentration, and awareness of internal states. Patients were taught a series of 12 yoga poses designed to stretch, tone, and relax the body and to help develop internal awareness (Benson, 1977). Participants were advised to stretch slowly and gently while focusing attention on the areas being stretched to avoid injury or strain. Between poses, they were directed to relax. Afterward, participants were taught a progressive relaxation

technique of sequentially tensing and relaxing specific muscle groups. Following the progressive relaxation, they were taught three breathing techniques. After this, they were asked to sit in a comfortable upright position and to focus their attention (meditate) by repeating a nonsectarian or sectarian sound, phrase, or prayer chosen by each patient. Next, patients were directed to choose and maintain an image (picture, sound, idea, or feeling) of a healthy heart. Patients were asked to practice these stress-management techniques for at least 1 hour each day.

Smoking Cessation and Aerobic Exercise

Experimental-group patients were required to quit smoking to enter the study, and the one smoker in the experimental group did so. Patients were individually prescribed exercise levels according to a baseline treadmill heart rate, metabolic (MET) level, and perceived exertion. Following the retreat and throughout the year, the patients were asked to exercise for a minimum of 3 hours per week and to spend a minimum of 30 minutes per session exercising within their target heart rates. During the biweekly meetings, the patients participated in an hour-long exercise session.

Group Discussion

The twice-weekly group discussions provided social support to help patients adhere to the life-style-change program and to decrease their sense of isolation. Sessions were led by a clinical psychologist who facilitated expression of feelings regarding interpersonal relationships at work and at home, communication skills, and strategies for maintaining adherence to the program. Group-support sessions were held for 1 hour on both Tuesday and Thursday evenings.

Adherence and Psychological Measures

Adherence Measures

The subjects' baseline and 1-year participation in exercise and stress-management activities were assessed by a questionnaire on the type, frequency, and minutes per week the subjects engaged in any type of exercise and any of the prescribed stress-management techniques. At baseline and 1 year, dietary intake was assessed by a 3-day history, which is considered representative of nutrient intake when weekend days are included. Nutrients examined included total fat, total cholesterol, saturated fat, polyunsaturated fat, protein, and calories.

Psychosocial Measures

General well-being was measured using Goldberg's 30-item scale, which has subscales to assess anxiety and depression, social facilitation, sense of coherence, and insomnia

(Goldberg & Hillier, 1979). Social support was assessed using two brief questionnaires that were successful in correlating with coronary artery disease severity in a sample of San Francisco Bay Area heart patients (Seeman & Syme, 1987). Sense of coherence was measured using a 13-item scale assessing the respondent's perceptions that their lives are comprehensible, manageable, and meaningful. Anger was measured using Spielberger's State and Trait Anger scales (Spielberger, Jacobs, Russel, & Crane, 1983). Type A behavior was assessed using the method developed by Friedman (Friedman & Powell, 1984). Participants were scored on 35 separate characteristics, which were divided into the two categories of time urgency and hostility.

Life-Style Changes After 1 Year

The experimental and control group did not differ on any life-style-adherence measure or on any psychosocial-status measure at baseline. After 1 year, the results indicated that the experimental group could be motivated to make comprehensive changes in life-style on a free-living basis (Ornish et al., 1990). Patients in the experimental group reduced fat intake from 30.8% to 7.0% of total calories, they increased their exercise from 20.2 to 37.2 min per day, and they increased their stress management from 6.3 to 77.7 min per day. Patients in the control group maintained their fat intake fairly evenly from 29.3% to 29.4% of total calories, they increased their exercise very little from 18.4 to 20.6 min per day, and they changed little their practice of stress management from 1.8 to 4.3 min per day.

The changes in life-style in the experimental group appeared to have had an effect on the coronary artery disease as measured by quantitative coronary angiography. The average percentage diameter stenosis decreased from 40.0% ($SD = 16.9$) to 37.8% ($SD = 16.5$) in the experimental group, yet progressed from 42.7% ($SD = 15.5$) to 46.1% ($SD = 18.5$) in the control group ($p = .001$, two-tailed). When only lesions greater than 50% stenosed were analyzed, the average percentage diameter stenosis regressed from 61.1% ($SD = 8.8$) to 55.8% ($SD = 11.0$) in the experimental group, but progressed from 61.7% ($SD = 9.5$) to 64.4% ($SD = 16.3$) in the control group ($p = .03$, two-tailed). Eighty-two percent of the patients in the experimental group showed average changes in the direction of regression of coronary atherosclerosis, whereas 53% of patients in the usual-care group had changes in the direction of progression of atherosclerosis.

Furthermore, in an analysis combining both the experimental and control groups, the degree of life-style change was directly and strongly correlated with changes in coronary atherosclerosis ($r = .68$). In fact, the difference in coronary atherosclerosis was completely accounted for by differences in life-style changes in the two groups.

Effects of Life-Style Changes on Psychosocial Status

At baseline, there were no significant differences between the experimental and control groups for any psychosocial measure. However, after 1 year, the comprehensive life-style improved the experimental group's psychosocial status as much as it did their cardiovascular status (Table 2 and Table 3).

Life-style change participants reported a much greater sense of coherence ($p =$ .002), suggesting that their lives became more meaningful, that they faced the difficulty of having heart disease with more manageability, and that they felt they could control their lives (see Table 2). This is consistent with what patients and their spouses say in the group meetings. In contrast, control patients reported less of a sense of coherence.

TABLE 2

Changes in Psychosocial Characteristics

	n^a	Baseline		12 Months		
		M	**SD**	**M**	**SD**	**p^b**
Sense of coherence						
Experimental	27	43.9	6.9	46.0	6.4	
Control	17	47.6	6.4	45.1	5.4	.0021
State anger						
Experimental	25	21.4	9.4	20.2	8.9	
Control	16	20.0	7.5	20.6	6.6	.4550
Trait anger						
Experimental	27	29.9	8.0	25.8	6.5	
Control	17	26.6	6.8	26.3	5.2	.0350
Social-support total						
Experimental	27	19.7	4.1	21.3	4.7	
Control	16	20.3	5.1	19.5	3.5	.0744
Instrumental social support						
Experimental	27	4.2	2.5	5.4	3.1	
Control	16	4.5	2.9	4.2	2.1	.0714
Social-support adequacy						
Experimental	27	15.4	2.5	15.8	2.8	
Control	17	15.8	3.6	15.3	2.5	.2715

Note: $^a n$ at baseline.
^{b}Probability levels are based on a one-between (group), one-within (pre-post) ANOVA.
Copyright by Larry Scherwitz. Reprinted by permission of Larry Scherwitz.

Experimental-group patients had a significant reduction in Trait Anger, compared with no change in the control group ($p = .04$), and the experimental-group patients reported a little more social support, whereas the control-group patients reported a little less social support after 1 year ($p = .07$). Overall, the life-style-change group appeared to feel better as evidenced by a very significant improvement in general well-being, with the Social Facilitation and Insomnia subscales contributing most to this effect ($p = .005, .02, .008$, respectively; see Table 3).

TABLE 3
Changes in Psychosocial Characteristics

	n^a	Baseline		12 Months		
		M	SD	M	SD	p^b
General well-being total						
Experimental	26	27.5	10.5	20.1	10.4	.0056
Control	17	23.9	9.0	25.5	13.8	
General well-being insomnia						
Experimental	26	5.8	2.5	4.0	2.2	.0087
Control	17	4.9	1.5	5.4	2.1	
General well-being social facilitation						
Experimental	26	4.1	1.8	2.8	1.7	.0225
Control	17	3.8	1.0	3.6	1.7	
General well-being anhedonia						
Experimental	26	3.8	1.3	3.3	1.8	.1776
Control	17	3.8	1.4	3.8	2.1	
General well-being depression						
Experimental	26	6.0	3.5	3.9	3.6	.0535
Control	17	4.7	3.6	5.2	5.2	
Total Type A score						
Experimental	27	35.3	12.0	25.8	10.7	.0685
Control	20	35.1	11.6	30.8	10.3	
Type A time-urgency component						
Experimental	27	25.7	8.8	19.9	7.2	.1907
Control	20	26.2	8.3	22.4	8.1	
Type A hostility component						
Experimental	27	9.5	5.6	5.9	5.3	.0381
Control	20	8.9	5.7	8.4	5.6	

Note: $^a n$ at baseline.
^{b}Probability levels are based on a one-between (group), one-within (pre-post) ANOVA.
Copyright by Larry Scherwitz. Reprinted by permission of Larry Scherwitz.

The Anxiety and Depression subscale also showed significant improvement for the experimental patients ($p = .05$), and the Anhedonia subscale showed a little, but not significant, improvement. The control group had somewhat lower general well-being, particularly in the Insomnia and the Anxiety and Depression subscales.

Despite the fact that the life-style program was not designed to reduce Type A behavior, the experimental group reduced their total Type A scores approximately a standard deviation, twice as much as the control group. More important, when compared with the control group, there was a significant reduction in the experimental group's hostility. The confidence that hostility was reduced by life-style changes is increased because the interviewer did not know the study design and was masked to experimental conditions, the assessments were made through direct observation, and the findings were consistent with similar reductions in the Spielberger Trait Anger measure, which did not change for the control group.

The results of this study suggest the surprising power of changing life-style. First, we were surprised by the subjects' excellent adherence to the program. We expected that adherence would be difficult because we asked patients to make more radical changes than any previous study. It appears that the benefits and the support patients experienced were powerful incentives for maintaining adherence to the program guidelines.

We think the reason patients maintained their adherence so well is that the program addressed the emotional and spiritual dimensions of the individual. We emphasized changing life-style, not out of fear of dying, but to increase the joy of living. More important, we provided participants the intimacy they were lacking. The 8 hours together each week resulted in an intense bonding of the participants with one another as well as with the staff. This feeling was fostered by the support-group meetings, where there was emphasis on altruism and the development of skills for getting in touch with and communicating these feelings. This helped patients feel the intimacy and expansion of being a part of something larger than themselves.

We are encouraged by the pervasive benefits of the program on patients' risk-factor levels, chest pain, exercise tolerance, coronary stenosis, and their overall psychosocial status. The study findings provide encouraging evidence that exercise, stress management, group support, and diet can alter hostility and other risk factors without direct therapeutic intervention on these factors.

In summary, the concept of life-style has promise in the identification of the mechanisms linking hostility to all-cause mortality. Although it is true that we must identify specific aspects of life-style and attempt to understand how they cohere, once this is done, we have a much better opportunity for dramatically increasing our predictiveness for cardiovascular and other diseases than by using a single-risk-factor approach. In addition, and even more encouraging, by changing life-style, we have an opportunity to alter not only the risk-factor status but the underlying causes of disease.

References

Abel, T. (1991). *Measuring health lifestyle in a comparative analysis: Theoretical issues and empirical findings.* Unpublished manuscript.

Abel, T., Cockerham, W., Lüschen, G., & Kunz, G. (1989). Health lifestyles and self-direction in employment among American men: A test of the spillover effect. *Social, Science, and Medicine, 28,* 1269–1274.

Antonovsky, A. (1967). Social class, life expectancy and overall mortality. *Milbank Memorial Fund Quarterly, 45,* 31–73.

Barefoot, J. C., Dahlstrom, W. G., & Williams, R. B., Jr. (1983). Hostility, CHD incidence, and total mortality: A 25-year follow-up study of 255 physicians. *Psychosomatic Medicine, 45,* 59–63.

Barefoot, J. C., Dodge, K. A., Peterson, B. L., Dahlstrom, W. G., & Williams, R. B., Jr. (1989). The Cook-Medley Hostility scale: Item content and ability to predict survival. *Psychosomatic Medicine, 51,* 46–57.

Benson, H. (1977). Systemic hypertension and the relaxation response. *New England Journal of Medicine, 296,* 1152–1156.

Dembroski, T. M., MacDougall, J. M., Costa, P. T., Jr., & Grandits, G. A. (1989). Components of hostility as predictors of sudden death and myocardial infarction in the multiple risk factor intervention trial. *Psychosomatic Medicine, 51,* 514–522.

Friedman, G. D., Cutter, G. R., Donahue, R. P., Hughes, G. H., Hulley, S. B., Jacobs, D. R., Jr., Liu, K., & Savage, P. (1988). CARDIA: Study design, recruitment, and some characteristics of the examined subjects. *Journal of Clinical Epidemiology, 41,* 1105–1116.

Friedman, M., & Powell, L. H. (1984). The diagnosis and quantitative assessment of Type A behavior: Introduction and description of the videotaped structured interview. *Integrative Psychiatry, 2,* 123–129.

Goldberg, D. P., & Hillier, V. F. (1979). A scaled version of the General Health Questionnaire. *Psychological Medicine, 9,* 139–145.

Hardy, J. D., & Smith, T. W. (1988). Cynical hostility and vulnerability to disease: Social support, life stress, and physiological response to conflict. *Health Psychology, 7,* 447–459.

Healthy People. (1979). *The Surgeon General's report on health promoting and disease prevention.* [DHEW (PHS) Publication No. 79-55071]. Washington DC: U.S. Government Printing Office.

Jacobs, D. R., Hahn, L. P., Haskell, W. L., Pirie, P., & Sidney, S. (1989). Validity and reliability of short physical activity history: CARDIA and the Minnesota Heart Health Program. *Journal of Cardiopulmonary Rehabilitation, 9,* 448–459.

Koskenvuo, M., Kaprio, J., Rose, R. J., Kesäniemi, A., Sarna, S., Heikkilä, K., & Langinvainio, H. (1988). Hostility as a risk factor for mortality and ischemic heart disease in men. *Psychosomatic Medicine, 50,* 330–340.

Leiker, M., & Hailey, B. J. (1988). A link between hostility and disease: Poor health habits? *Behavioral Medicine, 14,* 129–133.

Marmot, M. G., Kogevinas, M., & Elston, M. A. (1987). Social/Economic status and disease. *Annual Review of Public Health, 8,* 111–135.

Marx, K. (1960). *Politische schriften* [Political writings] (Vol. 1) (H. Lieber, Ed.). Stuttgart, Federal Republic of Germany: Cotta.

McDonald, A., Van Horn, L., Slattery M., Hilner, J., Braag, C., Caan, B., Jacobs, D., Liu, K., Hubert, H., Gernhoffer, N., Betz, E., & Havlik, D. (in press). The CARDIA dietary history: Development and implementation. *Journal of the American Dietetic Association.*

Navarro, V. (1986). *Crisis, health, and medicine.* New York: Tavistock Publications.

Ornish, D., Brown, S. E., Scherwitz, L. W., Billings, J. H., Armstrong, W. T., Ports, T. A., McLanahan, S. M., Kirkeeide, R. L., Brand, R. J., & Gould, K. L. (1990). Can lifestyle changes reverse coronary heart disease?: The Lifestyle Heart Trial. *Lancet, 336,* 129–133.

Ornish, D. M., Scherwitz, L. W., Doody, R. S., Kesten, D., McLanahan, S. M., Brown, S. E., DePuey, E. G., Sonnemaker, R., Haynes, C., Lester, J., McAllister, G. K., Hall, R. J., Burdine, J. A., & Gotto, A. M. (1983). Effects of stress management training and dietary changes in treating ischemic heart disease. *Journal of the American Medical Association, 249,* 54–59.

Patel, C., Marmot, M. G., Terry, D. J., Carruthers, M., Hunt, B., & Patel, M. (1985). Trial of relaxation in reducing coronary risk: Four year follow up. *British Medical Journal, 290,* 1103–1106.

Sallis, J. F., Haskell, W. L., Wood, P. D., Fortmann, S. P., Rogers, T., Blair, S. N., & Paffenbarger, R. S., Jr. (1985). Physical activity assessment methodology in the Five-City Project. *American Journal of Epidemiology, 121,* 91–106.

Scherwitz, L., Ornish, D., Sparler, S., & Brown, S. (1991). *Effects of lifestyle changes on psychosocial factors in the San Francisco lifestyle heart trial.* Manuscript submitted for publication.

Scherwitz, L., Perkins, L., Chesney, M., & Hughes, G. (in press). Cook-Medley Hostility scale and subsets: Relationship to demographic and psychosocial characteristics in young adults in the CARDIA Study. *Psychosomatic Medicine.*

Scherwitz, L., Perkins, L., Chesney, M., Hughes, G., Sidney, S., & Manolio, T. (1991). *Cook-Medley Hostility scale and health behaviors in young adults: The CARDIA Study.* Manuscript submitted for publication.

Seeman, T. E., & Syme, S. L. (1987). Social networks and coronary artery disease: A comparison of the structure and function of social relations as predictors of disease. *Psychosomatic Medicine, 49,* 341–354.

Shekelle, R. B., Gale, M., Ostfeld, A. M., & Paul, O. (1983). Hostility, risk of coronary heart disease, and mortality. *Psychosomatic Medicine, 45,* 109–114.

Slater, C., & Carlton, B. (1985). Behavior, lifestyle, and socioeconomic variables as determinants of health status: Implications for health policy development. *American Journal of Preventive Medicine, 1,* 25–33.

Smith, T. W., & Allred, K. D. (1989). Blood pressure responses during social interaction in high- and low-cynically hostile males. *Journal of Behavioral Medicine, 12*, 135–143.

Smith, T. W., & Frohm, K. D. (1985). What's so unhealthy about hostility? Construct validity and psychosocial correlates of the Cook and Medley Ho scale. *Health Psychology, 4*, 503–520.

Smith, T. W., Pope, M. K., Sanders, J. D., Allred, K. D., & O'Keeffe, J. L. (1988). Cynical hostility at home and work: Psychosocial vulnerability across domains. *Journal of Research in Personality, 22*, 525–548.

Spielberger, C. D., Jacobs, G., Russell, S., & Crane, R. S. (1983). Assessment of anger: The State-Trait Anger scale. In J. N. Butcher & C. D. Spielberger (Eds.), *Advances in personality assessment, Vol. 2*. Hillsdale, NJ: Erlbaum.

Stoner, S. B. (1988). Undergraduate marijuana use and anger. *Journal of Psychology, 122*, 343–347.

Syme, S. L., & Berkman, L. F. (1976). Social class, susceptibility and sickness. *Journal of Epidemiology, 104*, 1–8.

Veblen, T. (1989). *Theory of the leisure class*. New York: Macmillan.

Weber, M. (1972). *Wirtschaft und Gesellschaft* [Economy and society]. (5th rev. ed.). Tübingen: Mohr.

Wenzel, E. (1982). Perspectives of the WHO regional office for Europe. Health promotion and lifestyles. *Hygie, 1*, 57–60.

Wiley, J. A., & Comacho, T. C. (1980). Life-style and future health: Evidence from the Alameda County Study. *Preventive Medicine, 9*, 1–21.

Williams, R. B., Jr., Haney, T., Lee, K. L., Kong, Y., Blumenthal, J., & Whalen, R. E. (1980). Type A behavior, hostility, and coronary atherosclerosis. *Psychosomatic Medicine, 42*, 539–549.

CHAPTER 7

Behavioral Influences on Coronary Artery Disease: A Nonhuman Primate Model

Stephen B. Manuck, Jay R. Kaplan, Thomas B. Clarkson,
Michael R. Adams, and Carol A. Shively

M ost studies of behavioral influences on coronary heart disease adhere to one of two generic research strategies. The first involves epidemiologic investigation, which seeks to establish broad associations between putative risk factors and disease incidence and prevalence. The second strategy subsumes clinical studies, which when using sufficiently sensitive diagnostic technologies can offer a glimpse of underlying pathobiology as it is related to behavioral parameters of interest. As a result of research pursuing these two approaches, there is now much evidence that psychosocial factors contribute to the development of functional and clinical expressions of coronary disease, including angina pectoris, myocardial ischemia and infarction, and sudden cardiac death (Kamarck & Jennings, 1991; Manuck, Kaplan, & Matthews, 1986). There is also evidence that the behavioral attributes of individuals, particularly aspects of anger and its expression, are associated with the severity of coronary artery atherosclerosis observed among patients referred for diagnostic angiography (Manuck et al., 1986).

Preparation of this manuscript was supported, in part, by a grant from the National Institutes of Health (HL 40962).

Despite these advances, there are substantial limitations to human investigation that impede a deeper study into the origins and mechanisms of behavioral predisposition to coronary disease. These limitations relate to important aspects of coronary disease itself, including the processes that promote development of atherosclerotic lesions within coronary arteries. Particularly problematic is the fact that the natural history of atherosclerosis spans decades, rather than weeks, months, or years (as in the case of many infectious diseases), and for this reason, exceeds the scope of feasible longitudinal investigation. Even if investigators were prepared to devote decades to such study, ethical considerations would still preclude the angiographic evaluation of asymptomatic individuals. And should even these constraints be surmounted, diagnostic angiography itself is of limited value because it reveals only the extent of lesion present in the artery, not the cellular composition of plaque or its degree of complication. In consequence, factors affecting the progression of coronary artery atherosclerosis cannot be investigated satisfactorily in human beings in advance of the usual clinical manifestations of coronary heart disease.

A complementary research strategy pursued in the study of nearly all significant human diseases involves use of appropriate animal models. Among the most obvious advantages of studying animals are the experimental control afforded over pertinent environmental and dietary factors and the possibility of creating, in the laboratory, conditions that hasten the disease process. In addition, animal models permit preclinical identification of disease, as well as a more precise quantification of lesion characteristics than is feasible in patient populations. It is important to note, however, that not all species are good models of atherogenesis—some for reasons of gross morphology, some for metabolic reasons, and some because the lesions that do develop are dissimilar to those seen in human beings (Kaplan, Manuck, Clarkson, & Prichard, 1985). For example, many common features of atherosclerotic lesions in man, such as the presence of intimal plaques containing intracellular and extracellular lipid, macrophages, and smooth muscle cells, are rarely observed in rodents. Intimal lipid-containing lesions occur in other species (e.g., chickens and rabbits), but tend to predominate in small intramyocardial arteries rather than in proximal portions of the main-branch coronary arteries as in human beings. Fortunately, the nonhuman primates, particularly the macaques, develop lesions that are similar in their location and morphologic features to those seen in people and, therefore, do provide suitable models for the study of coronary artery disease (Armstrong, Trillo, & Prichard, 1980; Clarkson, 1980).

With respect to biobehavioral studies, selection of an appropriate animal model depends as much on the candidate species' behavioral and social features as on similarities to man in the morphologic and physiologic characteristics of its atherosclerosis (Kaplan et al., 1985). Current hypotheses regarding the behavioral antecedents of coronary heart disease are based on both the dispositional attributes of individuals (e.g., Type A behavior and hostility) and the social contexts in which these individuals find themselves (e.g., the degree of threat or situational challenge encountered). To prove relevant to such hypotheses, experimental studies must use species that are also sensitive to the influences of environmental perturbations and that possess behavioral repertoires of considerable complexity and individual variability. Here, too, nonhuman primates are particularly suitable for study; the elaborated patterns of antagonistic and affiliative interaction they exhibit are analogous to much of human social behavior and, in fact, subsume characteristics thought to confer an increased risk for coronary disease in man (e.g., competitiveness and aggression; Manuck, Kaplan, Muldoon, Adams, & Clarkson, 1991).

To date, there are relatively few animal studies of psychosocial factors in coronary artery disease, although the study of nonhuman primates has elucidated fundamental aspects of the natural history of coronary artery atherosclerosis. To illustrate the utility that animal models may also have for studying behavioral influences on coronary disease, the principal results of a series of investigations we have conducted on socially housed groups of male cynomolgus monkeys (*Macaca fascicularis*) are summarized briefly in this chapter (more extensive discussions of this research may be found in Manuck, Kaplan, Adams, & Clarkson, 1988; Manuck et al., 1991; and Manuck, Muldoon, Kaplan, Adams, & Polefrone, 1989).

In this work, it has been our intention to avoid the use of laboratory stimuli that perturb the animal by exposing it to acutely aversive events (e.g., shock), physical restraint, or manipulation of conditioning schedules. Rather, we have wished to evaluate the disease sequelae of relatively naturalistic social stressors, experiences that would not depart appreciably from the ordinary social ecology of the animal. In this regard, it may be noted that for much of their lives, male cynomolgus monkeys have a rather transitory social existence. As juveniles and young adults, males frequently reside in all-male bands that occupy the periphery of established heterosexual groupings. Monkeys from such peripheral bands often seek membership in an established group (to gain access to mates and other preferred resources) and do so by contesting the social positions of existing group members. This has occasioned one of the most frequent observations in field and laboratory primatology: that the appearance or introduction of strange animals to well-established social groupings temporarily disrupts social relationships and is associated with some intensification of antagonistic encounters as members seek to redefine their hierarchical (dominance) and affiliative relationships (Bernstein, Gordon, & Rose, 1974).

With respect to our own work, the disruptive influence of strangers on status relationships of socially grouped monkeys offers the basis for a naturalistic social challenge—namely, the periodic reorganization of social group memberships. Thus, in our first experiment, monkeys were assigned to one of two social conditions (Kaplan, Manuck, Clarkson, Lusso, & Taub, 1981). In the first or unstable social condition, monkeys lived in five-animal social groups, the memberships of which were redistributed every 1-to-3 months for a period of 22 months. The remainder of animals, assigned to a stable social condition, lived for the same period in five-member social groups of fixed membership. Also evaluated was the relative rank or social status of individual monkeys, on the basis of the observed outcomes of each animal's agonistic encounters with all other members of the same social group. Monkeys ranked either first or second in their respective groups were identified as socially dominant monkeys, whereas lesser ranked animals were designated subordinates. Interestingly, dominance rankings were quite stable over the course of the experiment and equally so among animals assigned to the unstable and stable social conditions. Finally, all monkeys were fed a moderately atherogenic (high fat) diet, and routine measurements were made of the animals' serum lipid concentrations (total serum cholesterol and high density lipoprotein cholesterol), blood pressure, and ponderosity over the course of the study.

Results of this investigation revealed that coronary artery-atherosclerosis, measured at the completion of the study by standard morphometric techniques, was greatest among socially dominant animals that had been housed in unstable social groups. Indeed, unstable–dominant monkeys developed nearly twice the coronary atherosclerosis that was seen among their subordinate counterparts or among similarly dominant animals assigned to the stable social condition. Relative to conditions of stable social housing, then, periodic reorganization of social groups promotes development of atherosclerosis, but does so only among animals of high social status (that is, in the more competitive, dominant monkeys). Although the behavioral demands of retaining preeminence in an unstable social environment may potentiate atherogenesis, subordinate animals remain relatively unaffected by recurrent changes in group membership. Perhaps this is because only social dominance is actively contested when new groups form, social subordination being retained by default.

Because the influence of dominance and social environment on atherosclerosis in this experiment was also independent of concomitant variability in animals' blood pressures or serum lipid concentrations, it is unclear exactly how these behavioral parameters contribute to atherogenesis. One prominent mechanistic hypothesis derives from psychophysiological studies of human subjects, which have shown that (a) individuals vary greatly in the magnitude of the cardiovascular responsivity to stress; and (b) persons thought to be behaviorally predisposed to coronary disease (e.g., Type A and "high" hostile individuals) exhibit heightened cardiovascular reactions to frustrating laboratory tasks or other behavioral challenges (Manuck & Krantz, 1986). In turn, these observations have prompted speculation that an exaggerated cardiovascular or neuroendocrine (e.g., sympathoadrenal) reactivity to stress promotes atherogenesis (Manuck et al., 1986). To examine this hypothesis, we recorded animals' heart rates at rest and during exposure to a standard laboratory challenge involving a stylized "threat of capture" (Manuck, Kaplan, & Clarkson, 1983). Like human beings, monkeys differ appreciably in their cardiac reactivity, as evaluated in response to this stimulus. This interindividual variability also permitted a partition of the animals into clearly differentiated groups of high- and low-heart-rate-reactive monkeys. Comparisons of these groups showed the coronary artery atherosclerosis of high-heart-rate reactors to be significantly greater than that of their low-reactive counterparts. The high reactors were also more aggressive than low-heart-rate-reactive monkeys, as documented in social observations made during the experiment. Hence, these findings provide initial evidence that severity of atherosclerosis is greatest among monkeys that show the largest cardiac reactions to stress, and such reactivity is in turn associated with variability in animals' aggressive potential.

It is probable that the heightened heart-rate responsivity of high-reactive animals reflects influences of the sympathetic nervous system on the heart. If so, it follows that administration of a beta-adrenoreceptor blocking agent should inhibit the behavioral exacerbation of atherosclerosis. We tested this hypothesis by administering propranolol hydrochloride to monkeys for 26 months, during which period, they were housed in periodically reorganized social groups and fed an atherogenic diet (Kaplan, Manuck, Adams, Weingand, & Clarkson, 1987). Control animals were treated identically, but did not receive propranolol, and again, all monkeys were evaluated for social dominance. Treatment with propranolol did not affect the behavior or serum lipid concentrations of either dominant or subordinate animals. With respect to atherosclerosis, however, dominant monkeys in the untreated condition developed approximately twice the extent of lesion seen in the coronary arteries of subordinate animals, closely replicating the relationship described earlier for monkeys assigned to the parallel (unstable) social condition of our first experiment. Yet social dominance did not potentiate atherogenesis among the propranolol-treated animals; indeed, the mean atherosclerosis of treated dominant monkeys approximated that of both treated and untreated subordinate animals. Beta-adrenergic blockade is, therefore, protective against atherosclerosis, albeit only among behaviorally predisposed (dominant) monkeys.

Finally, it is important to determine when in the natural history of atherosclerosis behavioral factors influence lesion development most significantly. In one study germane to this question, we observed that our psychosocial manipulation promoted atherogenesis even among monkeys fed a low-fat–low-cholesterol diet modeled on recommendations of the American Heart Association (Kaplan, Manuck, Clarkson, Lusso, Taub, & Miller, 1983). Not surprisingly, the extent of atherosclerosis seen under these dietary conditions, even among the most affected animals, was rather minimal, characterized primarily by so-called *fatty streaking* and the initial development of fibrous plaques. Because the extent of artery involvement was quite limited in this experiment, however, it may be concluded that predisposing behavioral factors are pathogenic (at least) in the early stages of atherogenesis.

But how early are predisposing behavioral factors pathogenic? There is now much agreement that the atherosclerotic process is initiated when some form of injury is sustained by the innermost layer of the artery, the endothelium, which acts as a barrier between the lumen of the artery and the artery wall (Ross, 1981). Composed of a single layer of cells, the normal endothelium shows limited permeability to macromolecules, such as the lipoproteins, and in this way, prevents deposition of lipid into the coronary artery. When the endothelium is injured, however, a number of proatherogenic events occur that foster an accumulation of lipids and the proliferation of smooth muscle cells in the artery wall (Davies, 1986; Schwartz, Campbell, & Campbell, 1986). With respect to behavior, our most recent evidence indicates that the social disruption of monkeys results in significant endothelial dysfunction and injury, as documented by autoradiographic evidence of endothelial cell turnover and replacement in both the aorta and coronary arteries (Strawn et al., 1991). Such injury also predominates at arterial locations having a predilection for development of atherosclerosis and may be prevented by administration of a beta-adrenergic blocking agent (metoprolol). It appears, then, that psychosocial factors can trigger the very first events in atherogenesis and that this is achieved by activation of the sympathetic nervous system and occurs in areas that tend later to be associated with significant lesion development.

Summary

At the outset, we noted that both epidemiologic and human clinical investigation suggest that behavior is implicated in coronary-disease risk and, in patient populations, it may be associated with extent of angiographically documented atherosclerosis. The foregoing studies of male cynomolgus monkeys add appreciably to our understanding of the behavioral ante-cedents of coronary disease and provide experimental evidence not obtainable in human subjects. To summarize, these studies demonstrate that psychosocial factors do contribute to the development of coronary artery atherosclerosis, as defined morphometrically. More spe-cifically, recurrent reorganization of social-group memberships promotes atherogenesis among monkeys fed a cholesterol-containing diet, but does so only in animals that maintain positions of social dominance. Behavioral influences on atherosclerosis are independent of variability in blood pressure and serum lipid concentrations and may be seen even among otherwise well-protected animals (i.e., monkeys fed a low-fat–low-cholesterol diet). In addi-tion, animals exhibiting the greatest heart-rate reactivity have more extensive coronary artery atherosclerosis and are more aggressive behaviorally than monkeys that show a less-pro-nounced cardiac responsivity to stress. This finding is consistent with the hypothesis that exaggerated cardiovascular reactions to behavioral stimuli increase risk for coronary artery disease. Moreover, chronic administration of a beta-adrenergic blocking agent, propranolol hydrochloride, fully prevents the exacerbated coronary artery atherosclerosis characteristic of autonomically intact, dominant animals living in unstable social environments. This result indicates that behavioral influences on atherosclerosis are mediated by the sympathetic ner-vous system. And last, psychosocial stress causes injury to the endothelium of coronary ar-teries (again via sympathetic activation), encouraging speculation that the behavioral exacerbation of coronary artery disease begins even in the earliest events of atherogenesis.

References

Armstrong, M. L., Trillo, A., & Prichard, R. W. (1980). Naturally occurring and experimentally induced atherosclerosis in nonhuman primates. In S. S. Kalter (Ed.), *The use of nonhuman primates in cardiovascular diseases.* Austin, TX: University of Texas Press.

Bernstein, I. S., Gordon, T. P., & Rose, R. M. (1974). Aggression and social controls in rhesus monkey (*Macaca mulatta*) groups revealed in group formation studies. *Folio Primatologia, 21,* 81–107.

Clarkson, T. B. (1980). Symposium summary. In S. S. Kalter (Ed.), *The use of nonhuman primates in cardiovascular diseases* (pp. 452–473) Austin, TX: University of Texas Press.

Davies, P. F. (1986). Vascular cell interactions with special reference to the pathogenesis of atherosclerosis. *Laboratory Investigations, 66*, 5–24.

Kamarck, T. W., & Jennings, J. R. (1991). Biobehavioral factors in sudden cardiac death. *Psychological Bulletin, 109*, 42–75.

Kaplan, J. R., Manuck, S. B., Adams, M. R., Weingand, K. W., & Clarkson, T. B. (1987). Inhibition of coronary atherosclerosis by propranolol in behaviorally predisposed monkeys fed an atherogenic diet. *Circulation, 76*, 1364–1372.

Kaplan, J. R., Manuck, S. B., Clarkson, T. B., Lusso, F. M., & Taub, D. B. (1981). Social status, environment, and atherosclerosis in cynomolgus monkeys. *Arteriosclerosis, 2*, 359–368.

Kaplan, J. R., Manuck, S. B., Clarkson, T. B., Lusso, F. B., Taub, D. B., & Miller, E. W. (1983). Social stress and atherosclerosis in normocholesterolemic monkey. *Science, 220*, 733–735.

Kaplan, J. R., Manuck, S. B., Clarkson, T. B., & Prichard, R. W. (1985). Animal models of behavioral influences on atherogenesis. In E. S. Katkin & S. B. Manuck (Eds.), *Advances in behavioral medicine. Vol. 1* (pp. 115–163). Greenwich, CT: JAI Press.

Manuck, S. B., Kaplan, J. R., Adams, M. R., & Clarkson, T. B. (1988). Effects of stress and the sympathetic nervous system on coronary artery atherosclerosis in the cynomolgus macaque. *American Heart Journal, 116*, 328–333.

Manuck, S. B., Kaplan, J. R., & Clarkson, T. B. (1983). Behaviorally induced heart rate reactivity and atherosclerosis in cynomolgus monkeys. *Psychosomatic Medicine, 45*, 95–108.

Manuck, S. B., Kaplan, S. B., & Matthews, K. A. (1986). Behavioral antecedents of coronary heart disease and atherosclerosis. *Arteriosclerosis, 6*, 2–14.

Manuck, S. B., Kaplan, J. R., Muldoon, M. F., Adams, M. R., & Clarkson, T. B. (1991). The behavioral exacerbation of atherosclerosis and its inhibition by propranolol. In P. McCabe. N. Schneiderman, T. Field, & J. Skylar (Eds.), *Perspectives on behavioral medicine* (pp. 51–72). Hillsdale, NJ: Erlbaum.

Manuck, S. B., & Krantz, D. S. (1986). Psychophysiologic reactivity in coronary heart disease and essential hypertension. In K. A. Matthews, S. B. Weiss, T. Detre, T. Dembroski, B. Falkner, S. B. Manuck, & R. B. Williams, Jr. (Eds.), *Handbook of stress, reactivity and cardiovascular disease* (pp. 11–47). New York: Wiley-Interscience.

Manuck, S. B., Muldoon, M. F., Kaplan, J. R., Adams, M. R., & Polefrone, J. M. (1989). Coronary artery atherosclerosis and cardiac response to stress in cynomolgus monkeys. In A. W. Siegman & T. M. Dembroski (Eds.), *In search of coronary-prone behavior: Beyond Type A* (pp. 207–227). Hillsdale, NJ: Erlbaum.

Ross, R. (1981). Atherosclerosis: A problem of the biology of arterial wall cells and their interactions with blood components. *Arteriosclerosis, 1*, 293–311.

Schwartz, S. M., Campbell, G. R., & Campbell, J. H. (1986). Replication of smooth muscle cells in vascular disease. *Circulation Research, 58*, 427–444.

Strawn, W. B., Bondjers, G., Kaplan, J. R., Manuck, S. B., Schwenke, D. C., Hansson, G. K., & Clarkson, T. B. (1991). Endothelial dysfunction in response to psychosocial stress in monkeys. *Circulation Research, 68*, 1269–1279.

EDITOR'S NOTE

The following two commentaries illustrate some of the issues that grow out of the preceding chapters on hostility. The first, by Burns and Katkin, draws attention to broader issues of construct validity and urges caution. The second, by Kaplan, Manuck, and Shumaker, discusses an intriguing puzzle regarding psychosocial factors and cholesterol.

Commentary to Part Two: Hostility and the Coronary-Prone Personality

John W. Burns and Edward S. Katkin

P rovoked initially by the clinical observations and epidemiological findings of Friedman and Rosenman (1959; Rosenman et al., 1964) on the Type A behavior pattern, much research has come to focus on what is believed to represent the most coronary-prone dimension of the Type A pattern—hostility (Williams & Barefoot, 1988). As Barefoot noted (this volume), the proliferation of research on Type A behavior was plagued continually by problems of definition and assessment; these problems could also undermine current research on the role of hostility in the etiology of coronary heart disease (CHD). The refinement of the assessment of hostility and the gathering of evidence in support of the construct validity of the Cook-Medley Hostility (Ho) scale, as outlined by Barefoot and by Smith and Christensen in their chapters, are crucial first steps toward avoiding some of these difficulties. However, we believe that a number of issues regarding the definition, measurement, and conceptualization of hostility have not yet been addressed adequately.

This research was supported in part by a fellowship (1F31MH09836) from the National Institute of Mental Health awarded to John W. Burns and a grant (89-01-3G) from the American Heart Association awarded to Edward S. Katkin.

SI-Derived Coding Schemes Versus the Ho Scale

Hostility, as defined by methods using the structured interview (SI), need not be related to hostility as defined by self-report instruments such as the Ho scale. Indeed, the Potential for Hostility component of the SI method for assessing Type A behavior appears to be only modestly correlated ($r = .37$) with scores on the Ho scale (Dembroski, Mac-Dougall, Williams, Haney, & Blumenthal, 1985). It is not clear to what extent hostile-style scores on the Hostile Behavior Index of Barefoot's Interpersonal Hostility Assessment Technique (IHAT) are related to scores on the Ho scale. However, Barefoot reported (this volume) that the Hostile Behavior Index was not correlated significantly with the IHAT assessment of the hostile content of an interviewee's speech (i.e., Self-Report Hostility), the category apparently most analogous to responses on the Ho scale. Although the Self-Report Hostility component of the IHAT and the Ho scale are not identical measures, these results, nonetheless, imply that the hostile style measured by the IHAT may differ significantly from hostility defined via the Ho scale.

Conceptual ambiguities regarding the hostility construct may develop from the differences between SI- and Ho-defined hostility, and it is likely that these ambiguities could parallel those that arose around the Type A construct from discrepancies in assessment using the SI versus the Jenkins Activity Survey (JAS). If SI-derived indexes and the Ho scale are not equivalent measures, then individuals defined as hostile by the IHAT may not possess the personality characteristics that would be attributed to hostile individuals on the basis of the results of construct-validity studies using the Ho scale. For instance, even though scores on the Ho scale appear to be inversely related to social support (Smith & Frohm, 1985), the Hostile Behavior Index of Barefoot's IHAT may not be so related. Conversely, inferences regarding Ho-defined hostility may be inaccurately drawn on the basis of findings using the SI to assess hostility.

If SI-based coding schemes and the Ho scale are not equivalent measures, then it is possible that they exhibit different relationships with CHD criteria. For example, Barefoot reported that the Hostile Behavior Index of the IHAT bears a strong association with the severity of coronary artery disease (CAD); the Ho scale, however, appears to be inconsistently related to CHD (Barefoot, Dahlstrom, & Williams, 1983; McCranie, Watkins, Brandsma, & Sisson, 1986). Given that SI and self-report measures appear to overlap only moderately, it is possible that the dimensions of the SI-based measures that tap coronary proneness may be unrelated to the self-report measures. Thus, the coronary proneness tapped by the IHAT may be poorly described in terms of the global hostility construct represented by the Ho scale. It may prove necessary to investigate the construct validity of SI-derived measures of hostility directly to see whether the findings converge appropriately with those using the Ho scale.

Hostility and the Coronary-Prone Personality

The trait of hostility, like Type A behavior, is probably not synonymous with the coronary-prone personality; as others have similarly argued (e.g., Friedman & Booth-Kewley, 1987), coronary proneness appears to be a broader construct than any one trait. But as Barefoot noted, there has not been a "comprehensive definition of hostility"; therefore, it has been difficult for investigators to identify core features of a hostility construct, and it has been difficult to distinguish hostility from other constructs. Without such a definition, hostility may be used to characterize a wide range of psychological phenomena. Thus, it is conceivable that investigators may start from a notion that hostility is associated with CHD, empirically find and retain predictors or correlates of disease, and then refer to those measures as indexes of hostility, because they are associated with disease, even if they only vaguely resemble the hostility construct that was the starting point of the research. Thus, if the definition of hostility becomes too closely identified with coronary proneness or coronary-disease severity, not only does the concept of hostility lose specificity, but the exploration of the possible multidimensional nature of the coronary-prone personality could be compromised.

This potential loss of definitional specificity may be illustrated by recent efforts to clarify the coronary-prone nature of hostility. It has been hypothesized that, because hostility appears to be a multidimensional construct (e.g., Costa, Zonderman, McCrae, & Williams, 1986), some dimensions may be more predictive of disease criteria than others. Thus, attempts have been made to identify the subcomponents of the Ho scale (e.g., Barefoot, Dodge, Peterson, Dahlstrom, & Williams, 1989) and the Buss-Durkee Hostility Scale (Siegman, Dembroski, & Ringel, 1987) most predictive of CHD. Such strategies entail a narrow focus on those subcomponents of self-report instruments associated with disease, disregarding those that are not so associated. However, this largely empirical approach seems to assume that the subcomponents that emerge as significant predictors of CHD can best be understood with reference to a global hostility construct.

Another illustration is provided by Barefoot's attempt to refine the assessment of hostility as defined by the Ho scale, while attempting to maximize the predictive utility of the construct vis-à-vis CAD severity. Although the whole Hostile Behavior Index of the IHAT was related significantly to CAD severity, Barefoot reported that the Indirect Challenge category was the component most predictive of CAD severity. Characterized by Barefoot in chapter 2 of this volume as "... by far the most subtle ... and the most difficult for the untrained observer to recognize," Indirect Challenge is "... not overtly confrontational" (p. 24). Although this concept could conceivably tap a type of suppressed, indirectly expressed hostility, it is not immediately obvious that it does; nor has evidence been reported that links Indirect Challenge to a global construct of hostility.

Our point is not to deny that hostility plays an important, even essential, role in a coronary-prone personality, but it is to emphasize that all that appears to be coronary prone is not necessarily a part of the hostility construct. Without a firm definition of hostility, it is difficult to tell where hostility ends and other traits that are also predictive of CHD begin. Moreover, by focusing so closely on and interpreting so much in terms of hostility, we may lose appreciation for the multidimensional nature of the coronary-prone personality. Scattered evidence suggests that psychological factors such as anxiety and depression may predict CHD criteria independently (e.g., Booth-Kewley & Friedman, 1987; Friedman & Booth-Kewley, 1987; Carney et al., 1987; Zyzanski, Jenkins, Ryan, Flessas, & Everist, 1976). At the very least, these findings argue for the use of a multidimensional approach to the study of coronary proneness, which could identify traits with additive relationships to CHD criteria. According to such a notion of coronary proneness, coronary risk could increase in proportion to the number of coronary-prone traits an individual possesses.

Additionally, interactive relationships between traits may be associated with CHD (e.g., Fontana et al., 1989). Fontana et al. (1989) showed that a sample of hostile coronary patients reported high dependency needs, whereas hostile noncoronary patients did not. Although the published analyses merely implied an interaction, the results suggest that potentially complex interrelationships among traits should be considered in the prediction of CHD. Thus, the coronary-prone personality may comprise not only traits having independent effects on CHD, but also, as Fontana et al. (1989) suggested, traits that potentiate the effects of other traits, so that, for example, the predictive utility for CHD of the combination of hostility and high dependency needs exceeds the sum of the individual associations.

The suggestion that the interaction among traits may be a more useful predictor of disease proneness implies that we may need to develop research strategies that are more dynamically based. Price's (1982) model of Type A behavior is noteworthy in this respect.

According to this model, the (Type A) coronary-prone person is dependent on the approval of others to maintain a sense of self-worth, and thus is especially vulnerable to criticism. Hostility, as part of a dynamic, can be seen as a defense against "... the anticipated pain of being criticized for being 'wrong'" (Price, 1982, p. 107). Thus, it may become necessary to develop dynamic personality profiles of individuals, focusing on the manner in which expressive as well as defensive traits interact to result in differing degrees of coronary-disease proneness. A more dynamic strategy would admittedly be more difficult to pursue and would require considerably more effort than the traditional trait-identification approach. Indeed, assessment may be further complicated by considering, as Barefoot suggests (this volume), that the expression of certain traits may be manifested differently depending on the situation in which they are elicited. Nonetheless, entertaining dynamic factors in the study of coronary proneness, despite its increased costs and difficulties, may provide greater payoffs than the investigation of a series of discrete traits.

Underlying Mechanisms

Whenever the association of hostility and coronary disease is discussed, great care is usually taken to avoid making definitive causal inferences from correlational data. Nevertheless, it is not unreasonable to assume that most investigators in the field share a common interpretive bias that hostility, anger, or some other toxic trait is a causal factor in coronary disease or at least contributes to some other more directly causal factor. As Goldband, Katkin, and Morell (1979) noted in a discussion of the relationship between the Type A behavior pattern and CHD, it is essential to demonstrate linkage among personality factors, pathophysiological mechanisms, and disease if one is interested in a causal analysis, because, ultimately, any model that postulates an association between a personality trait or a behavior pattern and disease must be able to demonstrate a final common pathophysiological path to the disease end point.

Many investigators have asserted that the final common path to coronary disease is likely to be excessive catecholaminergic reactivity (Obrist, 1981; Wright, Contrada, & Glass, 1985). Williams, Barefoot, and Shekelle (1985) specifically postulated that hostile individuals are likely to experience higher levels of serum catecholamines and generally greater levels of cardiovascular response to environmental stress than nonhostile individuals. Yet, as Smith and Christensen noted in their chapter, a number of studies have failed to find any relationship between scores on the Ho scale and cardiovascular responses to laboratory stressors. Recent findings (e.g., Suarez & Williams, 1989) suggest that a more productive research strategy must focus on the complex dynamics of Person × Situation interactions and should evaluate a variety of dispositions that may, under appropriate environmental conditions, result in cardiovascular hyperreactivity. To the extent that a variety of psychological dispositions may match up with the reactivity-eliciting characteristics of different situations, those individuals who show many of such dispositions would be more likely to exhibit greater cardiovascular reactivity across events than those showing fewer dispositions. If this analysis is cogent, then the focus on single traits, such as hostility or Type A behavior, represents only one dimension of what must be a multidimensional analysis of traits, situations, and physiological reactivity. Support for this view may be inferred from recent data of Burns and Katkin (1991), who found that the interaction of dimensions of anger expression (Anger-in × Anger-out) was associated with cardiovascular reactivity during a reaction-time task featuring harassment, but not during the same reaction-time task emphasizing social evaluation.

A final note of caution is in order here. It is now widely accepted that the link between personality and coronary disease is excess cardiovascular activation; yet there is little clear evidence to demonstrate that excess cardiovascular reactivity is a significant risk factor. Not only must we learn more about the intricacies of the relationship between hostility and cardiovascular reactivity, but we need to learn considerably more than we currently know about the relationship between reactivity and risk for disease before we can comfortably conclude that hostility (or any other personality factor) is truly a risk factor for CHD.

References

Barefoot, J. C., Dahlstrom, W. G., & Williams, R. B., Jr. (1983). Hostility, CHD incidence and total mortality: A 25-year follow-up of 255 physicians. *Psychosomatic Medicine, 45,* 59–63.

Barefoot, J. C., Dodge, K. A., Peterson, B. L., Dahlstrom, W. G., & Williams, R. B., Jr. (1989). The Cook-Medley Hostility scale: Item content and ability to predict survival. *Psychosomatic Medicine, 51,* 46–57.

Booth-Kewley, S., & Friedman, H. S. (1987). Psychological predictors of heart disease: A quantitative review. *Psychological Bulletin, 101,* 343–362.

Burns, J. W., & Katkin, E. S. (1991, March). *Anger, hostility, anxiety and cardiovascular reactivity to different stress conditions.* Paper presented at the meeting of the Society for Behavioral Medicine, Washington, DC.

Carney, R. M., Rich, M. W., teVelde, A., Saini, J., Clark, K., & Jaffe, A. S. (1987). Major depressive disorder in coronary artery disease. *American Journal of Cardiology, 60,* 1273–1275.

Costa, P. T., Jr., Zonderman, A. B., McCrae, R. R., & Williams, R. B., Jr. (1986). Cynicism and paranoid alienation in the Cook-Medley Hostility scale. *Psychosomatic Medicine, 48,* 283–285.

Dembroski, T. M., MacDougall, J. M., Williams, R. B., Jr., Haney, T. L., & Blumenthal, J. A. (1985). Components of Type A, hostility, and anger-in: Relationship to angiographic findings. *Psychosomatic Medicine, 247,* 219–233.

Fontana, A. F., Kerns, R. D., Blatt, S. J., Rosenberg, R. L., Burg, M. M., & Colonese, K. L. (1989). Cynical mistrust and the search for self-worth. *Journal of Psychosomatic Research, 33,* 449–456.

Friedman, H. S., & Booth-Kewley, S. (1987). Personality, Type A behavior, and coronary heart disease: The role of emotional expression. *Journal of Personality and Social Psychology, 53,* 783–792.

Friedman, M., & Rosenman, R. H. (1959). Association of specific overt behavior pattern with blood and cardiovascular findings. *Journal of the American Medical Association, 169,* 1286–1296.

Goldband, S., Katkin, E. S., & Morell, M. A. (1979). Personality and cardiovascular disorder: Steps toward demystification. In I. G. Sarason & C. D. Spielberger (Eds.), *Stress and anxiety. Vol. 6* (pp. 351–369). Washington, DC: Hemisphere Publishing.

McCranie, E. W., Watkins, L. O., Brandsma, J. M., & Sisson, B. D. (1986). Hostility, coronary heart disease (CHD) incidence and total mortality: Lack of association in a 25-year follow-up study of 478 physicians. *Journal of Behavioral Medicine, 9,* 119–125.

Obrist, P. A. (1981). *Cardiovascular psychophysiology: A perspective.* New York: Plenum Press.

Price, V. A. (1982). *Type A behavior pattern: A model for research and practice.* New York: Academic Press.

Rosenman, R. H., Friedman, M., Straus, R., Wurm, M., Kostichek, R., Hahn, W., & Werthessen, N. T. (1964). A predictive study of coronary heart disease. *Journal of the American Medical Association, 189,* 113–124.

Siegman, A. W., Dembroski, T. M., & Ringel, N. (1987). Components of hostility and the severity of coronary artery disease. *Psychosomatic Medicine, 49,* 127–135.

Smith, T. W., & Frohm, K. D. (1985). What's so unhealthy about hostility? Construct validity and psychosocial correlates of the Cook and Medley Ho scale. *Health Psychology, 4,* 503–520.

Suarez, E. C., & Williams, R. B., Jr. (1989). Situational determinants of cardioavascular and emotional reactivity in high and low hostile men. *Psychosomatic Medicine, 51,* 404–418.

Williams, R. B., Jr., & Barefoot, J. C. (1988). Coronary-prone behavior: The emerging role of the hostility complex. In B. K. Houston & C. R. Snyder (Eds.), *Type A behavior pattern: Research, theory, and intervention* (pp. 189–211). New York: John Wiley.

Williams, R. B., Jr., Barefoot, J. C., & Shekelle, R. B. (1985). Health consequences of hostility. In M. A. Chesney & R. H. Rosenman (Eds.), *Anger and hostility in cardiovascular and behavioral disorders* (pp. 173–185). Washington, DC: Hemisphere Publishing.

Wright, R. A., Contrada, R. J., & Glass, D. C. (1985). Psychophysiological correlates of Type A behavior. In E. S. Katkin & S. B. Manuck (Eds.), *Advances in behavioral medicine. Vol. 1* (pp. 39–88). Greenwich, CT: JAI Press.

Zyzanski, S. J., Jenkins, C. D., Ryan, T. J., Flessas, A., & Everist, M. (1976). Psychological correlates of coronary angiographic findings. *Archives of Internal Medicine, 136,* 1234–1237.

Commentary to Part Two: Does Lowering Cholesterol Cause Increases in Depression, Suicide, and Accidents?

Robert M. Kaplan, Stephen B. Manuck, and Sally Shumaker

Editor's Note: This commentary by Kaplan, Manuck, and Shumaker is not directly concerned with hostility and so deserves a brief introduction. Efforts to establish causal links among hostility, coping, and health are strengthened when likely physiological mediating mechanisms are identified. In the case of cardiovascular disease, elevated serum cholesterol is a well-known physiological risk factor. However, attempts to improve longevity by reducing serum cholesterol have produced unusual and puzzling results, possibly related to hostility and coping.

This interesting commentary is thus included in this book because (a) of the possible association between lowered cholesterol and hostility; (b) the paper makes important methodological and statistical points; and (c) the national, clinical implications are so important. Kaplan, Manuck, and Shumaker are all senior researchers in health psychology with a wealth of relevant experience.

Note: Based on a Discussion Group at the University of California, Health Psychology Network, Lake Arrowhead, CA, November 17, 1990

C holesterol lowering has become a national obsession. A national campaign on cholesterol lowering has begun with the support of prestigious federal agencies, including the National Institutes of Health. Simultaneously, the private sector has promoted lower cholesterol in the marketing of a wide variety of products. Although several consensus conferences (Expert Panel, 1988) strongly back the cholesterol-reduction campaign, there are also some dissenters (Moore, 1989).

At the heart of the controversy is the effect of cholesterol reduction on total mortality. In the following sections, we will briefly review the total-mortality issue, the public-policy interpretations of the data, and some potential explanations for the failure to find that cholesterol reduction extends the life expectancy. We will conclude with suggestions for future research.

The Total-Mortality Issue:

There is clear evidence that the United States and other Westernized countries have experienced an epidemic of deaths because of coronary heart disease. Furthermore, epidemiologic studies have clearly identified elevated serum cholesterol as a risk factor for early coronary-heart-disease deaths. Serum cholesterol is an abundant lipid that is primarily produced endogenously, but can also be systematically influenced by dietary practices. Perhaps the best demonstration of the relationship between serum cholesterol and mortality was the follow up of those screened for Multiple Risk Factors Intervention Trial (MRFIT). In this study, 356,222 men between the ages of 35 and 57 years were given standardized serum-cholesterol assessments. Six years later, mortality was evaluated, and there was a strong and systematic relationship between serum cholesterol and mortality within each age group. Furthermore, there appeared to be no threshold effect, suggesting that the lower the cholesterol, the lower was the probability of dying. These results cast doubt on current stagies of screening and treating only those in the highest cholesterol categories (Stamler, Wentworth, & Neaton, 1986).

Cholesterol can be reduced either through dietary or exercise interventions (McCann, Retzlaff, Walden, & Knopp, 1990), through drugs that bind bile acids, or through drugs that interfere with the endogenous production of cholesterol. Because high cholesterol is associated with deaths from coronary heart disease, it has been assumed that cholesterol reduction will reduce the probability of heart-disease deaths. Several major studies have investigated the relationship between cholesterol lowering and the probability of deaths from coronary heart disease. Perhaps the best U.S. study was the Lipid Research Clinics Coronary Primary Prevention Trial. In this multisite clinical trial, men were screened for serum-cholesterol levels. Those above the 95th percentile for the general population were rescreened. If they remained high, they were put on a diet to determine if they could reduce their cholesterol through dietary interventions. Those who did not respond to diet were then randomly assigned to use either a placebo or cholestyramine, a drug that binds bile acids and interferes with the production of cholesterol. The trial was large, involving over 3,800 participants. After 7 years of follow up, there was a significant reduction in deaths from coronary heart disease among those randomly assigned to the cholestyramine treatment (Lipid Research Clinics Program, 1984).

A similar result was obtained in another large study conducted in Helsinki, Finland. The Helsinki Heart Study evaluated a cholesterol-lowering drug called Gemfibrozil (Frick, et al., 1987). In the Helsinki study, 2,051 men were randomly assigned to take Gemfibrozil twice daily, while another 2,030 were given a placebo. After 6 years, 19 of the men in the placebo groups had died of ischemic heart disease, while only 14 of those in the drug-treated group had died. This significant difference led the authors to conclude that Gemfibrozil caused a 26% reduction in ischemic-heart-disease deaths. The 26% is calculated as follows: In the drug group .68% = 14/2051 died, while in the placebo group .93% = 19/2030 died of ischemic heart disease. The actual difference is about ¼ of 1%. However, the ratio (.0068/.0093) subtracted from 1.0 yields about a 26% reduction. Furthermore, the total number of deaths in the Gemfibrozil group was actually higher than those in the placebo group (45 vs. 42).

In both the lipid research and the Helsinki studies, there was one peculiar finding. Although each study demonstrated a reduction in deaths from coronary heart disease, neither study demonstrated a significant increase in life expectancy for those using cholesterol-lowering drugs. Reductions in deaths from heart disease were compensated for by increases in deaths from other causes. In both the lipid research and the Helsinki studies, the category of deaths that compensated for decreases for heart disease was accidents, suicides, and violence.

More recently, Muldoon, Manuck, and Matthews (1990) reviewed all primary prevention trials on lipid-lowering drugs. They discovered that, aggregated across studies, there was a significant benefit of cholesterol reduction for deaths associated with heart disease. However, there was an even stronger effect of cholesterol lowering on increases in deaths from nondisease causes. Across studies, the effects of cholesterol lowering on heart disease are inconsistent. However, the effects of cholesterol lowering on nondisease deaths occurs in all studies.

Another recent meta-analysis considered the value of cholesterol lowering for those who have already suffered a myocardial infarction (Rossouw, Lewis, & Rifkind, 1990). This review of six trials offered a more positive assessment of cholesterol lowering. However, the review was unable to substantiate a benefit of cholesterol lowering for total mortality. Across studies, there was a small but significant decrease in deaths from cardiovascular disease ($p<.05$), a nonsignificant decrease in cancer deaths, and a strong increase in noncardiovascular deaths ($p<.001$). The review of secondary prevention trials was unable to break out noncardiovascular, noncancer deaths to determine if the increase was because of accidents and violence. Overall, however, the effects of cholesterol lowering on total mortality were nonsignificant.

Are These Findings a Fluke?

One of the major issues is whether the compensatory deaths are a fluke? Clearly, there is a biological mechanism to account for the relationship between cholesterol reduction and deaths from coronary heart disease. The effect of cholesterol lowering on becoming an accident or suicide victim is less clearly identified with a specific behavioral or biological mechanism. One potential explanation is that cholesterol reduction causes some change in mood or behavior that predisposes individuals to these negative outcomes.

What might these potential mechanisms be? To date, we know of very few potential explanations. There are some neurochemical possibilities. In laboratory rats, for instance, modification of dietary fat appears to alter fluidity and cholesterol content of cell membranes in the central nervous system, with effects on maze learning, pain threshold, and physical activity (Coscina, Yehuda, Dixon, Kish, & Leprohon-Greenwood, 1986; Kessler, Kessler, & Yehuda 1985, 1986; Yehuda, Leprohon-Greenwood, Dixon, & Coscina, 1986). And in one study, monkeys fed a diet low in saturated fat and cholesterol (modeled on American Heart Association recommendations) were found to be more aggressive than control animals consuming a diet high in fat and cholesterol (Kaplan & Manuck, 1990). Results of several clinical investigations also suggest a link between serum cholesterol concentrations and aggressive behavior in human beings. Among adolescent boys with attention deficit disorder (ADD), individuals who were also diagnosed as having an aggressive conduct disorder had significantly lower fasting serum cholesterol than subjects with ADD alone (Virkkunen & Penttinen, 1984). Others have reported an association of low-serum-cholesterol concentration with poorly internalized social norms and low self-control (Jenkins, Hames, Zyzanski, Rosenman, & Friedman, 1979). Similarly, criminal offenders remanded for mental evaluation by court order and diagnosed as having antisocial personality disorders have been found to have lower serum-cholesterol concentrations than persons with other types of personality disorders or population-based means for individuals of comparable age (Virkkunen, 1979). In other studies, low cholesterol has been associated with alcohol-related violence, suicidal attempts, and undersocialized aggressive conduct disorder among homicidal offenders (Virkkunen, 1983a, 1983b).

At present, we are uncertain about the reliability of the increase in nondisease deaths in lipid-lowering trials. Furthermore, the explanation for the effect is unknown. However, several potential mechanisms need to be evaluated.

Public Policy Issues

The evidence on the relationship between serum cholesterol and mortality is puzzling. On the one hand, there have been national policies that endorse the reduction of cholesterol, even though the evidence that cholesterol reduction improves survival has been lacking (National High Blood Pressure Education Program, 1990). Indeed, there is as much evidence that cholesterol reduction causes increases in accidents, suicides, and violence as there is that cholesterol reduction decreases the chances of dying from coronary heart disease. The cholesterol-reduction literature is also troubled by other inconsistencies between results and policies. For example, nearly all studies in the literature used only male subjects (e.g., The Coronary Primary Prevention Trial). Additionally, these male subjects were above the 95th percentile in the population for serum cholesterol, and those who responded to a dietary intervention were excluded from the trial. Nevertheless, the interpretations of the trial results have been generalized to both men and women, to those at all cholesterol levels, and to dietary as well as pharmaceutical interventions. We raise questions about the correspondence between current data and public policy.

Directions for Future Research

The relationship between cholesterol reduction and behavioral outcomes needs more investigation. Several questions deserve prompt attention. For example, does cholesterol reduction affect neurotransmitters? Does cholesterol reduction affect physical activity, anger, and fighting? How does cholesterol reduction affect mood, cognitive functioning, etc.?

There are many potential behavioral mechanisms that might explain the relationship between cholesterol reduction and nondisease deaths. For example, cholesterol reduction may affect a cognitive or attentional process. Thus, those on cholesterol-lowering regimens may be more prone to accidents. Another possibility is that cholesterol reduction affects some biological process that results in greater anger, rage, or depression. Although confusing, the literature on cholesterol reduction suggests exciting possibilities for future research.

References

Coscina, D. V., Yehuda, S., Dixon, L. M., Kish, S. J., & Leprohon-Greenwood, C. E. (1986). Learning is improved by a soybean oil diet in rats. *Life Sciences, 38,* 1789–1794.

The Expert Panel. (1988). Report on the national cholesterol education program. Expert panel on detection, evaluation, and treatment of high blood cholesterol in adults. *Archives of Internal Medicine, 148,* 36–69.

Frick, M. H., Elo, O., Haapa, K., Heinonen, O. P., Heinsalmi, P., Helo, P., Huttunen, J. K., Kaitaniemi, P., Koskinen, P., & Manninen, V. (1987). Helsinki Heart Study: Primary-prevention trial with gemfibrozil in middle-aged men with dyslipidemia: Safety of treatment, changes in risk factors, and incidence of coronary heart disease. *New England Journal of Medicine, 312,* 1237–1245.

Jenkins, C. D., Hames, C. G., Zyzanski, S. J., Rosenman, R. H., & Friedman, M. (1979). Psychological traits and serum lipids. I. Findings from the California psychological inventory. *Psychosomatic Medicine, 31,* 115–128.

Kaplan, J. R., & Manuck, S. B. (1990). The effects of fat and cholesterol on aggressive behavior in monkeys. *Psychosomatic Medicine, 52,* 226–227 [abstract].

Kessler, A. R., Kessler, B., & Yehuda, A. (1985). Changes in the cholesterol level, cholesterol-to-phospholipid mole ratio, and membrane microviscosity in rat brain induced by age and a plant oil mixture. *Biochemistry and Pharmacology, 34,* 1120–1121.

Kessler, A. R., Kessler, B., & Yehuda, S. (1986). In vivo modulation of brain cholesterol level and learning performance by a novel plant lipid: Indications for interactions between hippocampal-cortical cholesterol and learning. *Life Sciences, 38,* 1185–1192.

Lipid Research Clinics Program. (1984). The Lipid Research Clinic's Coronary Primary Prevention Research Trial Results. *Journal of the American Medical Association, 251,* 351–374.

McCann, B. S., Retzlaff, B. M., Walden, C. E., & Knopp, R. H. (1990). Dietary intervention for coronary heart disease prevention. In S. A. Shumaker, E. B. Schron, & J. K. Ockeen (Eds.), *The handbook of health behavior change* (pp. 191–215). New York: Springer.

Moore, T. J. (1989). *Heart failure.* New York: Random House.

Muldoon, M. F., Manuck, S. B., & Matthews, K. A. (1990). Lowering cholesterol concentrations and mortality: A quantitative review of primary prevention trials. *British Medical Journal, 301*, 309–314.

National High Blood Pressure Education Program and National Cholesterol Education Program. (1990). *Working group report on management of patients with hypertension and high blood cholesterol* (DHHS/NIH, NHCBI Publication No. 90-2361).

Rossouw, J. E., Lewis, B., & Rifkind, B. M. (1990). The value of lowering cholesterol after myocardial infarction. *New England Journal of Medicine, 323*, 1112–1119.

Stamler, J., Wentworth, D., & Neaton, J. D. (1986). Is the relationship between serum cholesterol and risk of premature death from coronary heart disease continuous or graded? Findings in 356,222 primary screenees of the Multiple Risk Factor Intervention Trial (MRFIT). *Journal of American Medical Association, 256*, 2823–2828.

Virkkunen, M. (1979). Serum cholesterol in antisocial personality. *Neuropsychobiology, 5*, 27–30.

Virkkunen, M. (1983a). Serum cholesterol levels in homicidal offenders. *Biological Psychiatry, 10*, 65–69.

Virkkunen, M. (1983b). Insulin secretion during the glucose tolerance test in antisocial personality. *British Journal of Psychiatry, 142*, 598–604.

Virkkunen, M., & Penttinen, H. (1984). Serum cholesterol in aggressive conduct disorder: A preliminary study. *Biological Psychiatry, 19*, 435–439.

Yehuda, S., Leprohon-Greenwood, C. E., Dixon, L. M., & Coscina, D. V. (1986). Effects of dietary fat on pain threshold, thermoregulation and motor activity in rats. *Pharmacology, Biochemistry and Behavior, 24*, 1775–1777.

PART THREE

The Coping Perspective

CHAPTER 8

Inhibition as the Linchpin of Health

James W. Pennebaker

T he linchpin of a wagon wheel is that straight piece of metal or wood inserted at the end of the axle to prevent the wheel from falling off. Although a relatively unsung mechanical invention, the linchpin is critical to the functioning of the wagon or cart. Without it, the wheel quickly becomes wobbly and rolls off in a random direction. With each linchpin intact, the wheels of the wagon are able to move in exactly the same direction in an efficient way. This chapter is, in a sense, an ode to the linchpin.

Within health and social psychology, a number of basic processes analogous to the wheel, motor, and shape of the psychobiological wagon have been identified. Reinforcement and drive-reduction models have helped to define the direction and intensity of behaviors. Cognitive models have begun to explain how the organism thinks about and rationalizes stimuli and behaviors. Recent genetic and personality-trait approaches outline the biological boundaries that predispose organisms to behave in certain ways.

Central to all of these models is the assumption that the organism is able to behave in relatively coordinated ways toward particular goals over extended periods of time. To

The research reported in this chapter was funded by National Science Foundation grants BNS 9001615 and BNS 9021518.

accomplish this, the organism must quickly learn to inhibit competing behaviors, thoughts, and perhaps even emotions. To maintain behaviors over time, the linchpin of inhibition must remain intact.

Inhibition can be construed as both an automatic and a controlled process. Consider the ways that automatic forms of inhibition have been examined within the field of psychology. At the neural level, certain neurotransmitters and neurons function to inhibit random or irrelevant firing of nerve cells. In visual and auditory perception, the firing of one group of cells may block the firing of adjacent cells in order to enhance contrast, as in lateral inhibition. On the muscular level, reciprocal inhibition allows one group of muscles to contract while antagonistic muscles relax. Pavlov (1927) explained extinction of a conditioned response and spontaneous recovery to inhibitory processes. Inhibition has also played prominent roles within the areas of verbal learning and neurosciences. Particular brain regions such as the hippocampus and frontal lobes are largely devoted to the inhibition of behaviors.

More relevant to the current chapter are forms of controlled or active inhibition. Active inhibition occurs when the individual must consciously or effortfully hold back particular behaviors, thoughts, or feelings. Varieties of active inhibition have been discussed since the time of Freud and serve as the bases of socialization. Bowel and bladder control, when first attempted by children around the age of 2 years, initially require conscious attention and self-control. Urges among adolescents to rape and pillage must also be inhibited. Indeed, for individuals to function in the social world, they must learn to inhibit selfish desires and behave in socially defined ways. Interestingly, these forms of inhibition are initially conscious and active but, with time and practice, become automatic and passive.

Whether we are dealing with bladder control or good manners, some degree of inhibition is required. Usually, the processes of inhibition are highly adaptive for both the individual and the society at large. However, there can be an insidious side to inhibition as well. As discussed later, inhibition can be effortful, anxiety provoking, and, ultimately, it can be seen as a physical-health risk. In this chapter, I first point to evidence that suggests that inhibition is associated with a variety of health problems. The second part of the chapter deals with the reasons why individuals are often forced to inhibit their thoughts, feelings, and behaviors in maladaptive ways. The final section is devoted to a naturalistic study on the 1989 Loma Prieta Earthquake wherein the ongoing forces of social inhibition have been mapped over time.

Inhibition and Health: A Theory of Inhibition and Confrontation

Since 1983, I have been working on a general theory of inhibition and confrontation that is still evolving. Currently, the theory is based on the idea that to inhibit or hold back one's thoughts, feelings, or behaviors requires work. In the short run, the work of inhibition can be measured by increases in autonomic nervous system activity, such as heightened skin-conductance levels (SCL) (i.e., hand perspiration). Over time, the work of inhibition can be viewed as a form of stress (e.g., Selye, 1976). The effects of long-term, low levels of this stress can create or exacerbate illness and health problems.

A particularly dangerous form of inhibition can be seen among individuals who have suffered a trauma about which they cannot talk to others. Not talking about the trauma can be a never-ending form of inhibition and stress. Accordingly, requiring individuals to talk about upsetting experiences or in some way translate them into language should result in reductions in autonomic nervous system activity and, over time, improvements in physical health.

Across several questionnaire studies, we have found that individuals who have suffered any type of major trauma in childhood are far more likely to become ill if they never talked about the trauma. For example, we have consistently found that individuals who have had a childhood trauma and who have not talked about it are more likely to visit a physician in the 4 months following the administration of the questionnaire than students who have had comparable traumas, but who have talked about them (Pennebaker, 1989). Similar findings emerged with a sample of 200 corporation employees in terms of their reporting objective health problems, including cancer and hypertension (Pennebaker & Susman, 1988).

A particularly important aspect of the various correlational studies is that the confiding–health relationship appears to be independent of various demographic markers such as socioeconomic status (SES) and sex as well as traditional notions of social support. In fact, when we partial out the effects of friendship-network size, the confiding–health relation becomes slightly stronger (Pennebaker & Susman, 1988). Having had a trauma about which one cannot confide *and* having a close friendship network may place an additional burden on the individual. That is, he or she may have to actively hold back to a greater degree with friends than without them.

The Benefits of Talking and Writing About Traumas

Although not the main focus of this chapter, it is important to mention briefly that the flip side of inhibition, a state we variously refer to as disinhibition, a letting-go state, or opening up, can be healthy. We conducted several laboratory experiments with normal college students and other groups wherein we required them to write or talk about traumatic experiences. In the studies, volunteers were randomly assigned to disclose traumas or superficial topics for 15 to 20 minutes per day for 3 to 4 consecutive days. Those assigned to disclose traumas were encouraged to let go and explore their deepest thoughts and feelings.

The paradigm was quite powerful. Almost half of the participants cried. They disclosed shocking secrets that they had never told anyone before. While disclosing, many evidenced profound changes in voice characteristics and handwriting. Also, SCL dropped among those who disclosed the most personal and emotional experiences (see Pennebaker, 1990, for summary of effects and complete citation list).

In the various studies, those individuals who wrote about traumas subsequently visited physicians less than controls. All results were based on actual health records. A more recent study found that writing about traumas was also linked with improvements in immune function. That is, disclosure improved t-lymphocyte activity and reduced physician visits. Most recently, we found that writing about ongoing upsetting experiences (entering college) improved health for 4 to 5 months after writing. The writing paradigm, then, had finite positive health effects (Pennebaker, Kiecolt-Glaser, & Glaser, 1988; see also a study by Spiegel, Bloom, Kraemer, & Gottheil, 1989, with breast-cancer patients). Finally, in a recent study with 33 survivors of the Holocaust, we found that talking about the Holocaust in depth in our laboratory was associated with health improvements up to 1.5 years after the study (Pennebaker, Barger, & Tiebout, 1989).

When and Why Can Inhibition Be Unhealthy?

In most cases, inhibitory processes are healthy and adaptive. As noted earlier, active inhibition is primarily a problem when individuals desire to talk abut an upsetting experience, but are unable to do so. In these cases, inhibition can cause or exacerbate health problems for at least three interrelated reasons:

1. The work of holding back. As noted earlier, actively restraining ongoing thoughts, feelings, and behaviors is physiological work. In the short run, behavioral inhibition has been demonstrated by increases in autonomic nervous system activity

(e.g., Fowles, 1980) and central nervous system activity in the septal and hippo-campal regions (Gray, 1975) and cerebral cortical areas (Luria, 1980). Actively re-straining thoughts (e.g., Wegner, 1989) and the expression of emotions (e.g., Buck, 1984) have also been linked to heightened autonomic activity.

The inhibition of behaviors, thoughts, and emotions over long periods has been tied to illness episodes and immune-system difficulties. It should be noted that the long-term inhibition–illness relation is far more difficult to establish in unambigu-ous terms compared with short-term laboratory studies. Nevertheless, research in the personality domain, for example, indicates that young children who are labeled as socially and emotionally inhibited have more health and sleep problems, ele-vated cortisol levels, and other physiological upheavals traditionally viewed as risky (e.g., Kagan, Reznick, & Snidman, 1988). Among adult samples, individuals who reported experiencing greater long-term conflicts over goals and ambivalence concerning emotional expression are more likely to visit physicians for illness (Emmons & King, 1988; King, Emmons, & Woodley, in press).

2. Not talking about upsetting experiences impedes the natural cognitive processes that promote health. Typically, when individuals face emotionally powerful events, they talk about them to others. One benefit of translating an experience into lan-guage is that it helps to organize and assimilate the event (e.g., Horowitz, 1976). Once an event is encoded in a language format—or at least not just an image for-mat—it can be summarized and better understood (see Harber & Pennebaker, in press, for summary of the literature). Inhibition, then, can be insidious in that this organizing process is impeded, thus prolonging the deleterious effects of the trauma.

3. Actively attempting to suppress thoughts and feelings about traumas increases cognitive interference and work. Individuals who would like to talk about a trauma, but are unable to do so, typically find themselves thinking about, dreaming about, and living with the trauma much of the time (cf. Nolen-Hoeksema, 1990). The degree to which a person is cognitively living with a trauma should be directly related to cognitive time and effort devoted to the trauma. It is commonly known, for example, that the individuals who have faced upsetting experiences report greater difficulties concentrating and working on complex tasks.

Interestingly, the act of thought and emotion suppression further interferes with cognitive processes. Gilbert, Krull, and Pelham (1987), for example, found that when individuals are told to actively ignore interfering stimuli, they are less able to process complex information. Wegner (1989), in an important line of studies, demonstrated that people are unable to suppress thoughts. Furthermore, when given instructions to suppress thoughts, not only are the forbidden thoughts more accessible, but other cognitive information is not fully processed.

To summarize, inhibition can affect psychological and physical health following upsetting experiences in a number of direct and indirect ways. Although I have not reviewed the substantial literature in the psychosomatic field, there is little doubt that active inhibition can be toxic under some circumstances. (For a thorough review of the psychosomatic effects of inhibition, see Traue & Pennebaker, in press).

Social Constraints That Drive Inhibitory Processes

In 1989, I was asked to give a series of talks to groups of parents who had recently experienced the death of a child. I was particularly struck by how trivial most of health psychology research sounds when attempting to help grieved individuals cope with an overwhelming trauma. By talking to the parents, I learned that one of their major adjustment problems involved their friends' behaviors. That is, relatives, friends, and acquaintances seemed to avoid the bereaved parents. Perhaps they did not know what to say, did not want to think about the tragedy, or even feared that they would remind the bereaved parents of the death. Whatever was occurring in their friends' minds was ultimately constraining the bereaved parents' options to talk about the death even if they had wanted to.

The act of not talking about a trauma can result from overt social constraints. That is, I may not talk about my own personal upheavals because you won't allow it. Over the last 2 years, my students and I have been examining this possibility with a variety of samples.

Listening to the Traumas of Others Can Be Stressful

Whereas talking about upsetting experiences can be physically and psychologically healthy, listening to other people's upheavals may not be. The literature on burnout, for example, suggests that individuals who hold jobs that require empathic responses but that have very little control to ameliorate the suffering of others are most likely to become emotionally blunted and dissatisfied with their jobs, and they are most likely to report a variety of physical complaints (cf. Maslach, 1982).

Recently, we had 66 college students watch 1 of 33 videotapes of Holocaust survivors telling about their personal experiences in Nazi concentration camps during World War II (Shortt & Pennebaker, 1991). While watching the videotapes, the students' SCL and heart rate (HR) were continuously monitored. The same autonomic measures were collected from the Holocaust survivors themselves during their interviews. We were then able to correlate SCL and HR between the speaker and listener over time on a case-by-case basis. Overall, we found a negative correlation between speaker and listener on the SCL measure. That is, the more that the Holocaust survivor let go and disclosed horrible experiences, the more that the listener's SCL increased. Hearing about traumas is itself traumatic.

Although the effects were modest, they fit in with a number of interesting findings emerging from the social-support literature. It is well documented, for example, that having a strong social-support network in the midst of a trauma is physically beneficial for the one facing the trauma (Cohen & McKay, 1984). What is less well publicized is that those who are providing the social support have *more* health problems during this same time (Coyne et al., 1987; Kessler, McLeod, & Wethington, 1985).

Extrapolating from this research, it is easy to understand why people shy away from distressed friends. Talking with someone who has faced a horrible experience and who is continuing to cope with it can be burdensome. The distressed individual often wants to talk about the trauma or, at least, may think about it frequently. Whether the bereaved friend talks about the trauma or simply thinks about it, the standard social-interaction rules will be disrupted.

The Art of Social Constraint

Recently, my students and I have become interested in learning how social-constraint mechanisms become engaged in normal interaction. This research, which has been inspired by previous work in the general area of social physics (Knowles, 1978), has examined how groups of individuals subtly shun a group member who is perceived to be different.

In one recent study, three groups of seven students participated in 30-min "parties" wherein they stood in a fixed area and talked. Approximately 4 m above them, a video camera recorded their locations on a minute-by-minute basis. On entering the party room, a party mask was placed on each person. The mask, which was made of white plastic, covered the entire face, but had holes for the eyes and mouth. Five of the seven masks were blank. The remaining two had facial expressions drawn on them: one was a happy expression, and the other was an angry expression. No one knew what their own masks looked like. In fact, at the end of the study, everyone in all the groups thought they had on a plain white mask.

Most interesting is what happened to the people wearing the angry masks. In all three groups, the angry-masked (AM) people were gradually excluded from the group. When the AM subjects spoke, no one looked at them. Those standing adjacent to the AM subjects slowly stepped in front of the AMs, forcing the AMs further away from the group center. In fact, the AMs stood almost 2 ft further from the group center than any other members.

Not only were the AM subjects verbally and physically excluded from each of the groups, but they reported feeling most isolated, nervous, and lonely. The irony was that none of the AM subjects attributed their isolation to their masks. In their own minds, they had become outcasts because of their own shortcomings. The subtlety of this effect was highlighted by the fact that 88% of the other subjects reported that they did not treat the AM subjects differently—indeed, almost half claimed not to have really noticed the mask differences.

This experiment, of course, is a pale analogy of the social processes that must occur in the real world with people who have faced a traumatic experience. It does illustrate, however, how quickly and subtly social constraints can take over and affect the interaction quality of those perceived as different.

Inhibition and Social Constraint Following an Earthquake

When the original inhibition–confrontation theory was formulated, I assumed that people would be least likely to talk about traumas that were socially unacceptable. For example, people would feel free to discuss openly something like the death of a friend, but not a personal sexual trauma. The rationale was that a socially unacceptable trauma would be something that could bring on humiliation, embarrassment, or even punishment from others. Socially acceptable traumas, on the other hand, could be shared without possible social censure. This distinction is becoming less convincing as more studies are conducted.

On October 17, 1989, a large earthquake shook the San Francisco Bay area. The quake, which registered 7.2 on the Richter scale, resulted in wide-scale damage and the loss of over 60 lives. The October quake along the Loma Prieta fault was not completely unexpected and certainly not a socially unacceptable trauma. Within days of the earthquake, Kent Harber of Stanford University, a group of students, and I had begun studying the social and health effects that followed (Pennebaker & Harber, 1991).

Since the earthquake, we have interviewed by phone over 1,000 residents of San Francisco, Sacramento, Los Angeles, and Dallas concerning their perceptions of their own psychological, social, and physical health. Phone calls were made using standard random-digit dialing techniques between 6:00 and 9:00 p.m. weeknights during the following weeks after the quake: 1, 2, 3, 6, 8, 16, 28, and 50. In addition, we were able to collect crime and health data from police and health departments in San Francisco and Sacramento.

Although we are still analyzing data, some fascinating effects are emerging that are relevant to our understanding of inhibition and social constraint. Perhaps the most important discovery is that coping and social behaviors change substantially over time. During the first 3 weeks after the quake, for example, the majority of San Francisco residents reported talking and thinking about the quake quite frequently; 3 weeks after the quake, approximately 70% reported thinking about it at least three times a day, and 50% reported talking about it three times a day (10% and 6% of nonarea residents reported thinking and talking about the quake at these levels during the same time).

By 6 weeks after the quake, however, things had changed substantially. Among Bay Area citizens, almost 30% continued to think abut the quake at least three times daily, but only 4% were talking about it. Their not talking about the quake does not reflect uninterest. We also asked residents how much they would like to talk about the quake and how much they would like to hear other people tell about it. Beginning at 3 weeks after the quake (but not before), 80% of Bay Area residents reported that they would like to talk about the quake, whereas less than 60% reported that they would like to hear about it. Indeed, about 4 weeks after the quake, T-shirts began appearing in the affected areas that read, "Thank you for not sharing your earthquake experience."

During the 3 to 8 weeks after the earthquake, the social dynamics had shifted. A sizable percentage of residents reported thinking but not talking about the earthquake. Even though many people wanted to talk about the quake, fewer wanted to listen to other people's stories about it. During this same period, some other social shifts occurred that may reflect the underlying anxiety that people probably felt about the earthquake. As depicted in Figure 1, there was a sharp increase in self-reported arguments that people had with family members and coworkers. Even more striking were the San Francisco police data concerning the number of assaults for the months following the earthquake compared with the assaults the year previously. As seen in Figure 2, assaults were almost 10% higher in the 2 months after the quake compared with the previous year. By 3 months, however, assault rates returned to the 1988 levels. (Note that the mean number of assault reports per month in San Francisco is about 1,000).

Although our health records from area hospitals are not yet complete, self-reports of health problems are showing similar patterns. Specifically, almost 50% of Bay Area residents reported feeling sick in the 3 to 8 weeks after the quake compared with 30% of the controls. By 12 weeks after the earthquake, almost 40% of both Bay Area and nonarea residents reported feeling sick at least once in the prior week.

Summary and Implications: Linchpin or Hub?

In this chapter, I have briefly discussed the importance and, in some cases, the dangers of inhibition. As a construct in psychology and health, inhibition has historically been acknowledged but not examined thoroughly. There is little doubt that inhibitory processes

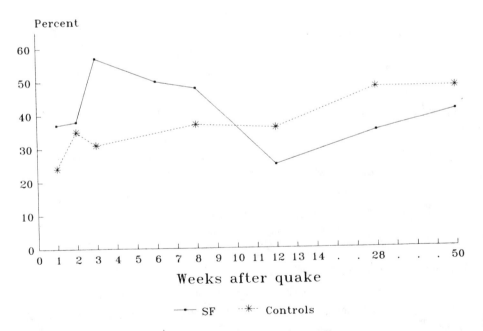

FIGURE 1   Percentage of respondents in San Francisco (SF) versus those in control cities who reported having at least one argument with a family member or coworker in the previous week.

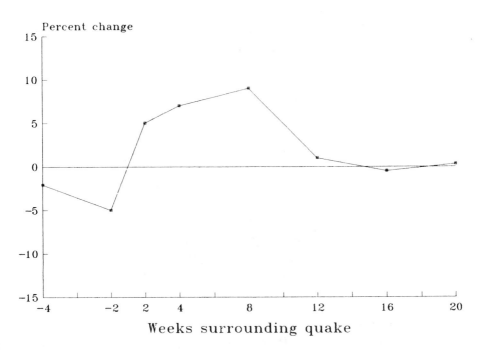

FIGURE 2   Percentage change in aggravated assaults from the year before to the year of the Loma Prieta Earthquake in San Francisco.

have a genetic component, underlie much of socialization, and make socialization and a long life possible. However, there is also evidence that suggests that inhibition of behaviors, thoughts, and feelings can, under some circumstances, be a health risk.

We are currently living in an era that highlights the possible health danger of virtually everything in our environment. Red meat, fish, shellfish, spices, coffee, alcohol, driving, sitting, running, and just about anything else we might want to eat, drink, or do is potentially toxic. Just how dangerous is inhibition? Is it safer than, say, smoking three packs of cigarettes a day? How about hang gliding?

In the grand scheme of things, not talking with others following a trauma probably increases the probability of illness to some degree. Hang gliding after the death of a loved one, however, would probably be more dangerous. We must not lose sight of the fact that many—perhaps most—people cope with traumas fairly well. The work of Wortman and Silver (1989), for example, suggests that perhaps only 30 to 40% of people would ever be at much risk for health problems following a trauma, even if they did not talk about it.

Future research must now begin to put inhibition and other health risks (e.g., hostility, Type A, hang gliding) in some perspective.

References

Buck, R. (1984). *Communication and emotion.* New York: Guilford Press.

Cohen, S., & McKay, G. (1984). Social support, stress, and the buffering hypothesis. A theoretical analysis. In A. Baum, S. E. Taylor, & J. E. Singer (Eds.), *Handbook of psychology and health: Vol. 4. Social psychological aspects of health* (pp. 253–268). New Jersey: Erlbaum.

Coyne, J. C., Kessler, R. C., Tal, M., Turnbull, J., Wortman, C. B., & Greden, J. F. (1987). Living with a depressed person. *Journal of Consulting and Clinical Psychology, 55,* 347–352.

Emmons, R. A., & King, L. A. (1988). Personal striving conflict: Immediate and long-term implications for psychological and physical well-being. *Journal of Personality and Social Psychology, 54,* 1040–1048.

Fowles, D. C. (1980). The three arousal model: Implications of Gray's two-factor learning theory for heart rate, electrodermal activity, and psychopathy. *Psychophysiology, 17,* 87–104.

Gilbert, D. T., Krull, D. S., & Pelham, B. W. (1987). Of thoughts unspoken: Behavioral inhibition and social inference. *Journal of Personality and Social Psychology, 55,* 685–694.

Gray, J. (1975). *Elements of a two-factor theory of learning.* New York: Academic Press.

Harber, K. D., & Pennebaker, J. W. (in press). Overcoming traumatic memories. In S. A. Christianson (Ed.), *The handbook of emotion and memory.* New York: Guilford Press.

Horowitz, M. J. (1976). *Stress responses syndromes.* New York: Jasob Aronson.

Kagan, J., Reznick, J. S., & Snidman, N. (1988). Biological bases of childhood shyness. *Science, 240,* 167–171.

Kessler, R. C., McLeod, J. D., & Wethington, E. (1985). The costs of caring: A perspective on the relationship between sex and psychological distress. In I. G. Sarason & B. R. Sarason (Eds.), *Social support: Theory, research, and applications* (pp. 491–506). Dordrecht, The Netherlands: Martinus Nijhoff.

King, L. A., Emmons, R. A., & Woodley, S. (in press). The structure of inhibition. *Journal of Research in Personality.*

Knowles, E. S. (1978). The gravity of crowding: Application of social physics to the effects of others. In A. Baum & Y. M. Epstein (Eds.), *Human response to crowding* (pp. 183–219). Hillsdale, NJ: Erlbaum.

Luria, A. R. (1980). *Higher cortical functions in man* (2nd ed.). New York: Basic Books.

Nolen-Hoeksema, S. (1990). *Sex differences in depression.* Stanford, CA: Stanford University Press.

Maslach, C. (1982). *Burnout: The cost of caring.* Englewood Cliffs, NJ: Prentice-Hall.

Pavlov, I. (1927). *Conditioned reflexes.* New York: Oxford University Press.

Pennebaker, J. W. (1989). Confession, inhibition, and disease. In L. Berkowitz (Ed.), *Advances in experimental social psychology, Vol. 22* (pp. 211–244). New York: Academic Press.

Pennebaker, J. W. (1990). *Opening up: The healing power of confiding in others.* New York: Morrow.

Pennebaker, J. W., Barger, S. D., & Tiebout, J. (1989). Disclosure of traumas and health among Holocaust survivors. *Psychosomatic Medicine, 51,* 577–589.

Pennebaker, J. W., & Harber, K. (1991). *The psychological effects of the Loma Prieta Earthquake: A preliminary report.* Unpublished manuscript, Southern Methodist University, Dallas.

Pennebaker, J. W., Kiecolt-Glaser, J. K., & Glaser, R. (1988). Disclosure of traumas and immune function: Heath implications for psychotherapy. *Journal of Consulting and Clinical Psychology, 56,* 239–245.

Pennebaker, J. W., & Susman, J. R. (1988). Disclosure of traumas and psychosomatic processes. *Social Science and Medicine, 26,* 327–332.

Selye, H. (1976). *The stress of life.* New York: McGraw-Hill.

Shortt, J. W., & Pennebaker, J. W. (1991). *Talking versus hearing about Holocaust experiences.* Unpublished manuscript, Southern Methodist University, Dallas.

Spiegel, D., Bloom, J. R., Kraemer, H. C., & Gottheil, E. (1989). Effects of psychosocial treatment of patients with metastatic breast cancer. *Lancet, ii:* 888–891.

Traue, H., & Pennebaker, J. W. (Eds.). (in press). *Inhibition as a risk factor for health.* Heidelberg, Federal Republic of Germany: Hogrefe & Huber.

Wegner, D. (1989). *White bears and other unwanted thoughts.* New York: Viking Press.

Wortman, C., & Silver, R. C. (1989). The myths of coping with loss. *Journal of Consulting and Clinical Psychology, 57,* 349–357.

CHAPTER 9

The Repressive Personality and Social Support

Robert A. Emmons

M odels of personality and personality functioning, although playing an increasingly important role in understanding health and disease, have yet to be fully exploited. Several of the contributors to this volume point to the pathological effects of the personality dispositions of chronic anger, hostility, and inhibition. Kobasa (1990) recently chided the field for focusing on cold, cognitive constructs, such as hardiness and optimism, at the expense of psychodynamically oriented concepts, such as repression, conflict, and projection. Echoing her sentiments, Erdelyi (1990) stated that "It is perhaps time that academic psychology simply correct the overemphasis of the merely intellective and incorporate into its corpus conflict-fraught spheres of cognitive functioning" (p. 27). Hence, the examination of these constructs is timely. Given that health has been dominated by cognitive approaches, this volume is significant in that it is an example of the attention now being drawn to the more primitive emotions and motivations relevant to psychosomatic disease. Unfortunately, what is lacking in much current work on personality and disease is a strong conceptual base. The complexities of intrapsychic functioning are receiving insufficient attention. Distorted operationalization of psychodynamic constructs, for instance, equating *anger-in* with repressed

I would like to thank Rebecca Eder for her very insightful comments on an earlier draft of this paper.

hostility (Siegel, this volume) leads to a misrepresentation of psychodynamic hypotheses. This distortion also can lead to the erroneous conclusion that hypotheses offered by psychosomatic theorists such as Alexander (1950) have little validity when in fact the hypotheses were not adequately tested.

Researchers in the field of personality and health have expressed displeasure over the atheoretical nature with which the personality concept has been treated (Friedman, 1990; Maddi, 1990). The classic example of this is undoubtedly the Type A construct. Although research flourished in the absence of a compelling theoretical framework, the concept has been dissected so that it no longer resembles its former self. Undaunted, researchers studying the health consequences of anger and hostility are following in these atheoretical footsteps. Much attention has been directed away from theoretical conceptions of hostility and instead toward methodological and assessment nuances. The latter is commendable, but as Cronbach and Meehl (1955) elegantly pointed out, construct validity is a theoretical enterprise involving hypothesis testing derived from a theory of the construct. The atheoretical nature of constructs such as Type A, hostility, and anger makes the construct-validation process an exercise in futility.

My purpose within these pages is to attempt to link the psychodynamic construct of repression with the social context within which it operates, that is, the level and quality of social support. As many contributors to this volume point out, there is a need to examine constructs such as repression and hostility with respect to the social context within which these processes operate, rather than in isolation. There has been much research on the intrapsychic processes of the repressive personality style, but relatively little research on the ramifications of such a style for interpersonal functioning. A consideration of the interpersonal consequences of repression may be useful for understanding the mechanisms by which this style confers a risk for physical disease. In doing so, I hope also to demonstrate how research in the area of personality and health can profit by incorporating personality theory, and I shall use aspects of psychodynamic theory as an example.

The characteristics of the repressive personality style or repressive coping style have been recently reviewed (Bonanno & Singer, 1990; Weinberger, 1990); thus, I will not elaborate on this literature here. Repressors are individuals who chronically defend themselves against negative affects, particularly anger and anxiety, and who deny experiencing distress even in the face of objective signs indicating that they are distressed. Repressors are believed to be at a risk for developing a number of physical diseases, particularly neoplastic disease (Jensen, 1987). Eysenck (1988) speculated that there exists a personality that is essentially opposite to that of the Type A individual, a Type C or repressive personality, that is not at risk for cardiovascular disease, but rather for cancer.

Several mechanisms have been proposed to explain why repressive individuals are more susceptible to physical disease. These include neuroendocrine–immune-system interactions such as the opioid-peptide hypothesis (Jamner, Schwartz, & Leigh, 1988), as well as differences in health-related behaviors. Because of their tendency to ignore threatening information, repressors are likely to delay seeking medical treatment, and they are not likely to notice or interpret inner sensations as signals of potentially serious diseases. These explanations have been summarized by Schwartz (1983) and Weinberger (1990).

An alternative yet unexplored explanation involves the repressive individual's social environment. There is reason to believe that repressors may be less likely to seek out and profit from social support in their environment. Social support is a major form of coping; thus, one reason for the repressor's seeming inability to deal with stress is due to deficiencies in this domain. There is a large literature documenting the protective buffering effects of social support in the face of stress (Cohen & Wills, 1985). Although the effects of the repressive style for interpersonal functioning have not been as thoroughly explored as their intrapsychic processes, findings suggest that repressors are likely to experience difficulties in interpersonal functioning. Summarizing several studies, Bonanno and Singer (1990) concluded that repressors tend to be preoccupied with issues of relatedness and are troubled by dependency and ambivalence in relation to others. Weinberger (1990) noted that repressors have difficulties in the areas of self-assertion and empathy and are characterized by an inaccurate perception of not only their own but also others' behavior. Because of their ambivalence in personal relations, repressors tend to avoid deep interpersonal involvements. Plante and Schwartz (1990) proposed that repressors tend to engage in solitary leisure activities (e.g., running) where social interaction is avoided. Selection of solitary activities serves as a means of coping with interpersonal dysfunctions.

Given that interpersonal relations may be problematic for repressive individuals, what are the actual mechanisms by which they are less likely to enjoy the buffering effects of social support? There is a host of possibilities. Revenson (1990) suggested two avenues by which personality may be linked with social support. Personality may directly determine social support. Sociable individuals, for example, receive (and give) more support than unsociable individuals. Indirectly, a given personality disposition may determine a person's need for social support: for example, a person with a strong need for affiliation requires more support than does a person with a low need; however, merely possessing the need does not automatically guarantee that such desired support will be forthcoming.

Direct processes are probably in operation for repressive individuals. Given that repressors are less likely to communicate distress, it will be more difficult for others to determine when the individual is in need of support. Repressors tend to be emotionally unexpressive and less likely to engage in self-disclosure behaviors that are likely to elicit reciprocation. They are also more likely to be ambivalent about expressing emotion (King & Emmons, 1990). Their lack of complexity in their representations of themselves and others (Lane & Schwartz, 1987) makes it difficult for them to achieve empathic awareness.

There are also a number of indirect processes in operation for repressive people. Close relationships inevitably involve conflictual interactions, and the repressive individual, having difficulty dealing with conflict in a nonthreatening, nondefensive manner, is going to be less likely to develop loving and intimate relationships with others. His or her ambivalence over entering into relationships may partially stem from the desire to avoid this type of inevitable conflict. An excessive concern with social approval and with how he or she is perceived by others may also lead to difficulty in the area of conflict resolution. Lastly, given the repressor's tendency to avoid dealing with threat (as evidenced in his or her delay in seeking medical attention), it is plausible that the repressor will delay seeking social support until the stressor has reached a catastrophic level. Under stress, the repressor's fragile coping system becomes critically weakened, lowering the chances for the successful recruitment of social support. Ironically and unfortunately for repressors, it is under conditions of high stress that the health-protective effects of support appear to be strongest (Cohen & Wills, 1985).

Given the repressive individual's apparent inability to fully obtain and profit from social support, the question becomes how this deficit arose. What sort of environmental or biological events produced this deficiency? I believe that the answers to these questions may be found in object-relations and attachment theory. In particular, the distinction between anaclitic and introjective personality configurations (Blatt, 1990; Blatt & Shichman, 1983) may be a useful theoretical tool for thinking about the links between the repressive style and interpersonal functioning and, consequently, social support.

Blatt (1990) proposed two primary personality types or configurations, which emerge as a function of the amount of emphasis placed on one of two developmental tasks. These two developmental tasks are (a) establishing mature and satisfying interpersonal relationships and (b) establishing a coherent, realistic, and positive sense of self. Healthy development involves a dialectical integration of these two tendencies. This is certainly not a new distinction; variations of it can be seen in Bakan's (1966) concepts of communion and agency, McAdams's (1985) motivational lines of intimacy and power, and Angyal's (1951) polarities of surrender and autonomy. Several object-relations theorists, such as Mahler, Kohut, and Fairbairn, emphasized that the transition from a state of dependence to increasing autonomy is the primary goal of human development (Eagle, 1984, for a good introduction to these positions). Blass (1990) went beyond these other formulations, however, by proposing a scheme for organizing psychopathologies when one of the developmental lines is exaggerated, relative to the other. Anaclitic depression, conversion, and psychosomatic and dissociative disorders are posited to involve preoccupation with issues of relatedness, whereas paranoia, obsessive–compulsive disorders, introjective depression, and narcissism involve preoccupations with issues of control and self-definition.

It is also important to take into consideration the nature of the defenses or coping styles within each formation. Defenses within the anaclitic formation are avoidant (denial and repression), with the goal being to maintain peace and harmony. The defenses within the introjective style are counteractive (projection, reaction formation, and intellectualization) in order to maintain a sense of control and mastery (Blatt, 1990). At first glance, it might seem paradoxical that an individual primarily concerned with interpersonal relatedness would have difficulty with social support. Keep in mind, however, that it is a concern with relatedness driven by dependency and ambivalence at the expense of self-definition that renders it pathological. It is precisely this type of individual who is most likely to be devastated by the inability to successfully obtain the desired social support. Zuroff and Mongrain (1987) found that anaclitic or dependent individuals were at a greater risk for depressive affect associated with negative interpersonal events than were individuals primarily concerned with self-definition. Similarly, Davis (1990) noted that the impaired ability of repressors to experience negative affect does not occur for all negative emotions. Although defending against anger and anxiety, repressors do not report less sadness or depression, affects typically associated with loss or separation. These affects, then, indicate domains of vulnerability for the repressive individual.

The literature on attachment styles and defensive processes suggests a link between early developmental experiences and the repressive personality style. Cassidy and Kobak (1988), citing Main, Bowlby, Ainsworth, and other prominent attachment theorists, proposed that avoidance is a defense against maternal rejection and a lack of maternal emotional expression. Avoidance is a means by which negative emotions in relation to the attachment figure is handled. To express anger at the attachment figure is to risk rejection; to become dependent and demanding is to invite a similar fate. Avoidance then becomes a strategy used to reduce this conflict and to regulate affect. An impairment in affective communication in the parent–child relationship leads to the child's inability to recognize, understand, and organize his or her affective experiences (Cassidy & Kobak, 1988), resulting in the attenuation of affect that is so prototypic of the repressive personality. Furthermore, there is evidence that this avoidant defense is linked with problematic interpersonal behaviors, including hostility, aggressiveness, and a lack of empathy (Kobak & Sceery, 1989), qualities also characteristic of repressors. Interestingly, there is a dissociation between these behavioral observations of avoidant individuals and their subjective reports. In their self-reports, they tend to minimize distress, vulnerability, and conflict. Given this pattern, it is not surprising then that these individuals could be expected to have difficulty with social support. Cassidy and Kobak (1988) recognized this possibility when they concluded that "Especially during times of stress or transition, the avoidant individual's inability to gain comfort from others or use emotion to share and reflect upon experience may result in symptomatic behavior" (p. 316). The avoidant style, then, would appear to have much in common with the anaclitic configuration, even though these two literatures have not yet been integrated. Seen in the light of the object-relations theories mentioned earlier, repressive defenses can be viewed as strategies for coping with disturbances arising from the separation–individuation task.

Bonanno and Singer (1990) recently presented a model in which the anaclitic and introjective styles map onto the repression–sensitization dimension. They reviewed a host of evidence suggesting commonalities between the repressive and anaclitic styles, particularly the positive self-presentational style and concern over evaluation by others. Blatt and Shichman (1983) also referred to the passivity and compliance of the anaclitic style, qualities also characteristic of the repressive personality. Similar to Eysenck's continuum of Type C and Type A styles noted earlier, the anaclitic and introjective styles appear to be risk factors for neoplastic and cardiovascular disease, respectively. Bonanno and Singer viewed these styles as opposites on a dimension that they labeled *interpersonal relatedness versus self-esteem*. I would take exception, though, with their pitting one tendency against the other: it is more useful to view these as separate dimensions rather than opposites on a single continuum.

Although there are both theoretical and empirical reasons for believing that repressive individuals are less likely to benefit from social support than nonrepressors, there is no research to my knowledge that has tested such speculations. Future research in this area should focus on the multidimensional nature of social support. As Thoits (1982) showed, social support can be characterized in terms of types, amounts, sources, and structures of the support network. The possibility of bidirectional causality should also not be overlooked: chronic deficiencies in social support may lead a person to become more repressive and inhibited. The behaviors and emotions elicited in significant others by the repressive individual are important determiners of the individual's emotional and cognitive state. Blatt and Shichman (1983) stated that the demandingness of the dependent individual may often lead to the rejection that is so desperately feared. The necessity of taking into account the relationship style of the repressor's partner was demonstrated in a study by Zuroff and de Lorimier (1989). They found differences between dependent and self-critical women in terms of their actual and ideal romantic partners. Dependent (or repressive) women preferred partners with high needs for intimacy, whereas self-critical women tended to prefer men with high needs for achievement. These preferred relationships were also linked with satisfaction in their current relationships. Examining ongoing as well as ideal relationships in repressive individuals will help to pinpoint likely sources of support as well as problematic areas.

Understanding in this area will also be advanced by studying the person schemas underlying the maladaptive interpersonal patterns of the repressive individual. Previous research suggested that repressors possess a less-differentiated view of self and others (Weinberger, 1990). Yet little is known about the content of these representations. Although these schemas are largely unconscious, various techniques including thought sampling, psychophysiological methods, and the analysis of therapeutic protocols (Emmons & King, in press; Singer, 1988) can be used to explore the contents of these person schemas. Singer and Salovey (in press) identified markers for extracting schemas from materials derived from these sources. Identification of other schemas and schemas of the self in relation to others is a necessary first step in replacing inappropriate, maladaptive schemas with more adaptive ones. The examination of person schemas in repressive individuals is also a step in the direction of integrating information-processing models with psychodynamic theory, and linking theories about content with theories about processes (Horowitz, 1988).

Several contributors to this volume point to the need to include contextual factors in our theorizing about hostility and health. What tends to be underestimated, however, is the role that individuals play in creating and selecting these contexts. Smith (this volume; Smith & Anderson, 1986) presented a persuasive case for the need for transactional models of personality and environmental risk factors. Much like Type A or hostile individuals, repressors create and select situations and evoke reactions in others that serve to maintain this coping style over time. It is clear that a comprehensive understanding of the relation between the repressive coping style and social support must also be sensitive to contextual factors. The need to embed such models in theory, such as object-relations theory is also critical. Of course, there is no need to limit theorizing to psychodynamic models. These and other psychological theories should be supplemented, when appropriate, with biological and evolutionary perspectives. For instance, Barkow (1980) presented an anthropological perspective on hostility, and McGuire and Troisi (1990) offered an evolutionary interpretation of anger. Such theories can bring order to the often chaotic and inconsistent empirical findings of constructs such as the repressive style or hostility, while at the same time being couched in terms that permit the derivation of testable hypotheses. Such research would be significant for another reason, namely that it would link trait-based personality models with process-oriented models of stress and coping. All too often, research on personality and disease has emphasized one perspective over the other, with the result being an underestimation of the role that personality plays in health and disease. Our theories must be cognizant of developmental determinants, intrapsychic processes, and contextual factors affecting health and disease. Research that is informed by personality theory addressing these domains would represent progress toward rediscovering the "person" (Kobasa, 1990) in research on personality and disease.

References

Alexander, F. (1950). *Psychosomatic medicine: Its principles and applications.* New York: Norton.

Angyal, A. (1951). *Neurosis and treatment: A holistic theory.* New York: Wiley.

Bakan, D. (1966). *The duality of human existence: Isolation and communion in Western man.* Boston: Beacon Press.

Barkow, J. H. (1980). The anthropology of hostility. In L. J. Saul (Ed.), *The childhood emotional pattern and human hostility* (pp. 219–228). New York: Van Nostrand Reinhold.

Blatt, S. J. (1990). Interpersonal relatedness and self-definition: Two personality configurations and their implications for psychopathology and psychotherapy. In J. L. Singer (Ed.), *Repression and dissociation* (pp. 299–335). Chicago: University of Chicago Press.

Blatt, S. J., & Shichman, S. (1983). Two primary configurations of psychopathology. *Psychoanalysis and Contemporary Thought, 6,* 187–254.

Bonanno, G. A., & Singer, J. L. (1990). Repressive personality style: Theoretical and methodological implications for health and pathology. In J. L. Singer (Ed.), *Repression and dissociation* (pp. 435–470). Chicago: University of Chicago Press.

Cassidy, J., & Kobak, R. (1988). Avoidance and its relation to other defensive processes. In J. Belsky & T. Nezworski (Eds.), *Clinical implications of attachment* (pp. 300–323). Hillsdale, NJ: Erlbaum.

Cohen, S., & Willis, T. A. (1985). Stress, social support, and the buffering hypothesis. *Psychological Bulletin, 98,* 310–357.

Cronbach, L. J., & Meehl, P. E. (1955). Construct validity in psychological tests. *Psychological Bulletin, 52,* 281–302.

Davis, P. J. (1990). Repression and the inaccessibility of emotional memories. In J. L. Singer (Ed.), *Repression and dissociation* (pp. 387–404). Chicago: University of Chicago Press.

Eagle, M. N. (1984). *Recent developments in psychoanalysis: A critical evaluation.* Cambridge, MA: Harvard University Press.

Emmons, R. A., & King, L. A. (in press). Thematic analysis, experience sampling, and personal goals. In C. Smith (Ed.), *Thematic analysis for personality and motivation research.* New York: Cambridge University Press.

Erdelyi, M. H. (1990). Repression, reconstruction, and defense: History and integration of the psychoanalytic and experimental frameworks. In J. L. Singer (Ed.), *Repression and dissociation* (pp. 1–31). Chicago: University of Chicago Press.

Eysenck, H. J. (1988). Personality and stress as causal factors in cancer and coronary heart disease. In M. P. Janisse (Ed.), *Individual differences, stress, and health psychology.* New York: Springer-Verlag.

Friedman, H. S. (Ed.). (1990). *Personality and disease.* New York: Wiley.

Horowitz, M. J. (1988). Psychodynamic phenomena and their explanation. In M. J. Horowitz (Ed.), *Psychodynamics and cognition* (pp.3–20). Chicago: University of Chicago Press.

Jamner, L. D., Schwartz, G. E., & Leigh, H. (1988). Repressive coping predicts monocyte eosinophile and serum glucose levels: Support for the opioid-peptide hypothesis. *Psychosomatic Medicine, 50,* 567–577.

Jensen, M. R. (1987). Psychobiological factors predicting the course of breast cancer. *Journal of Personality, 55,* 317–342.

King, L. A., & Emmons, R. A. (1990). Conflict over emotional expression: Psychological and physical correlates. *Journal of Personality and Social Psychology, 58,* 864–877.

Kobak, R., & Sceery, A. (1989). Attachment in late adolescence: Working models, affect regulation, and perceptions of self and others. *Child Development, 59,* 135–146.

Kobasa, S. C. (1990). Lessons from history: How to find the person in health psychology. In H. S. Friedman (Ed.), *Personality and disease* (pp. 14–37). New York: Wiley.

Lane, R. D., & Schwartz, G. E. (1987). Levels of emotional awareness: A cognitive–developmental theory and its applications to psychopathology. *American Journal of Psychiatry, 144,* 133–143.

Maddi, S. R. (1990). Issues and interventions in stress mastery. In H. S. Friedman (Ed.), *Personality and disease* (pp. 121–154). New York: Wiley.

McAdams, D. P. (1985). *Power, intimacy, and the life story: Personological inquiries into identity.* New York: Guilford Press.

McGuire, M. T., & Troisi, A. (1990). Anger: An evolutionary view. In R. Plutchik & H. Kellerman (Eds.), *Emotion: theory, research, and experience* (Vol. 5, pp. 43–57). San Diego: Academic Press.

Plante, T. G., & Schwartz, G. E. (1990). Defensive and repressive coping styles: Self-presentation, leisure activities, and assessment. *Journal of Research in Personality, 24*, 173–190.

Revenson, T. A. (1990). All other things are not equal: An ecological approach to personality and disease. In H. S. Friedman (Ed.), *Personality and disease* (pp. 65–94). New York: Wiley.

Schwartz, G. E. (1983). Disregulation theory and disease: Applications to the repression/cerebral disconnection/cardiovascular disorder hypothesis. *International Review of Applied Psychology, 32*, 95–118.

Singer, J. L. (1988). Sampling ongoing consciousness and emotional experience: Implications for health. In M. J. Horowitz (Ed.), *Psychodynamics and cognition* (pp. 297–346). Chicago: University of Chicago Press.

Singer, J. L., & Salovey, P. (in press). Cognitive approaches to nuclear scenes, schemas, and scripts. In M. Horowitz (Ed.), *Person schemas and maladaptive interpersonal patterns.* Chicago: University of Chicago Press.

Smith, T. W., & Anderson, N. B. (1986). Models of personality and disease: An interactional approach to Type A behavior and cardiovascular risk. *Journal of Personality and Social Psychology, 50*, 1166–1173.

Thoits, P. A. (1982). Conceptual, methodological, and theoretical problems in studying social support as a buffer against life stress. *Journal of Health and Social Behavior, 23*, 145–159.

Weinberger, D. A. (1990). The construct validity of the repressive coping style. In J. L. Singer (Ed.), *Repression and dissociation* (pp. 337–386). Chicago: University of Chicago Press.

Zuroff, D. C., & de Lorimier, S. (1989). Ideal and actual romantic partners of women varying in dependency and self-criticism. *Journal of Personality, 57*, 825–846.

Zuroff, D. C., & Mongrain, M. (1987). Dependency and self-criticism: Vulnerability factors for depressive affective states. *Journal of Abnormal Psychology, 96*, 14–22.

CHAPTER 10

Social Withdrawal as a Short-Term Coping Response to Daily Stressors

Rena L. Repetti

I suggest in this chapter that social withdrawal immediately following exposure to a stressor can alleviate some of the negative aftereffects of the stressful encounter by returning the individual's mood, arousal, and energy to baseline levels. The description of a social withdrawal response differs in several ways from the paradigms that are currently popular in the coping literature. Withdrawal is conceptualized as a daily coping strategy that facilitates a *short-term recovery process.* It is therefore directed toward coping with the immediate residues of a stressful encounter, rather than with the long-term effects of the stressor or the precipitating stressor itself. Differences between short-term and long-term coping strategies account for the effectiveness of social withdrawal despite the known long-term benefits of social support. In addition, because withdrawal is viewed as an adaptive response to the *aftereffects* of a stressful encounter, it is expected to occur in a social situation that is disconnected from the stressor. Finally, in contrast to the usual assumption that coping involves a deliberate effort to manage a stressor, the social withdrawal response as described here does not necessarily involve a conscious intention to cope with the precipitating stressor nor

I would like to thank Howard Friedman, Joanne Wood, Arthur Stone, Eileen Kennedy-Moore, and Melanie A. Greenberg for their helpful comments on an earlier draft of this chapter.

even an awareness of a link with the stressor. Therefore, as discussed later, self-report assessment techniques may not be the most appropriate approach to use when studying social withdrawal as coping behavior.

In order to detect social withdrawal, one must observe a temporary change in the subject's typical behavior. Three possible dimensions of a social withdrawal response are discussed here: (a) an observable reduction in behavioral involvement and interest in others, (b) decreased emotional responsiveness to others, which may include less expression of both positive and negative emotion, and (c) a concomitant increase in self-focused attention.

A Working Model of the Functions of Social Withdrawal

The model presented here suggests that social withdrawal is an overdetermined response to stressful episodes. Specifically, it proposes that three common short-term outcomes associated with stress—negative affect, increased arousal, and fatigue—may be alleviated by a period of withdrawal immediately following the stressful encounter. Thus, the social withdrawal response should be observed in situations that follow the stressful event.

Negative Affect and Social Withdrawal

Most stressors have an immediate impact on individual subjective well-being, especially by increasing dysphoric mood. A growing body of research indicates that individuals use a variety of techniques to manage their emotional states and, in particular, to repair negative moods (Mayer, Salovey, Gomberg-Kaufman, & Blainey, 1991).

Social withdrawal may help to regulate emotional responses to stressors, which Lazarus and Folkman (1984) termed *emotion-focused coping.* Evidence from several different literatures suggests that social withdrawal can help to restore a more positive affective state. First, residual negative emotional states from a prior situation are sometimes associated with decreased social responsiveness in a new situation (Isen, 1984; Moore, Underwood, & Rosenhan 1984). Second, data from daily diary studies indicate that a period of solitude has a positive aftereffect on mood (Larson & Csikszentmihalyi, 1983). Third, negative mood states that commonly result from exposure to stressors, such as sadness, anxiety, and anger, appear to be associated with an increased focus on the self (Wood, Saltzberg, & Goldsamt, 1990; Wood, Saltzberg, Neale, Stone, & Rachmiel, 1990).

Several theorists speculated that the association between self-focused attention and dysphoric mood may reflect a process of self-regulation following a stressful event and that the period of self-focus may be transitory (Greenberg & Pyszczynski, 1986; Wood, Saltzberg, & Goldsamt, 1990). As mentioned earlier, a temporary shift in attention away from others and toward the self may sometimes be an important component of social withdrawal.

In addition, when individuals use distraction to relieve negative moods, some of the distracting behaviors may remove them from social interaction. Solitary nonarousing activities, such as reading, watching television, listening to music, or working on a crossword puzzle, can facilitate distraction both from thoughts about the stressful events and from any potentially stressful cues in the current environment. Thus, social withdrawal may help to restore a more positive affective state both directly and indirectly as part of some other effort at mood repair.

Increased Arousal and Social Withdrawal

Most theorists assume that the initial "fight or flight" response to a stressful situation or demand involves increased levels of sympathetic arousal (Selye, 1976). A purely mechanistic homeostatic model posits that, following the stressful encounter, arousal levels mechanically return to baseline levels. Frankenhaeuser and her colleagues identified a pattern of physiological unwinding, consisting of a gradual decrement in heart rate, blood pressure, and levels of circulating catecholamines that occurs after returning home from a stressful day at work (Frankenhaeuser, 1979, 1981). I would like to suggest that this unwinding response reflects more than a mechanistic–biologic process. Unwelcomed secondary effects of increased arousal may motivate individuals to facilitate a return to baseline levels of arousal and thereby enhance the automatic recovery process.

An individual might strive to reduce his or her arousal level for several reasons. High levels of arousal can interfere with performance (Anderson, 1990). In addition, the perception of autonomic arousal may amplify the intensity of emotional experiences (Chwalisz, Diener, & Gallagher, 1988). Therefore, negative mood states resulting from stressful encounters might be ameliorated by reducing perceived arousal levels. Zillmann and his colleagues (Bryant & Zillmann, 1979) found that residual excitation or arousal from a previous situation can intensify provoked aggressive behavior in a current (nonrelated) situation. This is another potential aftereffect of the increased arousal that remains after termination of a stressor. To illustrate the negative secondary outcomes that may be associated with increased arousal following a stressful episode, imagine a highly aroused mother after a particularly stressful day at work and a difficult drive home in heavy traffic. Research indicates that if she can relax and facilitate a return to baseline levels of arousal, she will enhance her performance of complex household tasks, diminish the intensity of her negative emotional state, and avoid overreacting in an aversive manner to her demanding child. Her own experience may have taught her the same lesson.

Social withdrawal and other behaviors that may sometimes require withdrawal, such as relaxation and distraction, can facilitate recovery from increased levels of arousal. Someone in a heightened state of arousal from stress may avoid social interaction because it would further increase arousal. For example, blood pressure and heart rate have been found to increase during couples' discussions of problems (Ewart, Taylor, Kraemer, & Agras, 1991) and during even simple social conversation (Lynch, Thomas, Paskewitz, Malinow, & Long, 1982). So just as the phobic person avoids anxiety-arousing stimuli, a stressed individual may withdraw from potentially arousing social stimuli in the environment. Relaxation lowers heart rate, blood pressure, and other indicators of arousal (Davidson & Schwartz, 1976), and in order to relax one typically withdraws from active participation in social interaction. Cognitive distraction also reduces arousal (Miller, 1980) and, as pointed out earlier, many solitary behaviors, such as watching television, can facilitate distraction.

Fatigue and Social Withdrawal
Stressors and efforts to cope with them require the expenditure of energy, often resulting in energy depletion and fatigue once the encounter has ended. Research indicates that physical exhaustion, even in response to everyday occurrences, is associated with reduced affective responsiveness (Thayer, 1989). Indeed, recovery from fatigue is probably best achieved in the absence of any social interaction. For example, someone who is tired or weakened by a stressful encounter often finds a quiet rest period, a nap, or a shower invigorating.

Once removed from a stressful situation, individuals may engage in behaviors to alleviate the physical and emotional residues of stress. Mood, arousal, and energy are nonindependent states that covary in response to stress (Thayer, 1989). The model and research evidence presented here suggest that recovery through mood repair, arousal reduction, and replenishment of energy can be facilitated by social withdrawal and behaviors that may entail withdrawal, such as distraction, relaxation, and rest. It is therefore reasonable to expect social withdrawal to be a common short-term response to stress.

Preliminary Evidence Regarding Social Withdrawal as a Short-Term Coping Response

There is preliminary evidence that social withdrawal immediately follows exposure to stressors. Repetti (1989) found that male air traffic controllers (ATCs) were more withdrawn from family interaction after stressful days at work. The daily report data indicated that after high-work-load days, husbands were more distracted and less involved and interested in social interaction with their wives. There was also evidence of decreased emotional responsiveness; the ATCs expressed less anger and engaged in fewer hostile behaviors during marital interactions that followed high-work-load shifts. It is important to point out that these findings do not simply reflect the effects of energy depletion. Controlling for self-reported fatigue after work did not change the relation between work load and marital behavior.

On the basis of data from the same study, Repetti (1991a) found that, for the subsample of ATC fathers of school-aged children, a day at work characterized by a high work load or negative social interactions with coworkers and supervisors was also followed by greater withdrawal from parent–child interactions. The fathers were less involved with their children both in a positive and helpful manner (such as helping with homework) and as disciplinarians (less reminding, yelling, and punishing) after stressful days at work. There was also less negative emotion expressed during father–child interactions.

Some of the ATC parent–child findings were recently replicated in an investigation that focused on mothers employed in a wide variety of occupations (Repetti, 1991b). For 1 week, at the end of each workday but before being reunited with their children, mothers completed surveys describing their day at work. Later each evening, each mother completed measures describing interactions with the target child that occurred between the time she left work and the time her child went to sleep. Preliminary findings indicated that, like the ATCs, on evenings after more demanding workdays these mothers were more withdrawn from their children. For example, they reported less playing, talking, and laughing with their children, less involvement with their children's activities and games, and less interest in what their children had to say. They described themselves as less responsive to their children and reported that between them there was a feeling of less warmth, less togetherness, and more disappointment.

The Absence of Social Withdrawal From the Coping Literature: Methodological Considerations

Although the findings summarized earlier suggest that withdrawal at home often follows stress at work, most subjects in stress and coping studies do not mention social withdrawal as a primary coping strategy. Coping inventories, therefore, generally do not include a separate social withdrawal scale, which is consistent with Stone and Kennedy-Moore's (this volume) observation that these scales may not represent the full domain of possible coping responses. Moreover, in most studies of daily coping, a subject is asked to use a self-report questionnaire to describe how he or she attempted to manage a problem that occurred that day or how he or she typically attempts to cope with daily stressors. This methodological approach precludes the possibility that the stressful event may have led the individual to alter his or her behavior (adaptively or maladaptively) in ways that he or she is not able to identify. Social withdrawal may be one response to stress that is not noticed by most people, perhaps because it is the absence of social behavior or because it requires one to observe a subtle qualitative change in social behavior rather than a proactive response to the event. Additionally, subjects may view their withdrawal from social interaction as secondary to some other coping response, such as watching television, resting, or reading the newspaper. This may explain why, as discussed later, social withdrawal items are often embedded within measures of avoidant coping styles.

Although social withdrawal may not be a salient response to stress, when behavior was assessed in the two studies described earlier without requiring the subject to interpret its link to earlier conditions at work, stress at work was clearly associated with increased withdrawal later at home. It may prove critical for researchers to design tests of the social-withdrawal hypothesis that do not require subjects to recognize a change in their level of social participation, to then connect that behavioral change to an earlier stressful encounter and, finally, to label their withdrawal as a separate coping response. Certain experimental designs, quasi-experimental designs, and passive observational methodologies (e.g., daily diary studies) may provide additional evidence that social withdrawal is a short-term response to stress. For example, changes in subjects' expressed preference for social interaction and their social behavior in naturalistic and analogue situations can be assessed following exposure to a stressor.

However, investigations of the proposed functions of social withdrawal are also needed in order to rule out the possibility that withdrawal is simply a symptom of stress. The only way to confirm that social withdrawal acts as an effective coping response is by observing actual reductions in negative mood, arousal, and fatigue. The research designs mentioned earlier might assess the rate at which the emotional and physiological residues of stress dissipate under conditions of social interaction and social isolation following exposure to a stressor.

Social Withdrawal and Avoidant Coping Strategies

The emotion-focused coping strategies described in the stress and coping literature include a general class of rejection or avoidant coping styles, such as denial, distraction, and repression, which may share some conceptual overlap with social withdrawal. Avoidant responses focus attention away from the stressor or one's psychological and somatic reactions to it (Suls & Fletcher, 1985). For example, the Avoidance subscale of the Impact of Events Scale includes items such as "I tried not to think about it," "I tried to remove it from memory," and "I tried not to talk about it" (Zilberg, Weiss, & Horowitz, 1982). In a study of the dimensionality of coping in older adults, Rohde, Lewinsohn, Tilson, and Seeley (1990) identified an Ineffective Escapism factor that had high loadings on items such as "Do something dangerous," "Wait for someone to help," and "Stay in bed." Related coping strategies include Pennebaker and colleagues' description of *inhibition* or *constraint*, in which people actively inhibit their desire to talk about or confront a traumatic event (Pennebaker & Susman, 1988), and Carver, Scheier, and Pozo's (this volume) studies of the effects of giving up or behavioral disengagement from pursuit of a goal.

The general avoidance–escapism–inhibition coping style usually refers to an internal psychological coping process that may or may not involve social withdrawal. On the one hand, most avoidance coping scales include social withdrawal items like "Keep away from people" (Rhode et al., 1990), "Avoided being with people in general," and "Wished that people would just leave you alone" (Amirkhan, 1990). On the other hand, avoidance coping may sometimes involve increased social activity. For example, one might avoid all opportunities to examine (through private thought or discussions with others) a stressful encounter by actively participating in distracting social events. Similarly, social withdrawal does not necessarily involve an escape from the problem or stressful situation at hand. During a period of social withdrawal, individuals may be attempting to distract themselves, or they may be using private time to actively problem solve or ruminate about the prior stressful situation. For example, self-focused attention, one possible component of social withdrawal, may help stressed individuals to actively analyze the stressful encounter and their emotional reactions to it. This, of course, is the opposite of avoidance.

Despite the differences between social withdrawal and avoidance as coping strategies, the partial areas of overlap between the two constructs may be a fruitful avenue for further investigation. It is important to know, for example, when withdrawn individuals are attempting to distract themselves from thoughts about a prior stressful encounter, when they are ruminating about the encounter, and when they are planning problem-solving strategies. These different cognitive coping strategies, each of which can be associated with social withdrawal, may have different short-term effects on dysphoric mood, arousal, and fatigue following exposure to the stressor. For example, evidence suggests that distraction facilitates remediation of depressive affect, but rumination interferes with mood repair (Morrow & Nolen-Hoeksema, 1990).

Long-term problems may result if social withdrawal is always associated with avoidant coping strategies. These strategies not only can interfere with the individual's use of problem-focused coping, but evidence suggests that they may also increase risk for long-term health problems. In the short-term, distraction and other blunting techniques (responses that involve psychologically absenting oneself from danger signals) minimize arousal and subjective distress (Miller, 1980). In a meta-analytic study, Mullen and Suls (1982) also found that, in the short run, focusing attention away from a stressor is associated with a variety of indicators of better physical adaptation, including less arousal and fewer physical symptoms. However, in the long run, a strategy of focusing attention on the stressor was associated with better health, including fewer illnesses and symptoms. Pennebaker and his colleagues also found that writing or talking about a traumatic event resulted in fewer health problems and improved functioning of the immune system (Pennebaker & Susman, 1988).

Long-Term Effects of Social Withdrawal

Not only may avoidant cognitive activities during periods of social withdrawal have different short-term and long-term implications for coping, but social withdrawal alone may be associated with different short-term and long-term outcomes. It has been argued here that social withdrawal can be an adaptive short-term response to the emotional and physiological residues of a stressful encounter. Yet, a long-term strategy of social withdrawal in the face of repeated or chronic stressors may lead, over time, to difficulties in interpersonal relationships. For example, the frequent withdrawal of one partner during marital interactions is associated with marital dissatisfaction (Christensen & Heavey, 1990). The same may be true of withdrawal from the parent–child relationship.

Consider, for example, the ATCs who withdrew from father–child interaction after high-stress days at work. When a desired period of self-focus and withdrawal is interrupted by a child's need for attention, a father probably finds himself less responsive to the child's demands and less tolerant of the child's noncompliant behavior. Moreover, more frequent periods of parental withdrawal are probably associated with more attention-seeking behavior by the child. When repeated day after day, a nonresponsive parenting style and a child's reaction to it may escalate into irritable or punishing parental behavior and, ultimately, a more aversive parent–child relationship.

In the ATC study, there were different short-term and long-term effects of social stressors at work that are consistent with this analysis. Although there was a same-day link between distressing social interactions at work and increased withdrawal at home, controllers who were part of work groups with chronically stressful social climates characterized the emotional tone of their relationships with a target child as more negative and less positive. Over 3 days, they reported more anger, hostility, and tension, and less closeness and warmth during father–child interactions (Repetti, 1991a). It is possible that, for these fathers under chronic stress at work, repeated patterns of social withdrawal at home partly accounted for their more aversive parent–child relationships.

In addition to its effects on family relationships, a sustained pattern of social withdrawal in response to chronic daily stressors may gradually erode an individual's social-support network (including both family and friends). In one study, people who had a desire to be left alone also reported that less social support was available to them (Evans,

Palsane, Lepore, & Martin, 1989). By reducing access to social-support resources, social withdrawal may indirectly impede an individual's ability to cope with chronic stressors.

Despite the social difficulties that may result from a dependence on social withdrawal as a coping response, there may be some long-term health benefits associated with withdrawal. A prolonged recovery from the negative affect, increased arousal, and fatigue of a stressful episode might underlie some of the deleterious health outcomes associated with stress. It has been suggested that a sustained physiological mobilization following exposure to a stressor can result in systemic damage both directly (e.g., ulcers) and indirectly (e.g., by depressing the effectiveness of the immune response) (Lazarus & Folkman, 1984). Exaggerated cardiovascular and neuroendocrine responses to stress are associated with an increased risk for hypertension and coronary heart disease (Krantz & Manuck, 1984; Matthews et al., 1986). If social withdrawal facilitates a speedy recovery from physiological arousal caused by stress, it may also help to reduce risk for these health problems. In addition, by facilitating mood repair, social withdrawal may interfere with a dysfunctional process in which sustained daily increases in dysphoric mood gradually lead to a deterioration in psychological functioning.

Individual Differences and Situational Factors

The extent to which social withdrawal immediately follows exposure to a stressor and the extent to which it is experienced as beneficial may partly depend on individual differences and situational factors. For example, individuals with avoidant coping styles may be more likely to withdraw because, in addition to its other effects, withdrawal can facilitate distraction and escape. Individual variability in the extent to which people are arousal avoidant and in the intensity of their responses to minor daily events may also influence the extent to which withdrawal follows stress (Larsen, Diener, & Emmons, 1986; Martin, Kuiper, Olinger, & Dobbin, 1987).

Similarly, certain types of social situations may limit opportunities for withdrawal, whereas others may abet withdrawal. Aspects of the social environment that follows the stressful encounter, such as the nature of one's relationships with others in the environment, others' behavior, and the importance of situational demands on the individual, most likely play a critical role in determining whether the individual withdraws from social interaction. The influence of social partners was highlighted in the ATC study through an analysis of the wives' emotionally supportive behaviors (such as being tolerant, patient, and cheerful, and providing comfort and sympathy). Differences in the likelihood of withdrawal were found when the ATCs' evenings were divided into high-spouse-support evenings and low-spouse-support evenings. Social withdrawal was correlated with earlier levels of work load only on the high-spouse-support evenings (Repetti, 1989). On days in which wives provided high levels of emotional support, both subjective and objective measures of that day's work load were associated with withdrawal at home that evening. However, this was not true for low-spouse-support evenings. These results suggest that some level of emotional support from a spouse may be a necessary condition for withdrawal to occur at home.

Sex Differences

Despite Repetti's (1991b) finding that women also withdraw from parent–child interaction after demanding workdays, investigators should explore possible sex differences in the extent to which withdrawal is used as a coping response. In a recent study, the physiological unwinding response was observed in male managers after a stressful day at work, but female managers did not show evidence of unwinding (Frankenhaeuser et al., 1989). This finding might reflect a sex difference in the tendency to use social withdrawal as a response to job stress. More generally, we know that women complain more about their male partners' withdrawal and emotional nonresponsiveness than men complain about this behavior in their female partners (Buss, 1989). Men are also more likely than women to withdraw during marital conflict (Christensen & Heavey, 1990).

Sex differences in the use of social withdrawal as a short-term coping response may in part represent differences in the demands and expectations inherent in the situations in which men and women are observed. Data from the ATC study indicated that, under conditions of high spouse support, men use withdrawal as a short-term response to daily job stress. However, the family responsibilities and level of support in the home environment of most employed wives may not allow them to withdraw as easily as the ATCs did when they return home from a hard day at work. Csikszentmihalyi and Graef (1980) found that men tend to rate most of their daily activities as more voluntary, especially cooking and childcare. Furthermore, evidence suggests that when their husbands have had a demanding day at work, wives compensate by increasing their work load at home, but that husbands do not respond in kind (Bolger, DeLongis, Kessler, & Wethington, 1989). Thus, men may feel freer to withdraw from daily household routines (including parenting) after a stressful day, and their wives may encourage withdrawal by providing an emotionally supportive environment and by assuming additional responsibilities for household chores.

Directions for Future Research

The proposed model of social withdrawal as a short-term strategy for coping with some of the physiological and emotional discomforts engendered by everyday stressors suggests a promising avenue for further investigation. Some of the model's predictions and supporting preliminary evidence are surprising. For instance, they contradict a popular assumption that more irritable behavior is a common immediate reaction to everyday stressors (e.g., kicking the dog after an argument with the boss at work). Another example is that, although a large research literature indicates that a high level of socially supportive interaction can be an enormously helpful coping resource, withdrawal from all social interaction may be an effective short-term coping strategy. Indeed, findings from the ATC study of job stress suggest that emotional support from a spouse functions precisely by creating a situation in which withdrawal can occur.

I would like to review and highlight four directions for future research on social withdrawal as a response to stress. First, innovative research strategies that do not require subjects to identify their coping behaviors should supplement self-report assessment techniques. Researchers can make inferences about short-term coping strategies by observing behaviors that follow exposure to stressors and relating those behavioral changes to concurrent changes in rates of emotional and physiological recovery. Second, future research should include assessments of cognitive activity during periods of withdrawal. This will help researchers to determine when withdrawal is a social concomitant of other coping strategies, such as avoidance. Third, future studies might identify those situational factors that facilitate and those that impede a withdrawal response, as well as investigate individual differences and sex differences in the proclivity to use withdrawal.

Fourth, the persistent use of social withdrawal to cope with chronic daily stressors may, over time, be associated with significant health-related outcomes. The possibilities range from long-term health benefits to problems in intimate relationships and reduced access to social-support networks. If future studies indicate that social withdrawal is an adaptive short-term response to daily stress, one challenge for health psychologists will be to design preventive interventions that maximize the short-term and long-term health benefits of withdrawal and minimize long-term damage to social relationships. One recommendation might be to create situations that afford a brief period of social withdrawal following predictable daily stressors. An example is setting aside a period of solitary time to unwind and recover after work.

References

Amirkhan, J. H. (1990). A factor analytically derived measure of coping: The coping strategy indicator. *Journal of Personality and Social Psychology, 59,* 1066–1074.

Anderson, K. J. (1990). Arousal and the inverted-u hypothesis: A critique of Neiss's "reconceptualizing arousal." *Psychological Bulletin, 107,* 96–100.

Bolger, N., DeLongis, A., Kessler, R. C., & Wethington, E. (1989). The contagion of stress across multiple roles. *Journal of Marriage and the Family, 51,* 175–183.

Bryant, J., & Zillmann, D. (1979). Effect of intensification of annoyance through unrelated residual excitation on substantially delayed hostile behavior. *Journal of Experimental Social Psychology, 15,* 470–480.

Buss, D. M. (1989). Conflict between the sexes: Strategic interference and the evocation of anger and upset. *Journal of Personality and Social Psychology, 56,* 735–747.

Christensen, A., & Heavey, C. L. (1990). Gender and social structure in the demand/withdraw pattern of marital conflict. *Journal of Personality and Social Psychology, 59,* 73–81.

Chwalisz, K., Diener, E., & Gallagher, D. (1988). Autonomic arousal feedback and emotional experience: Evidence from the spinal cord injured. *Journal of Personality and Social Psychology, 54,* 820–828.

Csikszentmihalyi, M., & Graef, R. (1980). The experience of freedom in daily life. *American Journal of Community Psychology, 8,* 401–414.

Davidson, R. J., & Schwartz, G. E. (1976). The psychobiology of relaxation and related states: A multi-process theory. In D. I. Mostofsky (Ed.), *Behavior control and modification of physiological activity* (pp. 399–442). Englewood Cliffs, NJ: Prentice-Hall.

Evans, G. W., Palsane, M. N., Lepore, S. J., & Martin, J. (1989). Residential density and psychological health: The mediating effects of social support. *Journal of Personality and Social Psychology, 57,* 994–999.

Ewart, C. K., Taylor, C. B., Kraemer, H. C., & Agras, W. S. (1991). High blood pressure and marital discord: Not being nasty matters more than being nice. *Health Psychology, 10,* 155–163.

Frankenhaeuser, M. (1979). Psychoneuroendocrine approaches to the study of emotion as related to stress and coping. In H. E. Howe, Jr., R. A. Dienstbier, J. R. Averill, J. V. Brady, M. Frankenhaeuser, C. E. Izard, S. S. Tomkins, & R. A. Dienstbier (Eds.), *Nebraska symposium on motivation.* Lincoln, NB: University of Nebraska Press.

Frankenhaeuser, M. (1981). Coping with stress at work. *International Journal of Health Services, 11,* 491–510.

Frankenhaeuser, M., Lundberg, U., Fredrickson, M., Melin, B., Tuomisto, M., Myrsten, A., Bergman-Losman, B., Hedman, M., & Wallin, L. (1989). Stress on and off the job as related to sex and occupational status in white-collar workers. *Journal of Organizational Behavior, 10,* 321–346.

Greenberg, J., & Pyszczynski, T. (1986). Persistent high self-focus after success: The depressive self-focusing style. *Journal of Personality and Social Psychology, 50,* 1039–1044.

Isen, A. M. (1984). Toward understanding the role of affect in cognition. In R. S. Wyer & T. K. Srull (Eds.), *Handbook of social cognition* (pp. 179–236). Hillsdale, NJ: Erlbaum.

Krantz, D. S., & Manuck, S. B. (1984). Acute psychophysiologic reactivity and risk of cardiovascular disease: A review and methodologic critique. *Psychological Bulletin, 96,* 435–464.

Larsen, R. J., Diener, E., & Emmons, R. A. (1986). Affect intensity and reactions to daily life events. *Journal of Personality and Social Psychology, 51,* 803–814.

Larson, R., & Csikszentmihalyi, M. (1983). The experience sampling method. In H. T. Reis (Ed.), *Naturalistic approaches to studying social interaction.* San Francisco: Jossey-Bass.

Lazarus, R. S., & Folkman, S. (1984). Coping and adaptation. In W. D. Gentry (Ed.), *Handbook of behavioral medicine* (pp. 282–325). New York: Guilford Press.

Lynch, J. J., Thomas, S. A., Paskewitz, D. A., Malinow, K. L., & Long, J. M. (1982). Interpersonal aspects of blood pressure control. *Journal of Nervous and Mental Disease, 170,* 143–153.

Martin, R. A., Kuiper, N. A., Olinger, L. J., & Dobbin, J. (1987). Is stress always bad? Telic versus paratelic dominance as a stress-moderation variable. *Journal of Personality and Social Psychology, 53,* 970–982.

Matthews, K. A., Weiss, S. M., Detre, T., Dembrowski, T. M., Falkner, B., Manuck, S. B., & Williams, R. B., Jr. (Eds.). (1986). *Handbook of stress, reactivity and cardiovascular disease.* New York: Wiley.

Mayer, J. D., Salovey, P., Gomberg-Kaufman, S., & Blainey, K. (1991). A broader conception of mood experience. *Journal of Personality and Social Psychology, 60,* 100–111.

Miller, S. M. (1980). When is a little information a dangerous thing? Coping with stressful events by monitoring versus blunting. In S. Levine & H. Ursin (Eds.), *Coping and health* (pp. 145–169). New York: Plenum Press.

Moore, B., Underwood, B., & Rosenhan, D. L. (1984). Emotion, self, and others. In C. E. Izard, J. Kagan, & R. B. Zajonc (Eds.), *Emotions, cognition and behavior.* New York: Cambridge University Press.

Morrow, J., & Nolen-Hoeksema, S. (1990). Effects of responses to depression on the remediation of depressive affect. *Journal of Personality and Social Psychology, 58,* 519–527.

Mullen, B., & Suls, J. (1982). The effectiveness of attention and rejection as coping styles: A meta-analysis of temporal difference. *Journal of Psychosomatic Research, 26,* 43–49.

Pennebaker, J. W., & Susman, J. R. (1988). Disclosure of traumas and psychosomatic processes. *Social Science and Medicine, 26,* 327–332.

Repetti, R. (1989). Effects of daily workload on subsequent behavior during marital interaction: The roles of social withdrawal and spouse support. *Journal of Personality and Social Psychology, 57,* 651–659.

Repetti, R. (1991a). *Short-term and long-term effects of perceived job stressors on father–child interaction.* Manuscript submitted for publication.

Repetti, R. (1991b, April). *Mothers also withdraw from parent–child interaction as a short-term response to increased load at work.* Paper presented at the biennial meeting of the Society for Research in Child Development, Seattle, WA.

Rohde, P., Lewinsohn, P. M., Tilson, M., & Seeley, J. R. (1990). Dimensionality of coping and its relation to depression. *Journal of Personality and Social Psychology, 58,* 499–511.

Selye, H. (1976). *The stress of life* (rev. ed.). New York: McGraw-Hill.

Suls, J., & Fletcher, B. (1985). The relative efficacy of avoidant and non-avoidant coping strategies: A meta analysis. *Health Psychology, 4,* 249–288.

Thayer, R. E. (1989). *The biopsychology of mood and arousal.* New York: Oxford University Press.

Wood, J. V., Saltzberg, J. A., & Goldsamt, L. A. (1990). Does affect induce self-focused attention? *Journal of Personality and Social Psychology, 58,* 899–908.

Wood, J. V., Saltzberg, J. A., Neale, J. M., Stone, A A., & Rachmiel, T. B. (1990). Self-focused attention, coping responses, and distressed mood in everyday life. *Journal of Personality and Social Psychology, 58,* 1027–1036.

Zilberg, N. J., Weiss, D. S., & Horowitz, M. J. (1982). Impact of event scale: A cross-validation study and some empirical evidence supporting a conceptual model of stress response syndromes. *Journal of Consulting and Clinical Psychology, 50,* 407–414.

CHAPTER 11

Conceptualizing the Process of Coping With Health Problems

Charles S. Carver, Michael F. Scheier, and Christina Pozo

M any chapters in this book concern ways in which psychological and behavioral qualities may have a causal influence on physical well-being. For example, dispositional hostility may predispose people to react physiologically to certain kinds of challenging situations in ways that contribute to the pathogenesis of cardiovascular disorders (see Barefoot, this volume; Smith, this volume). As another example, the tendency to suppress feelings and thoughts that are associated with distressing experiences may create strains within the body that render the person more vulnerable to later disease (see Pennebaker, this volume).

This chapter, in contrast, considers the opposite path of influence between these two classes of variables. That is, just as certain psychological qualities may contribute to health problems, serious health problems can also produce a wide variety of psychological and behavioral responses (cf. Kaplan, 1990). It is our position that these psychological and behavioral phenomena are important in their own right. Though it may be that they also play a role in subsequent physical disorder, we will not address that possibility here (for a broader statement see Taylor & Aspinwall, 1990).

Preparation of this chapter was supported by grants BNS90-11653 and BNS90-10425 from the National Science Foundation and grant PBR-61173 from the American Cancer Society.

We begin this chapter by making some very general points about the nature of coping. The issue taken up in this first section is how to think about the processes of coping within the framework of behavior in general. This issue has implications for what aspects of coping may be worth research attention. We then consider how the points made in the first section apply to research investigating the ways in which people cope with serious threats to their health, using two of our own studies for purposes of illustration. We close the chapter with a second look at issues in coping research.

Conceptualizing Coping

As is true of most contemporary analyses of stress and coping, our approach to thinking about coping leans heavily on the pioneering work of Richard Lazarus and his colleagues (e.g., Lazarus, 1966; Lazarus & Folkman, 1984). Their theory starts with the idea that the experience of stress is a transaction between the person and the situation, dependent on both rather than just one. Basic to this approach is the idea that the objective nature of the situation is less important as a determinant of the person's response than is the person's construal of the situation. A second principle of the Lazarus model is that people do not always respond reflexively and automatically to the situations they confront (or even as they construe them). Rather, people often weigh options and consider the consequences of different responses.

Stressful situations obviously vary in their characteristics. For example, some situations are potentially controllable despite being aversive, whereas others are less controllable. Such variations across situations may certainly have a systematic influence on how people attempt to deal with them. Similarly, people vary in their propensities to respond in particular ways (even to particular sorts of situations), and these individual differences presumably play a role in determining what coping tactics people use. Thus, there is plenty of room in this model for a full range of situational, personal, and interactional effects.

Stress Theory and Broader Models of Behavior

Several ideas that underlie this approach to coping have assumed a prominent place in more general theories of behavior. For example, it is common today to view the flow of human experience as an ongoing transaction between person and situation, a mutual influence that Bandura (1978) labeled *reciprocal determinism*. It is also widely held that people's actions are determined by their construals of situations rather than by the objective situations (e.g., Mischel, 1973, 1990; cf. Kelly, 1955). It is commonly argued as well that people anticipate the likely consequences of their actions before acting and that these anticipations or expectancies play an important role in determining what action occurs (e.g., Bandura, 1986; Carver & Scheier, 1981, 1990b; Kanfer & Hagerman, 1985; Kirsch, 1990).

In short, the Lazarus model of stress and coping shares several themes with current conceptions of general principles that underlie the self-regulation of behavior, though there are also differences in emphasis. Discussions of stress tend to emphasize actual or impending harmful or unpleasant events, whereas models of self-regulation tend to focus on issues concerning the impending nonoccurrence of positive events. Thus, a person can be threatened by sudden movement in a dark alley, the sound of a tornado, or the diagnosis of a major illness, but the person can also be threatened by doubt about receiving a sought-after promotion. This difference in emphasis (and it is only that) should not obscure the fact that the stress model and self-regulation models share a concern with how people respond to adversity or difficulty.

Let's take a closer look at these models of behavior in general with which we are comparing the Lazarus stress theory in order to consider their characteristics more fully. These models begin by assuming that behavior is goal directed (e.g., Pervin, 1983, 1989; for a review see Cantor & Zirkel, 1990). People have long-term and short-term goals, narrow and broad goals, plans for the attainment of goals, and strategies to use in implementing the plans. In this view of behavior, people's goals give form to their lives. In expectancy-value terms, goals are *values.*

Expectancies are people's degree of confidence of attaining their goals. When people have favorable expectancies for goal attainment, they continue their efforts in that direction. In many instances of human behavior, expectancies never become an issue, because the behavior occurs smoothly and without difficulty. When progress toward a goal slows, however, when there are difficulties (whatever their source), the level of the person's confidence becomes a more critical parameter.

When people's doubts about goal attainment are strong enough, the result is a tendency to disengage effort, to withdraw from pursuit of the goal, to give it up (see Figure 1). In Klinger's (1975) phrase, commitment to the incentive gives way to disengagement from it. We have tended to view these responses to adversity as forming a rough dichotomy (see also Klinger, 1975; Kukla, 1972; Wortman & Brehm, 1975). Though the dichotomous quality of these responses is not stressed in every theory, it

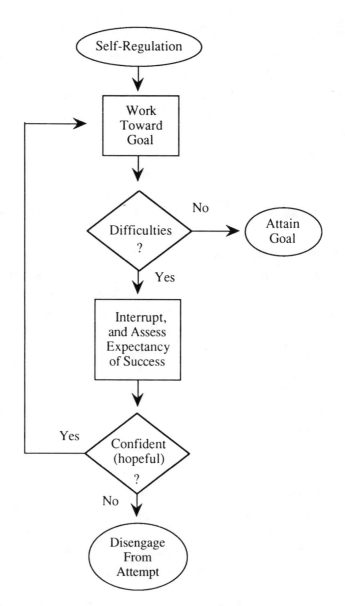

FIGURE 1   Flow diagram of three behavioral possibilities. (Sometimes behavior
proceeds unimpeded, leading to attainment of the desired goal.
Sometimes difficulties of one type or another cause behavior to be
interrupted and the person to evaluate (explicitly or implicitly) the chances
of successful goal attainment. Confidence leads to further effort;
sufficient doubt leads to a tendency to disengage.)

does seem to be true that a conceptual disjunction between continued striving and abandoning the struggle is an important feature of all such theories. Expectancy-based theories of behavior all incorporate the idea that people confronting obstacles either continue to try or give up.

The broad themes that we have sketched out here are reflected in a wide range of more specific constructs. Concepts such as helplessness, optimism, and pessimism (to name only a few) represent particular instances of the application of such broad principles (cf. Silver & Wortman, 1980). Helplessness (Seligman, 1975) is a case in which doubt about reaching desired goals is extremely strong, and the doubt is generalized not just to a single domain of action, but more broadly. Optimism is a case in which a person is confident not just about one aspect of life, but about the future more generally (Scheier & Carver, 1985, 1987). Similar qualities of confidence and doubt play a role in a variety of other constructs, such as learned resourcefulness (Rosenbaum, 1990), coherence (Antonovsky, 1987), and self-esteem (Brockner, 1988; Rosenberg, 1979).

Consequences of Effort and Disengagement

When issues of confidence and doubt are approached from the viewpoint of a general model of behavior, it rather quickly becomes apparent that both continued effort and giving up are functional aspects of behavior—when they occur in the right circumstances. Continued effort is adaptive in any situation where continued effort will eventually produce the desired outcome. In such cases, giving up prematurely works against the person. By one criterion at least (successful goal attainment), disengaging in such a situation is dysfunctional.

In situations where continued effort is futile, though, the sooner the person disengages from pursuit of the goal, the better. Giving up in these cases permits the person to take up an alternative goal and move forward with life. This is true whether the alternative goal is a lower aspiration in the same general domain or a new goal altogether. Thus, optimal functioning across a lifetime (or even a day) requires that the person sometimes stay locked onto goals and sometimes abandon them.

This view on the adaptive value of disengagement is easily applied to stressful situations involving loss. A loss (e.g., death of a loved one) renders one or more desired goals unreachable (e.g., continuing activities once engaged in with that person—cf. Millar,

Tesser, & Millar, 1988). At first, one remains committed to those goals. Over time, however, one is better served by disengaging from them rather than holding onto them (cf. Tait & Silver, 1989).

There are times, however, when the person is unable to disengage, where the disengagement response is prevented from being carried through (Figure 2). A person in this situation wants to give up but cannot. Sometimes this is because the goal from which the person wants to disengage has a direct link to his or her implicit definition of self. Disengagement from such a goal is disengagement from oneself. As an example, consider the person who wants a life involving a close relationship, but who has experienced constant frustration in trying to form such a relationship. This person may experience an impulse to give up the attempt. Expressing that impulse, however, would require great change in the superordinate goals of the self. This makes it very difficult to disengage from the behavioral goal, despite the impulse to do so.

Now consider the threat posed by serious illness. Such a threat can create a situation that is structurally similar to the one just described. The goal (or set of goals) is continuation of one's life as a healthy human being and all the activities that are thereby implied. The threat that is carried by the diagnosis of a life-threatening illness may imply that continuing one's present life on its current course is impossible, prompting a giving-up response with respect to that goal. Giving up in this case, however, means giving up on one's life. To manifest such a response would have very adverse consequences; it thus is extremely difficult to do.

To feel that it is impossible to continue to move toward a goal to which you are committed is a particularly untenable situation psychologically. In cases like this, the disengagement response, so useful in other circumstances, tears at the very fabric of the self. We have argued, for reasons more complex than need be addressed here, that this is precisely the situation in life that generates the greatest degree of emotional distress (Carver & Scheier, 1990a, 1990b).

Coping as Self-Regulation

The viewpoint on behavior sketched out in the preceding paragraphs is the view that we bring to the analysis of stress and coping. This more general view on behavior takes us somewhat beyond the framework of the Lazarus model of stress and coping, though we hasten to add that we see nothing in this view that contradicts the Lazarus model. We believe, however, that taking the broader view brings several points to mind that would not otherwise be as apparent.

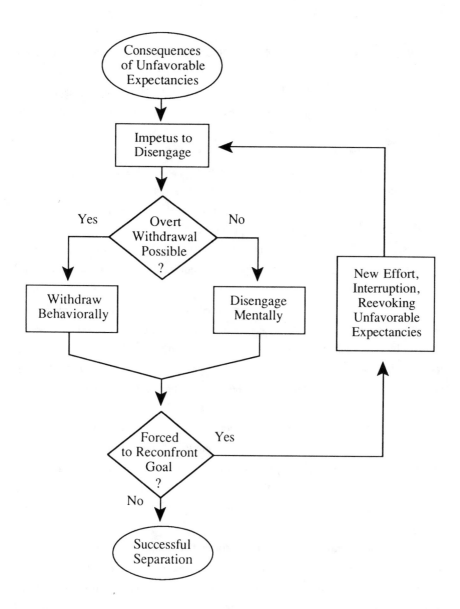

FIGURE 2 Flow diagram of consequences of unfavorable expectancies in various life circumstances. (When unfavorable expectancies prompt an impulse to disengage or give up, sometimes that impulse can be expressed fully and sometimes it cannot. If the person remains committed to the goal for some reason, circumstances will likely force the person to reconfront it and attempt again to move toward it. If the situation is no more favorable to doing so, however, the result is a cycle of sporadic effort and withdrawal, which is accompanied by heightened distress.)

For one thing, a goal-based approach suggests that many stressors are stressful because they threaten the attainment—or continued attainment—of important goals in the person's life. The more goals are threatened, and the more central those goals are to the overall sense of self and continuation of one's life's activities, the more stressful is the experience (cf. Millar et al., 1988). We think that many stressors in people's day-to-day experience constitute threats to the possibility of moving forward in desired activities of life (cf. Hobfoll, 1989). In this view, both the experience of stress and the processes of coping are embedded within the structure of self-regulation.

Taking this point of view has a number of implications. Most broadly, it implies that when one thinks about stress and coping in some particular context, one should also think about principles of self-regulation and their possible relevance to the situation under study. Two generalizations from the principles outlined earlier seem worth exploring further. First, given a severe-enough stressor, one can expect to see a dichotomy among people's responses to it, a dichotomy that is based on people's levels of confidence versus doubt. Some individuals will struggle to overcome the obstacle more than others. Some will be overwhelmed and will experience a tendency to give up on the goals with which the stressor is interfering. Second, when a person is doubtful enough to want to give up on something that cannot be given up on, that person can be expected to display deep distress.

These points also have some implications for how to go about conducting research on coping. One implication is that people's expectations for the future may be an important aspect of the overall psychological picture of the coping episode. Failure to assess one or another variable that falls in this general domain (and there are several such variables that one might assess) may mean disregarding an important determinant of people's coping processes.

Another implication derives from the notion that some responses to adversity work against success in coping. This notion implies that researchers should not focus solely on examining coping tactics that they expect to be useful and functional. It is every bit as important to study tactics you suspect are dysfunctional (e.g., Aldwin & Revenson, 1987; Holohan & Moos, 1985; Manne & Zautra, 1989; Rohde, Lewinsohn, Tilson, & Seeley, 1990; Warner & Rounds, 1989). It is important to determine what circumstances prompt the use of such tactics (and by whom), and it is also important to find out whether they are in fact dysfunctional. In thinking about a tactic's utility, of course, one must keep in mind that whether a tactic is functional or not may depend greatly on the situation being confronted (e.g., Folkman & Lazarus, 1988).

Commitment and Disengagement: One More Issue

Much of what we have said thus far about the contribution of self-regulation models to the analysis of stress and coping concerns processes at the point of disjunction between commitment and disengagement. Issues surrounding this disjunction seem to us to be critical to an understanding of effective and ineffective coping. There is a special case hidden within this discussion that we think is important to discuss more explicitly. This special case concerns the self-distraction and avoidance tactics that people often use when they want not to deal with problems they face. Such tendencies are also sometimes identified with the term *denial* (though the concept of denial is notoriously hard to pin down). At a minimum, these tactics reflect a temporary disengagement from problem-focused coping, and they may even reflect a disengagement from threatened goals.

It is often argued, quite plausibly, that self-distraction or avoidance coping can sometimes be useful because it gives the person a psychological breather, an opportunity to escape from the constant pressure of the stressful situation (cf. Miller, 1990; Repetti, this volume).[1] In the same way, it is often held that denial is adaptive in the short run, because it protects people from having to deal all at once with the implications of the problem they are confronting (Levine et al., 1987; Mullen & Suls, 1982; Suls & Fletcher, 1985). The usefulness of avoidance coping and denial has always been a matter of debate (Cohen & Lazarus, 1973; Klein, 1971; Meyerowitz, 1980; Weisman & Worden, 1976–1977), and the debate shows no clear sign of being settled. Sorting this question out is made more difficult by the fact that this family of coping tactics has several distinct manifestations. Though they are superficially similar in some ways, there are also differences among them that may be important.

To illustrate the breadth of this problem by an example, consider some of the ways in which denial and avoidance coping can be used by a woman who is at risk for breast cancer. Denial can play a role even before a threat is fully manifest, as a woman who wants to avoid considering the possibility of illness systematically avoids engaging in breast self-examination. There is no question that this manifestation of denial is dysfunctional to the extent that it interferes with early detection. Denial is also maladaptive at a stage when a threat has begun to emerge (for example, if a lump is noticed). In such a

---

[1] We should note a distinction between withdrawal of effort at goal attainment (described earlier) and the social withdrawal described by Repetti (1989, this volume). An air traffic controller sufficiently doubtful about performing adequately under conditions of high volume and poor visibility may withdraw goal-directed effort while on task. This response is what we focused on earlier. A controller who has been burdened by these conditions (not necessarily to the point of impaired effort) and needs time to recover from the experience may withdraw from an off-task activity such as social interaction. This response, which is one focus of Repetti's work, is quite different both in its origins and in its consequences.

situation, denial can slow the woman's help-seeking response, which can have obvious adverse consequences.

At the point where a diagnosis is made and the woman becomes aware of the disease, denial takes other forms, the effects of which are harder to judge. Denial now may mean denial of the life-threatening implications of the disease, denial of one's emotional reaction to the threat, avoidance of thinking about the situation, or active efforts at self-distraction from such thoughts or one's feelings of distress. Are these sorts of avoidance tactics adaptive or not? This question is difficult to answer, and it is likely to remain so, in part because many of these facets of denial and avoidance coping are hard to measure and thus hard to study. Some of them are subtle qualities of experience that are not easily spelled out in assessment devices and not easy for people to recognize in their own behavior. For this reason, these qualities are not likely to be measured easily by self-reports.

There are also conceptual difficulties in trying to specify whether a person's response does or does not imply denial. For example, if a woman says she is trying not to focus on her feelings of distress so that she can move beyond them to taking active steps forward, does that mean she is engaging in denial? If she says she is optimistic about her chances of recovery, does that mean she is engaging in denial? If she reports trying to derive something positive from the experience of having cancer, does that mean she is engaging in denial?

These questions are not easy to answer, but they are important. How best to conceptualize and interpret the cognitive tactics people deploy in confronting adversity is a broad issue that we feel deserves additional attention in the future.

Confronting Health Threats

We now turn to a brief description of certain aspects of two studies of our own in which subjects confronted serious threats to their health. These projects provide grounds for evaluating, in a preliminary way, the relevance to health-related settings of some of the ideas we outlined in the previous section of the chapter. One study examined the adjustment of men who were undergoing coronary artery bypass surgery (CABS). The other study examined the adjustment of women undergoing surgery for breast cancer. Both studies assessed aspects of psychological well-being as an outcome; the CABS study also incorporated some measures that were more behavioral. Both studies examined individual differences in expectancies as a predictor of outcomes, and both looked at aspects of coping, albeit assessed in very different ways.

CABS Patients

Subjects in the CABS study (Scheier et al., 1989) were men who were undergoing first-time nonemergency bypass surgery (see Scheier et al., 1989, for greater detail). Each subject was interviewed on the day prior to surgery, again 6 to 8 days after the surgery, and again 6 months later. The initial interview included a measure of optimism–pessimism called the Life Orientation Test or LOT (Scheier & Carver, 1985), a measure of mood, and a set of items intended to provide insight into what cognitive strategies subjects were using to cope with the upcoming surgery and its aftermath. The postsurgery interview repeated the mood measures and the items on coping. Also assessed at this stage was the subject's rate of recovery, both in terms of behavioral milestones and in terms of staff evaluations of progress. At 6 months postsurgery, subjects reported on their quality of life and on the extent and pace with which their life's activities had returned to normal.

The first question concerns the role of expectancies as predictors of subjects' reactions to the experiences they were undergoing. Expectancies in this study consisted of generalized expectancies for the future—optimism versus pessimism. As suggested by the theoretical analysis outlined earlier, pessimism was related to a variety of undesirable outcomes. For example, pessimists reported higher levels of hostility and depression on the day before surgery than did optimists. There was no difference on these particular mood variables postsurgery, but pessimists reported less relief and happiness postsurgery than did optimists.

This study did not incorporate a full measure of coping strategies, but several items were included to assess the use of certain cognitive tactics as ways of approaching (or avoiding) the issues surrounding the period of surgery. A number of differences on these items emerged as a function of optimism versus pessimism. Before the surgery, optimists were more likely than pessimists to report that they were making plans for the future and setting goals for their recovery. Optimists also tended to report being less focused on the negative aspects of their experience (their distress emotions and symptoms) than pessimists. Once the surgery was past, optimists were more likely than pessimists to report seeking out and requesting information about what the physician would be requiring of them during the months ahead. Optimists were also marginally less likely to report trying to suppress thoughts about their physical symptoms.

In sum, the pattern of psychological effects surrounding the optimism–pessimism variable is generally consistent with our earlier portrayal of the divergent responses that result from confidence and doubt. Optimists entered the surgery planning ahead to what life would be like on the other side, and a week after the surgery they were seeking additional information to prepare themselves to move forward. Pessimists entered the surgery more bound up in their distress, and afterward they seemed less gratified than optimists to have survived it without complication. Compared with optimists, the pessimists seemed far less ready to move forward and cope in an active, engaged way with the threat to their health and well-being that was posed by the diagnosis and surgery.

Along with these psychological differences, differences also emerged that were more behavioral in character. Optimists were quicker than pessimists to move forward in the recovery process, as measured both in terms of staff ratings of their recoveries and in terms of their behavioral milestones of recovery. The clearest evidence of the latter was the fact that optimists were up and walking around their rooms sooner after surgery than pessimists.

At the 6-month follow-up, subjects reported on the extent to which their lives had returned to normal in several domains and the rate at which this had taken place. Optimists were more likely to have reported having returned to vigorous exercise, and they were marginally more likely to have returned to full-time work. When a composite index was created from all the domains measured, optimism was associated with greater normalization of life activities. When a similar index was created for the rate of return to normal, optimism was also linked to faster normalization. These outcomes are very much what would be expected from the expectancy-based approach to behavior. Optimism was also related to reports of positive quality of life 6-months postsurgery.

Associations were also explored among responses to the coping items and outcome variables. Both before and after the surgery, the tendency to be focused on feelings of distress was correlated with the intensity of the distress emotions reported. Before surgery, but not afterward, the intensity of the emotions was also correlated with a tendency to report trying *not* to think about the feelings. Reports of making plans and setting goals for the future were associated with less distress, both concurrently and prospectively. That is, planning before surgery was predictive of lower distress levels 8 days later, even after controlling for earlier distress levels.

Planning and setting goals for recovery were associated with good outcomes in other respects as well. Both presurgery planning and postsurgery planning were associated with staff ratings of better progress toward recovery 1 week after surgery and also with self-rated satisfaction with the rate of progress made thus far. Planning for recovery also tended to be associated with shorter hospital stays after surgery. In contrast to this, focusing on one's distress (both before and after the surgery) went hand in hand with slower recovery. Focus on distress tended to be associated with slower progress toward walking after the surgery and with longer hospitalizations. Reports of trying *not* to think about distress postsurgery were correlated with staff ratings of poorer progress in recovery.

Other evidence about the adverse consequences of suppressing thoughts about distress comes from the 6-month follow-up. Subjects who reported trying not to think about their negative emotions on the day before surgery were less likely to have returned to work 6 months later, and less likely to have resumed vigorous exercise. Overall, their lives' activities were less likely to have returned to normal, and activities that had returned to normal had done so at a slower pace.

Although these findings are equivocal in a number of respects (e.g., many of the associations are concurrent), the pattern again is consistent with a picture in which people who actively take on the challenge of recovery are better off than those whose energy goes instead into focusing on their distress or trying to suppress it.

Breast Cancer Patients

The second study in which we have been involved looks at the adjustment process among a group of early-stage breast cancer patients. This study (Pozo et al., 1990) is still ongoing. The associations described here are those that emerged from preliminary analyses of a nearly complete sample. Subjects are women who have been diagnosed with Stage I or Stage II breast cancer. A diagnosis of Stage I or Stage II implies a relatively good prognosis, though the cancer clearly poses a threat to survival and health. In addition, the remedy for the disease is a disfiguring surgical procedure, which is often followed by adjuvant therapy that has unpleasant side effects. Thus, this experience incorporates many sources of potential distress.

Patients in this study are interviewed at the time of diagnosis, at which time optimism is assessed by the LOT. They are interviewed again the day before surgery and once again 7 to 10 days after surgery. Follow-up interviews are conducted 3 months later. All interviews beyond the initial one incorporate a measure of negative mood and a measure of coping tactics called the COPE (Carver, Scheier, & Weintraub, 1989). The COPE asks respondents to indicate the extent to which they have been engaging in each of a series of behavioral or cognitive tactics as a way of dealing with the stresses surrounding (in this case) the experience of diagnosis and surgery. At presurgery the patient indicates how much she used each tactic since learning she would need surgery, at postsurgery she refers to the time since surgery, and at follow-up she refers to the preceding month. The COPE is similar in many respects to such measures as the Ways of Coping (Lazarus & Folkman, 1984; see also Billings & Moos, 1981; McCrae, 1984; Stone & Neale, 1984), but it includes several additional scales.

During the period surrounding the surgery, optimism was associated with a pattern of reported coping tactics that revolved around accepting the reality of the situation, placing as positive a light on the situation as possible, trying to relieve the situation with humor, and taking active steps to do whatever there was to be done. By the time of the 3-month follow-up, some of these associations had weakened, though optimism was still significantly related to acceptance of the situation. In contrast to this picture of constructive coping, pessimism was associated with a pattern of overt (conscious) denial and reports of behavioral disengagement (giving up) during the period surrounding surgery. It is worth noting that reports of disengagement were infrequent overall, but the correlation of these reports with pessimism was quite substantial (around .50). This association remained strong even at the 3-month follow-up, though the link to denial largely disappeared by then.

The coping tactics that coalesced around optimism and pessimism were also strongly related to the distress that subjects reported. Positive reframing, acceptance, and the use of humor were all related inversely to self-reports of distress emotions, both before surgery and after. Denial and behavioral disengagement were positively related to distress at the same measurement points. By the 3-month point, the effect for reframing had fallen away, but a new association emerged, such that distress was positively correlated with mental disengagement (self-distraction). As might be expected from these correlations with coping, pessimism was associated with elevated distress at all three measurement points.

These findings form a pattern that is quite consistent with the reasoning outlined earlier in the chapter. Although disengagement is not at all common among these patients, it is a response with a good deal of emotional impact. The experience of giving up and also the attempt to escape from the reality of the situation are tied to higher levels of distress. Given the situation these women face, it is somewhat remarkable that acceptance of the reality of the situation is one of the strongest correlates of the relative *absence* of distress. It appears very much as though this response is tied to an effort to move forward rather than become mired in present unhappiness.

In the characterization of the pattern of coping and distress just outlined, the associations are concurrent, and thus are uninformative about the direction of causality. Additional information on this question is obtained by examining the effect of coping prospectively, that is, using coping at one stage to predict subsequent distress after controlling for earlier distress. Use of this tactic in this sample is less helpful than it might be, owing to the fact that distress is correlated quite highly across the three measurement points. As a result, once a control for initial distress is instituted, there is little room for prediction of subsequent distress. Nevertheless, two instances emerged in which coping at one point was related to distress at the next measurement point. Both instances fit well with the picture presented thus far. First, acceptance at presurgery predicted less distress at postsurgery. Second, disengagement at postsurgery predicted greater distress at the 3-month follow-up. Comparable prospective analyses exploring the possibility of reverse causality found that high levels of distress induced subsequent responses of three sorts. Distress postsurgery predicted higher reports of behavioral disengagement, mental disengagement, and seeking out of social support at the 3-month follow-up.

Similarities and Differences

The results of these two studies are similar in several ways though they differ in others. In both cases, subjects' generalized expectancies for the future were related to a variety of cognitive and behavioral outcomes that were consistent with our earlier portrayal of the structure of behavioral self-regulation. Optimistic patients showed evidence of accepting the reality of their situation, of actively confronting the threat posed by their illness and taking up the task of recovery. There is one salient difference between the studies' outcomes, however. Pessimism among the CABS patients was related to subjective distress before the surgery, but not afterward. Pessimism among the cancer patients, on the other hand, has been consistently related to subjective distress before surgery, afterward, and at the 3-month follow up.

We would speculate that this difference is at least partly attributable to differences in the situations faced by patients in the two studies. Among the CABS patients, the surgical procedure itself is the primary source of threat. If there are no complications from the surgery, recovery (though not free of effort) is a fairly straightforward matter. Indeed, when asked what effect the surgery would have on their underlying heart disease, over half of these men said that their disease would be gone after the surgery. Among the cancer patients, in contrast, two issues extend well beyond the surgery. First, recurrence of the cancer and the life threat that is thereby implied remains an acknowledged possibility (see, e.g., Peters-Golden, 1982). This in itself suggests that expectancies for the future are likely to play a role in the experience of distress well beyond the point of surgery. Second, the surgery changes the woman's body in an important way. This physical change itself constitutes a threat to the woman's self-image, and her expectancies for the future may play a role in how she deals with this aspect of the experience.

Coping Reconsidered

At this point, we would like to step back and consider some of the implications of these two studies—some of the points they seem to make and some of the questions they fail to answer. Most generally, the studies seem to bear out the usefulness of taking into account broad principles of self-regulation in predicting how patients will deal with health problems and in trying to identify what coping tactics are more useful and less useful. Having said that, however, we should note that evidence on the usefulness of various aspects of coping in response to these health crises is not as abundant as one might wish. In particular, although the pattern of coping qualities and outcomes is generally intelligible and consistent, the associations are mainly concurrent and thus equivocal about direction of causal influence. It was less common to find prospective effects in these studies. The lack of prospective effects in the cancer study is partially attributable to the relative stability of the outcome measure. Knowing this, however, does not help much in addressing the question of interest. Does coping influence adjustment, then, or do coping tactics merely covary with adjustment (cf. Aldwin & Revenson, 1987)? Are distress and coping qualities mutually intertwined reflections of something else? These questions are presently without firm answers, and more information will be needed before we can feel comfortable believing that coping has a causal influence on subsequent well-being.

Another question that these studies fail to answer concerns the comparative benefit of being an optimist versus being a pessimist. The theoretical model from which we have proceeded holds that confidence is more adaptive than doubt in situations where continued striving will ultimately produce desired outcomes. In theory, then, optimism is good whenever the threat can be met. But what about situations where struggling gets a person nowhere? What about threats that are so discrepant with one's worldview as to challenge the validity of that worldview? Some have suggested that optimists will not handle this sort of situation as well as pessimists (Tennan & Affleck, 1987). Expecting the best and finding themselves in an unmanageable situation, optimists may confront strains they are unprepared to handle. The impact may be less on pessimists, who enter the situation with lower expectations.

This is a reasonable hypothesis, and we are as interested as anyone else in how it will fare empirically. The two studies outlined here are not definitive, of course, at least in part because subjects in these studies were confronting situations that were potentially controllable by medical intervention. Still, there is at least one hint in the data that optimism confers benefits even in extreme circumstances. Specifically, among cancer patients optimism was related to self-reported acceptance of the situation, which in turn predicted low levels of distress. This acceptance response may be a more important psychological process than we have appreciated up to this point, and it seems worthwhile to give some additional thought to its meaning.

Acceptance means restructuring one's understanding of the situation one is in— assimilating a new reality (cf. Taylor, Collins, Skokan, & Aspinwall, 1989). In contrast, refusal to accept the reality of the problem (denial) means attempting to cling to a worldview that is no longer valid. Presumably reports of acceptance among these patients reflect the occurrence of a set of deeper and more extensive processes, in which the women are working through the experience in some way, integrating it into their evolving worldview rather than trying to isolate it from other aspects of their experience. Instead of running away from the problem these women seem to be coming to grips with it in one fashion or another. Indeed, such active attempts to come to grips with the problem may well be the mechanism for the beneficial effects of acceptance (cf. Pennebaker, this volume; Clark, 1991). By contrast, patients who report engaging in conscious efforts to deny the experience are thereby putting off psychological resolution, trying instead to escape from the problem's very existence. This difference between orientations appears to be important, in that it goes hand in hand with differences in distress.

This view on the nature of acceptance implies that it entails a kind of psychological flexibility. That is, accepting the reality of a diagnosis of cancer means adopting a view of one's situation in life that is very different from the view one held before. To attempt to deny the reality of the problem is an inflexible effort to force reality to conform to one's preexisting view. Inasmuch as reality does not often bend to this effort, the person trying to deny reality must continue to reconfront it until the denial diminishes.

Thus, acceptance as a facet of coping suggests taking an orientation to life in which one moves flexibly forward into whatever situation one encounters, whereas use of denial suggests an unwillingness to move forward into threatening situations.

This view of acceptance as a facet of coping suggests, in turn, the possibility that optimists may be more flexible than pessimists in their ability to assimilate harsh realities. It is obvious, of course, that evaluation of this possibility will require additional research. It is by no means clear, for example, that the association between optimism and acceptance would remain strong in situations that are even more adverse than described here—for example, if the diagnosis were one that carried a poorer prognosis. For the present, then, this issue remains unsettled, awaiting additional data.

References

Aldwin, C. M., & Revenson, T. A. (1987). Does coping help? A reexamination of the relation between coping and mental health. *Journal of Personality and Social Psychology, 53*, 337–348.

Antonovsky, A. (1987). *Unraveling the mystery of health: How people manage stress and stay well.* San Francisco: Jossey-Bass.

Bandura, A. (1978). The self system in reciprocal determinism. *American Psychologist 33*, 344–358.

Bandura, A. (1986). *Social foundations of thought and action: A social cognitive theory.* Englewood Cliffs, NJ: Prentice-Hall.

Billings, A. G., & Moos, R. H. (1981). The role of coping responses and social resources in attenuating the stress of life events. *Journal of Behavioral Medicine, 4*, 139–157.

Brockner, J. (1988). *Self-esteem at work: Research, theory, and practice.* Lexington, MA: Lexington Books.

Cantor, N., & Zirkel, S. (1990). In L. A. Pervin (Ed.), *Handbook of personality: Theory and research* (pp. 135–164). New York: Guilford Press.

Carver, C. S., & Scheier, M. F. (1981). *Attention and self-regulation: A control-theory approach to human behavior.* New York: Springer-Verlag.

Carver, C. S., & Scheier, M. F. (1990a). Origins and functions of positive and negative affect: A control-process view. *Psychological Review, 97*, 19–35.

Carver, C. S., & Scheier, M. F. (1990b). Principles of self-regulation: Action and emotion. In E. T. Higgins & R. M. Sorrentino (Eds.), *Handbook of motivation and cognition: Foundations of social behavior* (Vol. 2, pp. 3–52). New York: Guilford Press.

Carver, C. S., Scheier, M. F., & Weintraub, J. K. (1989). Assessing coping strategies: A theoretically based approach. *Journal of Personality and Social Psychology, 56*, 267–283.

Clark, L. F. (1991). *Stress and the cognitive–conversational benefits of social interaction.* Unpublished manuscript, Purdue University.

Cohen, F., & Lazarus, R. S. (1973). Active coping processes, coping dispositions, and recovery from surgery. *Psychosomatic Medicine, 35,* 375–389.

Folkman, S., & Lazarus, R. S. (1988). Coping as a mediator of emotion. *Journal of Personality and Social Psychology, 54,* 466–475.

Hobfoll, S. E. (1989). Conservation of resources: A new attempt at conceptualizing stress. *American Psychologist, 44,* 513–524.

Holohan, C. J., & Moos, R. H. (1985). Life stress and health: Personality, coping, and family support in stress resistance. *Journal of Personality and Social Psychology, 49,* 739–747.

Kanfer, F. H., & Hagerman, S. M. (1985). Behavior therapy and the information-processing paradigm. In S. Reiss & R. R. Bootzin (Eds.), *Theoretical issues in behavior therapy* (pp. 3–33). New York: Academic Press.

Kaplan, R. M. (1990). Behavior as the central outcome in health care. *American Psychologist, 45,* 1211–1220.

Kelly, G. A. (1955). *The psychology of personal constructs.* New York: W. W. Norton.

Kirsch, I. (1990). *Changing expectations: A key to effective psychotherapy.* Pacific Grove, CA: Brooks/Cole.

Klein, R. A. (1971). A crisis to grow on. *Cancer, 28,* 1660–1665.

Klinger, E. (1975). Consequences of commitment to and disengagement from incentives. *Psychological Review, 82,* 1–25.

Kukla, A. (1972). Foundations of an attributional theory of performance. *Psychological Review, 79,* 454–470.

Lazarus, R. S. (1966). *Psychological stress and the coping process.* New York: McGraw-Hill.

Lazarus, R. S., & Folkman, S. (1984). *Stress, appraisal, and coping.* New York: Springer.

Levine, J., Warrenburg, S., Kerns, R., Schwartz, G., Delaney, R., Fontana, A., Gradman, A., Smith, S., Allen, S., & Cascione, R. (1987). The role of denial in recovery from coronary heart disease. *Psychosomatic Medicine, 49,* 109–117.

Manne, S. L., & Zautra, A. J. (1989). Spouse criticism and support: Their association with coping and psychological adjustment among women with rheumatoid arthritis. *Journal of Personality and Social Psychology, 56,* 608–617.

McCrae, R. R. (1984). Situational determinants of coping responses: Loss, threat, and challenge. *Journal of Personality and Social Psychology, 46,* 919–928.

Meyerowitz, B. E. (1980). Psychosocial correlates of breast cancer and its treatments. *Psychological Bulletin, 87,* 108–131.

Millar, K. U., Tesser, A., & Millar, M. G. (1988). The effect of a threatening life event on behavior sequences and intrusive thought: A self-disruption explanation. *Cognitive Therapy and Research, 12,* 441–458.

Miller, S. M. (1990). To see or not to see: Cognitive informational styles in the coping process. In M. Rosenbaum (Ed.), *Learned resourcefulness: On coping skills, self-control, and adaptive behavior* (pp. 95–126). New York: Springer.

Mischel, W. (1973). Toward a cognitive social learning reconceptualization of personality. *Psychological Review, 80,* 252–283.

Mischel, W. (1990). Personality dispositions revisited and revised: A view after three decades. In L. A. Pervin (Ed.), *Handbook of personality: Theory and research* (pp. 111–134). New York: Guilford Press.

Mullen, B., & Suls, J. (1982). The effectiveness of attention and rejection as coping styles: A meta-analysis of temporal differences. *Journal of Psychosomatic Research, 26,* 43–49.

Pervin, L. A. (1983). The stasis and flow of behavior: Toward a theory of goals. In M. M. Page & R. Dienstbier (Eds.), *Nebraska symposium on motivation* (Vol. 31, pp. 1–53). Lincoln: University of Nebraska Press.

Pervin, L. A. (1989). *Goal concepts in personality and social psychology.* Hillsdale, NJ: Erlbaum.

Peters-Golden, H. (1982). Breast cancer. Varied perception of social support in the illness experience. *Social Science & Medicine, 16,* 483–491.

Pozo, C., Carver, C. S., Robinson, D. S., Ketcham, A. S., Legaspi, A., Moffat, F., & Scheier, M. F. (1990). Unpublished raw data.

Repetti, R. L. (1989). Effects of daily workload on subsequent behavior during marital interaction: The roles of social withdrawal and spouse support. *Journal of Personality and Social Psychology, 57,* 651–659.

Rohde, P., Lewinsohn, P. M., Tilson, M., & Seeley, J. R. (1990). Dimensionality of coping and its relation to depression. *Journal of Personality and Social Psychology, 58,* 499–511.

Rosenbaum, M. (Ed.). (1990). *Learned resourcefulness: On coping skills, self-control, and adaptive behavior.* New York: Springer.

Rosenberg, M. (1979). *Conceiving the self.* New York: Basic Books.

Scheier, M. F., & Carver, C. S. (1985). Optimism, coping, and health: Assessment and implications of generalized outcome expectancies. *Health Psychology, 4,* 219–247.

Scheier, M. F., & Carver, C. S. (1987). Dispositional optimism and physical well-being: The influence of generalized outcome expectancies on health. *Journal of Personality, 55,* 169–210.

Scheier, M. F., Matthews, K. A., Owens, J. F., Magovern, G. J., Sr. Lefebvre, R. C. Abbott, R. A., & Carver, C. S. (1989). Dispositional optimism and recovery from coronary artery bypass surgery: The beneficial effects on physical and psychological well being. *Journal of Personality and Social Psychology, 57,* 1024–1040.

Seligman, M. E. P. (1975). *Helplessness: On depression, development, and death.* San Francisco: Freeman.

Silver, R. L., & Wortman, C. B. (1980). Coping with undesirable life events. In J. Garber & M. E. P. Seligman (Eds.), *Human helplessness: Theory and applications* (pp. 279–340). New York: Academic Press.

Stone, A. A., & Neale, J. M. (1984). New measure of daily coping: Development and preliminary results. *Journal of Personality and Social Psychology, 46,* 892–906.

Suls, J., & Fletcher, B. (1985). The relative efficacy of avoidant and non-avoidant coping strategies: A meta-analysis. *Health Psychology, 4,* 249–288.

Tait, R., & Silver, R. C. (1989). Coming to terms with major negative life events. In J. S. Uleman & J. A. Bargh (Eds.), *Unintended thought* (pp. 351–382). New York: Guilford Press.

Taylor, S. E., & Aspinwall, L. G. (1990). Psychological aspects of chronic illness. In G. R. VandenBos & P. T. Costa, Jr. (Eds.), *Psychological aspects of serious illness.* Washington, DC: American Psychological Association.

Taylor, S. E., Collins, R. L., Skokan, L. A., & Aspinwall, L. G. (1989). Maintaining positive illusions in the face of negative information. Getting the facts without letting them get to you. *Journal of Social and Clinical Psychology, 8,* 114–129.

Tennen, H., & Affleck, G. (1987). The costs and benefits of optimistic explanations and dispositional optimism. *Journal of Personality, 55,* 377–393.

Warner, G. C., & Rounds, J. B. (1989, August). *Stress, coping and adjustment to spinal cord injury.* Paper presented at the 97th annual convention of the American Psychological Association, New Orleans, LA.

Weisman, A. D., & Worden, J. W. (1976–1977). The existential plight in cancer: Significance of the first 100 days. *International Journal of Psychiatric in Medicine, 7,* 1–15.

Wortman, C. B., & Brehm, J. W. (1975). Responses to uncontrollable outcomes: An integration of reactance theory and the learned helplessness model. In L. Berkowitz (Ed.), *Advances in experimental social psychology* (Vol. 8, pp. 277–336). New York: Academic Press.

CHAPTER 12

The Influence of Familial and Interpersonal Factors on Children's Development and Associated Cardiovascular Risk

Barbara J. Tinsley

R ecent meta-analytic reviews suggest that negative affective states are related to the development of a broad range of diseases, including coronary heart disease (Friedman & Booth-Kewley, 1987; Taylor, 1990). As demonstrated repeatedly in this volume, studies have implicated the role of anger and hostility in the etiology of cardiovascular disease (Dembrowski & Williams, 1990).

An emerging focus of this area of inquiry is centered on familial childhood precursors of cardiovascular risk. A variety of family-related child antecedents have been identified as potential or demonstrated markers of both concurrent and predictive factors that are associated with later risk. These include genetic influences, intergenerational physiologic hyperreactivity, gender, personality and emotional characteristics (e.g., anger–hostility and performance styles), and a variety of other familial variables ranging from sociodemographic factors (e.g., socioeconomic status and ethnicity), structural factors (e.g., family size and ordinal position), and systems characteristics (e.g., parent–child interaction styles) (Thoresen & Pattillo, 1988). Moreover, a smaller group of these studies has examined the simultaneous interaction of these types of family risk-associated variables. For example, Matthews and her associates found that non-Type A mothers of children identified as exhibiting Type A behavior patterns (e.g., impatient, aggressive, chronically time urgent, competitive, and hostile) will impose more achievement pressure on them than non-Type A mothers of non-Type A children (Matthews, 1977; Matthews, Glass, & Richins, 1977).

However, two major limitations characterize this research area: (a) an overreliance on a direct-effects model, which represents the direct influence of one family member on another, and (b) insufficient attention to the delineation of the mechanisms by which these family-process risk factors influence cardiovascular risk status.

Beyond Direct-Effects Models

It has been acknowledged over the last decade that in order to understand family relationships, or more specifically, the impact of the family on child development, it is necessary to recognize the interdependence among the roles and functions of all family members. It is now assumed that families are best viewed as social systems. Consequently, to understand the behavior of one member of a family, the complementary behaviors of other members also need to be assessed. This perspective has encouraged developmental psychologists to move beyond the study of the mother–child relationship and its impact on child development to consider the impact of other family members (e.g., fathers, siblings, and extended family members) on children's development. With this viewpoint, the direct (e.g., parent–child interaction patterns) and indirect (e.g., parent–sibling and spouse interaction patterns) impacts of family interaction on children can be articulated (Parke & Tinsley, 1987).

Most of the studies of familial childhood factors implicated in later cardiovascular risk have used a direct-effects approach, whereby family members directly influence other family members (and their risk status) through interaction. However, as is the case in other domains of developmental analysis of the relationships between family influences and their impacts, models that limit examination to the direct effects of one family member on another are inadequate for understanding development. A variety of familial demographic, structural, and systemic factors can influence development indirectly, as well as directly. For example, in analyzing the impact of the marital relationship on parent–child interaction, a parent may influence a child through the mediation of another family member's impact (e.g., a father may contribute to the mother's positive affect toward her child by praising her caregiving ability). Another way in which one parent may directly influence a child's treatment by other agents is by modifying the child's behavior. Child-behavior patterns that develop as a result of parent–child interaction may in turn affect the child's treatment by other social agents. For example, irritable infant patterns induced by an insensitive and impatient mother may in turn make the infant more difficult for the father to handle and pacify. Thus, patterns developed in interaction with one parent may alter interaction patterns with another caregiver. In larger families, siblings can play a similar mediating role (Parke & Tinsley, 1987).

Although careful attention continues to be paid to elucidating the direct effects of familial childhood influences on subsequent cardiovascular risk (see Thoresen & Pattillo, 1988, for an excellent review of this research), very little evidence exists concerning the indirect effects of these influences on later risk and the mechanisms by which they may operate to mediate risk.

Mechanisms Involved in Mediating Risk

Four mechanisms have been identified that may mediate the effects of familial factors on children's concurrent and subsequent cardiovascular risk status. These mechanisms are modeling, other socialization mechanisms, the development of a general disease-prone personality in the context of the family, and negative emotional states producing pathogenic physiological changes (McCranie & Simpson, 1986; Taylor, 1990). All four of these mechanisms can mediate risk through both direct and indirect effects.

Modeling

The acquisition of internal values and overt behavior determined by parental role models is well-documented in the developmental literature. Using a direct-effects model, parents who are hostile and angry with their children are teaching these behaviors to the children. Children may learn and adopt similar behavior strategies by emulating and imitating the angry or hostile behavior of their parents. However, in combination with an indirect-effects perspective, parental modeling of anger and hostility becomes even more powerful. When children are exposed to parental anger or hostility directed at others, either within the family (e.g., siblings or spouses) or outside the family (e.g., parental peers and coworkers), the children are being provided an especially powerful model of these behaviors, particularly if the children perceive the angry or hostile behavior as successful or rewarding in achieving compliance. For example, a mother's experience of having to defend herself against physical aggression directed at her by a spouse may motivate her child-rearing goal (i.e., that her child be able to defend herself), and in turn, her behavior of initiating teasing interactions in which the child is given the opportunity to practice fighting back (Miller & Sperry, 1987). Another way in which indirect effects of familial modeling of anger and hostility indirectly affect children's acquisition of these behaviors is discussed by Cummings, Iannotti, and Zahn-Waxler (1985), who suggested that children's exposure to parent–parent angry and hostile behavior is associated with children's increased aggressiveness with peers. Modeling appears to be a promising mechanism for understanding the relationship between familial interpersonal behavior and children's behavior that leads to cardiovascular risk.

Other Socialization Mechanisms

In addition to modeling, children are socialized through a series of other mechanisms, including parental control practices, parental expectations, parental supervision and monitoring, household rules, family attitudes toward exposure to violence and anger, and familial endorsement of aggressive tactics for social problem solving. Parental socialization of children's emotional and social development are important direct influences on children's anger and hostile behavior. Children establish self-esteem, identity, coping styles, and emotional response patterns in the context of parent–child interaction during infancy and early childhood (Parke et al., 1989; Price, 1982). McCranie & Simpson (1986) suggested that children may adopt various Type A behaviors as a way of coping with negative emotional family environments, characterized by evaluative parental performance expectations and frequent criticism and disapproval. Parental behavior marked by hostile and punitive control may result in child anger and resentment, yielding Type A emotional characteristics (Friedman & Rosenman, 1974). However, children's self-identity is also influenced by a variety of indirect mechanisms originating in the family. For example, parents' interaction with other children in the home, characterized by evaluative parental performance expectation, criticism, and disapproval can have a negative impact on children's social and emotional development, even if not targeted toward them. Not only are they exposed to the negative interactions, but children in such situations may be the target of subsequent resentment and hostility by their siblings, who may perceive them as more favored.

Compelling evidence suggests that anger and hostility in the home environment have a significant role in children's psychosocial development (Cummings & Cummings,

1988). Most of this research has focused, in a direct-effects approach, on the negative impact of hostile parent–child interaction. However, from an indirect-effects perspective, researchers recently have been examining the role of observed familial angry and hostile interaction on children's socioemotional development. A series of studies by Cummings and his associates (Cummings, 1987; Cummings & Cummings, 1988), Katz and Gottman (in press), and a review by Grych and Fincham (1990) suggest that children's exposure as bystanders to parent–parent anger and hostility is a source of stress for children and shapes their emotional response patterns.

Cummings et al. (1985, 1987) reported that children's responses to familial background anger include covert feelings, physiological responses, overt emotional behavior, and social behavior. Furthermore, this research suggests that children's reported emotions and children's observable behavior in response to parent–parent anger are not always similar. Children may appear neutral, but report angry feelings during angry parental exchanges, whereas others appear moved by the hostility, yet report calm. Cummings et al. (1985, 1987) proposed that exaggerated emotional response is most evident in children *during* exposure to background anger, whereas increased aggressive behavior is most identifiable *after* exposure to anger.

Several studies have documented children's emotional responses to familial background anger. Data from these studies suggest that boys appear to demonstrate disturbance by increased aggressiveness, in contrast to girls, who become more withdrawn, anxious, or well behaved (Block, Block, & Morrison, 1981; Emery, 1982). Moreover, boys who are rated as more aggressive seem more likely to respond to adults' anger with their own anger (Klaczynski & Cummings, 1989). Thus, negative interactions between adults in a family may increase aggressiveness in children, especially if they already have aggressive tendencies.

Other research by Cummings (Cummings, Vogel, & Cummings, 1987) suggests that whether or not children have the opportunity to determine if background anger is resolved can affect children's emotional responses. Viewing hostile disagreements was reported by children to be the most negative and elicited the most "mad" feelings in children, and unresolved background anger was perceived by children as more negative and resulted in more hostile reactions in children (Cummings & Cummings, 1988).

In general, this line of research (Cummings et al., 1987) exploring the indirect effects of family members suggests that experiencing parent–parent anger is very stressful for children, resulting in distress and arousal and, eventually, patterns of overreactivity to anger in others. From an indirect-effects perspective, this tendency to overrespond to anger in others may contribute to patterns of response by others that increase the likelihood of aggression and aggressive response (Cummings & Cummings, 1988). For example, research by Dodge (1986) suggests that children who view hostility in the home environment may come to perceive hostile intent in otherwise ambiguous situations and respond in an inappropriately aggressive manner. Responding in this manner to ambiguous situations may then cause others to react aggressively and result in more frequent experiences of conflict in many contexts outside the family. These findings provide strong evidence linking familial emotional climate to children's socioemotional development, but they are limited in an important sense. Some of the studies use family contexts in identifying negative emotional factors in interactions that affect children. However, other studies use nonfamily adults in laboratory conflict situations as a stimulus for children's emotional reaction to anger and hostility. The findings of these studies cannot be generalized to the family situation without replicating these paradigms in family contexts (Grych & Fincham, 1990).

Marital conflict is not the only source for either direct or indirect socialization of children's emotional development in the context of the family. With a direct-effects perspective, sibling interaction provides many aspects of social comparison and stimulation that are important for identity formation and general intellectual and socioemotional development (Dunn, 1983; Dunn & Kendrick, 1982). However, siblings are important in children's emotional regulation from an indirect-effects viewpoint as well. Dunn and Munn (1985) studied conflict in families with 2-year-old children and found that children were responsive to mother–sibling conflict as well as conflict in which they were directly involved. Specifically, these researchers demonstrated that children responded differently to mother–sibling conflict depending on the topic of conflict. Conflicts about siblings' aggressive behavior led to negative affect in children in comparison with other types of conflict.

These studies in combination seem to support the conclusion that families in which children are exposed to anger and hostility have children who are angry, aggressive, and hostile, and this may increase children's later cardiovascular risk.

Development of a General Disease-Prone Personality

Personality can influence disease through physiological mechanisms; patterns of emotional responses can influence physiological responses, which can lead to illness. Examples of diseases that appear to be associated with emotional and physiological responses include asthma and cardiovascular disease. In combination with genetic propensities to these diseases (e.g., allergies, in the case of asthma), stressful life-style factors, age, and a person's emotional and physiological responses can be significant in eliciting illness, although the exact mechanisms by which these responses are translated into illness have not yet been adequately specified. Meta-analytic studies of the relationship between personality and disease suggest that personality variables must, at least, be considered as risk factors for illness (Friedman & DiMatteo, 1989). This model is derived from a direct-effects perspective, whereby a particular set of emotional and physiological reactions are seen as directly influencing the presence or absence of illness. An alternative indirect-effects viewpoint would suggest that parents, in socializing children's personalities, might indirectly impact on their illness risk. For example, child personality variables, such as their achievement motivation or aggressiveness, may be influenced by parents. Child behavior patterns stemming from such personality characteristics (e.g., acting out at school) may in turn affect the child's treatment by other social agents (e.g., peer rejection), which in turn, may exacerbate the link between the child's personality and proneness to illness.

Negative Emotional States Producing Pathogenic Physiological Changes

The most consistent evidence for a causal link between negative emotional states and pathology is found in the literature documenting the impact of stress on the immune system (Cohen & Williamson, 1991; Kiecolt-Glaser & Glaser, 1991). In adults, studies suggest that stressful events, such as the death of a loved one, depression, or perceived loss of control, appear to compromise immunity (Taylor, 1990). Although no research to date has directly implicated anger or hostility in immune-system malfunctions, anger and hostility are often associated with depression, coping with death, and loss of control. Comparable work with children is not available, and an assumption can only be made that the mechanisms linking negative emotions with immunosuppression in adults might be similar in children, which may not be the case.

Many stressful events occur within the context of the family, and it could be argued that the intensity of negative affect in family contexts supersedes the intensity of negative affect in most other contexts (Bradbury & Fincham, 1990). Thus, a direct-effects model could suggest that negative emotions (e.g., anger and hostility) generated in the context of the family could lead to compromise of the immune system in children. However, an indirect-effects model would go further to suggest that many other family events could influence children's immune functioning. In the case of parental divorce, for example, the change in parents' marital relationship may lead to negative mother–child interaction (Hetherington, 1989), which could be associated with negative emotional response in the child, and in turn, with inadequate immune-system performance.

Although little research has been accomplished with respect to children's physiological reactions to anger, it is known that high physiological response in children is related to less-expressive verbal responses. Boys (from ages 4 to 6) increasingly inhibit overt emotional responses, and girls continue to respond uninhibitedly (Buck, 1977; Buck, Miller, & Caul, 1974). Thus, if observing parent–parent hostility is related to physiological arousal, children (especially boys) who are exposed to hostility over a period of time in the family, may have a heightened risk for cardiovascular disease.

Thus, it appears that stressful family interaction may be physiologically harmful to children. However, recent evidence provided by Katz and Gottman (in press) suggests an intriguing alternative hypothesis. This research demonstrated that in intact marriages, it is better for children if parents engage in conflict when resolving marital differences than if they withdraw from each other. When parents are withdrawn from each other, children increase their expressions of anger and physiological responses indicating an inability to regulate affect. These researchers interpreted these findings by stating that perhaps conflictive marital interaction is perceived by children as active problem solving, especially if the children are privy to the resolution (Cummings, Vogel, & Cummings, 1987). Perhaps withdrawn couples are signaling to the children that the relationship is about to end, and this message is more stressful and causes greater negative physiological response than the message delivered by angry yet engaged parents (Katz & Gottman, in press).

Negative Emotional States Leading to Unhealthy Health Behavior

Descriptions of young children's personal behaviors when seeking medical attention and health maintenance are rare. Young children's routine or preventive health care visits are manifestations of parents' health behavior. For the most part, except for child-initiated school nurse visits, preschool-aged and school-aged children are taken to practitioners by adults when they, the children, are perceived by the adults to have an illness or an injury requiring professional attention. Children's self-initiated care occurs only under unusual circumstances. This is consonant with more general theories concerning parents' management of children's lives and the distinction between parent-initiated child behavior and child-initiated behavior (Hartup, 1979; Tinsley, 1991). From a direct-effects perspective, parental negative emotional states could result in inadequate attention to children's health behavior and needs. For example, maternal depression (Downey & Coyne, 1990) was implicated in a variety of maladaptive parenting behaviors. From a health perspective, maternal negative emotional states, such as depression, could result in infrequency in obtaining wellness services for children (including blood-pressure monitoring) and inadequate monitoring of daily preventive health behavior, including maintaining cardio-vascular-system-promoting nutrition.

Indirect effects of parental negative emotional states on children's health behavior can also be delineated. Maternal anger or hostility toward her physician or the health-services delivery system in general could lead to ignoring important symptomology, which in turn could result in maternal morbidity or mortality—a significant stressor in childhood. Parental inability to agree on a health-maintenance plan for children could result in an inappropriate level of it. Thus, a variety of direct and indirect effects of parental negative emotional states can influence children's health behavior and status.

Summary and Future Directions for Research

Several mechanisms that may account for the relationship between family-interaction patterns and children's cardiovascular risk status have been identified. Moreover, a distinction has been made between direct and indirect effects of these familial processes on risk. However, support for these mechanisms is insufficient to determine a model that represents the relationship of these variables, and further research is necessary to elucidate these links and their direction of causality. Several limitations mark the existing findings. Detailed, microanalytic models of the specific ways in which stressful events affect children's socioemotional development are necessary, and to date, not available. Contextual factors (e.g., the child's previous experience with negative affect) must be recognized as having potential significance in these relationships. Child developmental status is an important modifier of cognitive, emotional, and psychophysiological response to negative family affect and must be incorporated in models that represent these responses. Changes in children's ability to regulate emotion, interpret events, and cope have been demonstrated to occur with age, and vulnerability to family interpersonal cardiovascular risk factors should be linked to these changes.

Frequency, intensity, chronicity, content, and resolution style are all dimensions of negative family-interaction patterns that may mediate the effect of these factors on children's status. Family beliefs and attitudes concerning the appropriateness of exposing children to negative family affect are probably important as well. Other family factors outside the scope of this discussion are also modifiers of family affect, including genetic influences, family structure, socioeconomic status, and ethnicity. Child gender also appears to guide children's socioemotional and physiological responses to the family emotional climate (Cummings & Cummings, 1988; Grynch & Fincham, 1990; Katz & Gottman, in press; Thoresen & Pattillo, 1988).

It is clear that research exploring the relationships between emotions and health is maturing and is now a more fully contextualized issue. Child development, as influenced by the family, is an increasingly appropriate point of entry for understanding emotion and its contributions to health.

References

Block, J. H., Block, J., & Morrison, A. (1981). Parental agreement–disagreement on child-rearing orientations and gender-related personality correlates in children. *Child Development, 52*, 965–974.

Bradbury, T. N., & Fincham, F. D. (1990). Attributions in marriage: Review and critique. *Psychological Bulletin, 107*, 3–33.

Buck, R. (1977). Nonverbal communication accuracy in preschool children: Relationships with personality and skin conductance. *Journal of Personality and Social Psychology, 33*, 225–236.

Buck, R. W., Miller, R. E., & Caul, W. F. (1974). Sex, personality, and physiological variables in the communication of emotion via facial expression. *Journal of Personality and Social Psychology, 30*, 587–596.

Cohen, S., & Williamson, G. M. (1991). Stress and infectious disease in humans. *Psychological Bulletin, 109*, 5–24.

Cummings, E. M., Iannotti, R. J., & Zahn-Waxler, C. (1985). Influence of conflict between adults on the emotions and aggression of young children. *Developmental Psychology, 21*, 495–507.

Cummings, E. M. (1987). Coping with background anger in early childhood. *Child Development, 58*, 976–985.

Cummings, E. M., & Cummings, J. L. (1988). A process-oriented approach to children's coping with adults' angry behavior. *Developmental Review, 8*, 296–321.

Cummings, E. M., Vogel, D., & Cummings, J. S. (1987). *Children's responses to different forms of expression of anger between adults.* Unpublished manuscript.

Dembrowski, T. M., & Williams, R. B., Jr. (1990). Definition and assessment of coronary-prone behavior. In N. Schneiderman, P. Kaufmann, & S. M. Weiss (Eds.), *Handbook of research methods in cardiovascular behavior medicine* (pp. 139–156). New York: Plenum Press.

Dodge, K. A. (1986). A social information processing model of social competence in children. In M. Perlmutter (Ed.), *The Eighteenth annual Minnesota symposium on child psychology* (pp. 77–125). Hillsdale, NJ: Erlbaum.

Downey, G., & Coyne, J. C. (1990). Children of depressed parents: An integrative review. *Psychological Bulletin, 108*, 50–76.

Dunn, J. (1983). Sibling relationships in early childhood. *Child Development, 54*, 787–811.

Dunn, J., & Kendrick, C. (1982). Interaction between young siblings: Changes in patterns of interaction between mother and first born. *Developmental Psychology, 17*, 336–343.

Dunn, J., & Munn, P. (1985). Becoming a family member: Family conflict and the development of social understanding in the second year. *Child Development, 56,* 480–492.

Emery, R. E. (1982). Interparental conflict and the children of discord and divorce. *Psychological Bulletin, 92,* 310–330.

Friedman, H. S., & Booth-Kewley, S. (1987). The "disease-prone personality": A meta-analytic view of the construct. *American Psychologist, 42,* 539–555.

Friedman, H. S., & DiMatteo, M. R. (1989). *Health psychology.* Englewood Cliffs, NJ: Prentice-Hall.

Friedman, M., & Rosenman, R. H. (1974). *Type A behavior and your heart.* New York: Knopf.

Grynch, J. H., & Fincham, F. D. (1990). Marital conflict and children's adjustment: A cognitive–contextual framework. *Psychological Bulletin, 108,* 267–290.

Hartup, W. W. (1979). The social worlds of childhood. *American Psychologist, 34,* 944–950.

Hetherington, E. M. (1989). Coping with family transitions: Winners, losers and survivors. *Child Development, 60,* 1–14.

Katz, L. F., & Gottman, J. M. (in press). Styles of marital interaction and children's emotional development. In R. D. Parke & S. Kellam (Eds.), *Exploring family relationships with other social contexts.* Hillsdale, NJ: Erlbaum.

Kiecolt-Glaser, J. K., & Glaser, R. (1991). Behavioral influences on immune function: Evidence for the interplay between stress and health. In T. Field, P. McCabe, & N. Schneiderman (Eds.), *Stress and coping* (Vol. 2). Hillsdale, NJ: Erlbaum.

Klaczynski, P. A., & Cummings, E. M. (1989). Responding to anger in aggressive and non-aggressive boys: A research note. *Journal of Child Psychology and Psychiatry, 30,* 309–314.

Matthews, K. A. (1977). Caregiver–child interactions and the Type A coronary-prone behavior pattern. *Child Development, 48,* 1752–1756.

Matthews, K. A., Glass, D. C., & Richins, M. (1977). The mother–son observation study. In D. C. Glass (Ed.), *Behavior patterns, stress and coronary disease.* Hillsdale, NJ: Erlbaum.

McCranie, E. W., & Simpson, M. E. (1986). Parental child-rearing antecedents of Type A behavior. *Personality and Social Psychology Bulletin, 12,* 493–501.

Miller, P., & Sperry, L. L. (1987). The socialization of anger and aggression. *Merrill-Palmer Quarterly, 33,* 1–31.

Parke, R. D., MacDonald, K. B., Burks, V. M., Carson, J., Bhavnagri, N., Barth, J. M., & Beitel, A. (1989). Family and peer systems: In search of the linkages. In K. Kreppner & R. M. Lerner (Eds.), *Family systems and life-span development* (pp. 65–92). Hillsdale, NJ: Erlbaum.

Parke, R. D., & Tinsley, B. J. (1987). Family interaction in infancy. In J. D. Osofky (Ed.), *Handbook of infant development* (2nd ed.) (pp. 579–641). New York: John Wiley.

Price, V. A. (1982). *Type A behavior pattern: A model for research and practice.* New York: Academic Press.

Taylor, S. E. (1990). *Health psychology.* New York: Random House.

Thoresen, C. E., & Pattillo, J. R. (1988). Exploring the Type A behavior pattern in children and adolescents. In B. K. Houston & C. R. Snyder (Eds.), *Type A behavior pattern: Research, theory and intervention* (pp. 98–145). New York: John Wiley.

Tinsley, B. J. (1991). *Multiple influences on the acquisition and socialization of children's health attitudes and behavior: An integrative review.* Manuscript submitted for publication.

EDITOR'S NOTE

The following two commentaries address problematic issues regarding the assessment of coping. The first, by Stone and Kennedy-Moore, raises potential difficulties with the influential Lazarus and Folkman approach. In her reply, Folkman responds to these concerns.

Commentary to Part Three: Assessing Situational Coping: Conceptual and Methodological Considerations

Arthur A. Stone and Eileen Kennedy-Moore

W ithout valid and reliable assessment tools, there is little hope of achieving the goal of understanding how psychosocial factors affect health. Only if our instruments are reliable will we be able to detect existing relationships; only if our instruments are valid will be able to interpret our findings meaningfully. These issues are fundamental to any field of research, and, in the long run, attention paid to developing excellent assessment tools is always worth the effort.

In the area of coping, assessment has made tremendous advances. Assessment devices have progressed from a priori, and often unidimensional, specification of adaptive coping traits to multidimensional descriptions of specific coping efforts. Questionnaires developed by Folkman and Lazarus (1980, 1985), Pearlin and Schooler (1978), Billings and Moos (1981), Stone and Neale (1984), and Carver, Scheier, and Weintraub (i.e., the problem-oriented version of the COPE; 1989) represent the state of the art of situation-specific, self-report, coping assessment tools. In contrast to earlier measures, these situation-specific instruments allow empirical determination of cross-situational coping consistency and coping efficacy.

Our motivation for exploring these issues stems from the desire to understand how well current coping instruments are fulfilling their intended function and to identify areas for improvement. Numerous studies have shown that coping questionnaires are associated with psychological and physical outcomes of interest (e.g., Folkman, Lazarus, Dunkel-Schetter, DeLongis, & Gruen, 1986; Martelli, Auerbach, Alexander, & Mercuri, 1987; Vitaliano, Russo, Carr, Maiuro, & Becker, 1985), but most of these associations have been modest in magnitude. Additional refinement of instruments may strengthen the relationships observed between coping and outcomes and sharpen our ability to use information from these studies in clinical applications. Moreover, we believe that developing excellent situation-oriented coping instruments is critically important because of the unique qualities and functions that these measures have to offer. First, situation-oriented approaches minimize possible biases resulting from memory distortions or personal theories. Second, situation-oriented instruments could be used to empirically demonstrate the validity of trait coping measures. Third, and most important, testing the transactional theory of coping (Lazarus & Folkman, 1984), which posits that coping is a process that changes over time in response to changing appraisals of the person–situation interaction, necessitates assessment instruments that can capture situation-specific coping.

Our comments apply to both self-report measures and interviews assessing situation-specific coping, and they are drawn from our recent empirical studies and literature reviews (Stone, Greenberg, Kennedy-Moore, & Newman, 1991; Stone, Helder, & Schneider, 1988; Stone, Kennedy-Moore, Newman, Greenberg, & Neale, in press; Stone & Neale, 1984). The issues that we will now discuss concern coping-scale construction, usage, and interpretation.

Scale Construction

Issues in scale construction are important because how items are generated and which ones are included as opposed to which ones are excluded determine the quality and thoroughness of an assessment.

Item Generation

To our knowledge, only one situational coping instrument was developed that is based on a broad sampling of items. Pearlin and Schooler (1978) generated items for their coping inventory by interviewing a large, representative sample of subjects in an open-ended format, about their coping responses to problems in a variety of role areas. The items for the Folkman and Lazarus (1980) original coping scale were rationally derived or taken from previous research. Recently, there has been a trend toward developing coping scales by deductively choosing items from a variety of existing scales. Regardless of whether items are empirically or rationally developed, it is important to examine the comprehensiveness of the item pool. In most cases, we simply have no idea how adequately coping items sample the domain of possible coping responses. Thus, the possibility remains that we are overlooking important strategies, and additional research into the domain of coping is needed.

Item Selection

Situation-oriented coping measures have often been developed using factor-analytic procedures similar to those used in the construction of attitude or personality scales. These methods typically involve factor-analyzing responses to coping items and creating scales that are based on the resulting factors. People who agree with the attitude represented by the scale are expected to endorse many scale items, whereas those who do not are expected to endorse few items. An implication of this approach to scale construction is that if some items are missed or deleted, it is not important because the construct is still adequately represented by the remaining items on the scale.

Assessment of situation-specific coping, however, is conceptually more similar to behavioral observation than to measurement of attitudes or traits. Items making up situation-specific coping scales usually are discrete, nonoverlapping thoughts or behaviors that serve the same function (e.g., distraction). They are conceptually related in terms of their function, but are not necessarily expected to co-occur in a given period of time. This property is illustrated by an example from one of the most widely used coping measures, the Ways of Coping Inventory (WOC). There are many thoughts and actions that fall into the construct depicted by the "planful problem-solving" scale. However, indicating that one "changed something so things would turn out right," does not necessarily suggest that one also "came up with a couple of different solutions to the problem." In fact, if one particular coping item worked well for a particular problem, then it might be the case that no additional coping items from that scale would be required to handle the problem; only one coping item from the scale would be reported. Thus, it is not reasonable to expect that situation-oriented coping items will covary the way that items on attitude or personality scales do. This results in a conceptual dilemma: If we do not expect interitem covariation in a situation-oriented coping scale, then why are procedures that assume internal consistency used to construct coping scales?

Moreover, factor-analytic scale-development procedures have other properties that are undesirable for use in the coping area. Because the magnitude of item-factor loadings is used as an inclusion–exclusion criterion in scale construction, these procedures eliminate items that load on multiple factors or load poorly on factors. If a coping item happens to serve multiple functions, it will load on more than one factor scale, and thus may be eliminated from the scale because it is impure. Research using sorting procedures of coping items into their conceptual categories has shown that subjects often view particular coping items as serving multiple functions (Stone & Neale, 1984). For example, the item "Went shopping" could represent handling the problem directly or distracting oneself. Eliminating items composing a scale may affect not only reliability, but also scale validity, because the domain of coping responses is diminished.

An alternative approach to the assessment of situation-specific coping abandons the idea of assessing specific thoughts and behaviors used to handle problems and focuses on the endorsement of coping constructs (e.g., distraction), which are at a higher level of abstraction. An assessment instrument of this type would index each construct with multiple items and would probably be internally consistent as well as amenable to factor-analysis methods. An example of this approach is the COPE (Carver, Scheier, & Weintraub, 1989). Another approach is to have subjects endorse the use of a coping construct and then provide details of what was thought or done that is indicative of the construct (see Stone & Neale, 1984).

Use of Coping Questionnaires

A number of issues exist concerning how coping questionnaires are typically used in research. These issues may strongly influence and perhaps bias reports of the amount and type of coping used.

Opportunity to Cope

The length of time from when a problem first occurs to when coping is reported (or when the problem is resolved) defines a subject's *opportunity-to-cope* with the problem. Subjects whose problems occurred earlier within the reporting period assessed by the coping questionnaire or who have more enduring problems will necessarily have had more time in which to cope with those particular problems. They may report a greater amount of coping and perhaps more varied types of coping. This is an issue for monthly, weekly, and even daily time frames of coping assessment, but the longer the time frame, the more serious this potential problem (i.e., there is a bigger discrepancy in opportunity to cope in a monthly format, in which subjects' problem onsets can differ by up to 29 days, compared with a daily time frame, in which problem onsets can differ by only a matter of hours). To our knowledge, this issue has not been systematically examined.

One possible solution to this problem appears to be relatively straightforward: An adjustment of coping amounts could be computed, which is based on the duration of the problem or the time that a person had to cope with the problem. However, there are several potential shortcomings with this correction strategy. First, it assumes that it can be determined when a coping episode begins and ends. Although some problems do have a discrete beginning and end, others are more ambiguous in their onset and duration, which makes determining opportunity-to-cope difficult. Second, it assumes that people are determining coping amounts by summing their efforts. Yet it may be that people's coping reports are more globally descriptive of their efforts, rather than being truly additive. For instance, subjects may report that they used a particular strategy "a great deal" whether they used it often on 1 day of a 3-day problem or on all 3 days of a 3-day problem (this also relates to the following response scale discussion). Similarly, dividing coping scores by opportunity-to-cope assumes that the proportion of time spent using a strategy is the best way to characterize coping, but an argument could be made that absolute amounts are more meaningful. Is using a coping strategy for 1 day of a 7-day problem really less than using the same strategy for the entirety of a problem that lasts only 1 day? Research is needed to determine how subjects summarize their coping efforts over time and how to take opportunity-to-cope into account. Overall, we have little doubt that opportunity-to-cope affects the magnitude and diversity of coping reports, but we are not sure how.

Effort After Meaning

Although situation-specific coping measures were intended to assess coping efforts independently of coping efficacy, with most of the current measures, it is possible that subjects' knowledge of encounter resolution (i.e., success or failure) influences their reports of coping efforts. When coping questionnaires are used in a daily, weekly, or monthly format, some subjects will report on events that have already concluded and whose final resolution is known. Knowledge of how successfully a stressful event was resolved could bias both recall and labeling of coping efforts. If the coping strategy of "thinking about the problem" appeared successful, for example, subjects may label it as "problem-solving." If it was unsuccessful, they may label it as "rumination." We suspect that subjects are more likely to recall efforts that they believe produced a desired outcome compared with those they do not believe were successful. Prospective designs are needed to eliminate this potential "effort after meaning" bias (Brown & Harris, 1976) in coping research.

Coping Stages

One reason that situation-oriented coping measures were developed was to examine the hypothesis that coping efforts change over the course of a problem. Yet the majority of studies using these instruments do not examine variability across the stages of a problem. A notable exception to this is the Folkman and Lazarus (1985) study of coping during three stages of a college examination. One reason that coping stages need to be considered is because subjects might differ in their definition of the coping period, which could greatly influence reports of coping efforts. For example, given the problem "argument with a spouse," some people might define the coping period as simply a few minutes of heated discussion and report how they coped during those minutes. Others might define the coping period for "argument with a spouse" more broadly and report not only what they did during the argument itself, but also what they did during the build up of tension prior to the argument and how they worked out the problem over the next day or so. Thus, amount of reported coping may differ depending on the way that an individual defines the coping period. A second reason for considering coping stages is that different stages of a problem are likely to be associated with different types of coping (cf. Folkman & Lazarus, 1985). For instance, direct, problem-focused strategies are more probable during the acute stage of a problem, whereas contemplative strategies are more probable at a later stage. Unless the stages of a problem are considered in coping assessment, there is the possibility of confounding coping efforts and problem stages. What look like interindividual differences in the quantity and type of coping used may really be differences in the type of problem stages experienced.

There are some data to suggest that responses to coping instruments refer to problems that vary greatly in their stages and that subjects do not necessarily consider all stages of a problem when reporting their coping efforts. Stone et al. (1991) gave undergraduate subjects who had just completed the WOC a description of three possible stages of a stressful event: preparatory, acute, and recovery. Subjects were then asked (a) which, if any, of these stages (or other stages) existed for their stressful problem, and

(b) whether they had considered their coping efforts during each of the stages that they said existed for their problem while completing the WOC. We found that 56% of the subjects did not report their coping efforts for all of the stages that they said existed for their problem. Specifically, 50% of the subjects who said their problems had a preparatory stage also said they did not report their coping efforts during that stage, 20% did not report coping efforts during an existing acute stage, and 37% did not report coping efforts during an existing recovery stage. This differing comprehensiveness among subjects in reporting coping efforts almost certainly leads to error and could lead to bias if it is systematically related to the type of coping that is reported. However, this problem may be remedied by including specification of stages as part of the methodology of future coping studies. As with opportunity-to-cope discussed earlier, there may be some difficulty establishing exactly when particular stages of a problem begin or end, but our subjects seemed to have minimal difficulty identifying and thinking about stages at a more global level. Thus, although specification of stages may not be precise, we believe assessing them in some form is better than ignoring them entirely.

Scale Interpretation

The issues discussed next concern our understanding of summary scores derived from coping inventories and the conclusions we drew about any observed relationships between coping and outcomes.

Applicability of Items

Self-report, situation-specific coping instruments were intended to measure coping strategies that are applicable to a wide variety of problems, yet at face value, some of the items seem problem specific. For example, interpersonal strategies (e.g., "tried to get the person responsible to change his or her mind") seem relevant only to interpersonal problems, spiritual strategies (e.g., "found new faith" or "rediscovered what is important in life") seem relevant only to serious problems, and problem-solving strategies seem relevant only to problems that are to some extent controllable. If coping items are problem specific, then scale scores could have artificial limitations on their magnitudes, which could confuse the interpretation of coping efforts across different problems.

We recently tested whether the applicability of WOC coping items varied by problem type by asking undergraduate students who had completed the WOC about the relevance of strategies that they did not use to cope with the reported problem (Stone et al.,

1991). When subjects said they did not use an item, we asked, "Would it have been possible for you to use this strategy in this situation? Does it make sense when applied to your problem?" The number of applicable items did in fact vary by problem type.[1]

Differences in item applicability across problem types is not problematic at a descriptive level. A subject may have a lower score on a particular type of coping than another subject because of differential restriction on the number of items available on that coping scale; nonetheless, the first subject still did less coping. However, the number of applicable items may be a problem at a quantitative level because it suggests that there may be different ceilings for coping scores referring to different types of problems. This could, in turn, influence the interpretation of the relationship between coping and outcome, because spurious effects would emerge if problem type influences both the maximal score on a coping scale and the ultimate resolution of the problem. For example, suppose that people with serious problems (e.g., death of a loved one) have limited opportunities for problem-focused coping, and their problems also result in poor outcomes, whereas people with trivial problems (e.g., breakdown of a xerox machine) have numerous opportunities for problem-focused coping, and their problems usually have good outcomes. If we are not aware of the differential applicability of problem-focused coping across these two types of problems, we may erroneously conclude that more problem-focused coping produces better outcomes, when in fact the problem content produced both the amount of problem-focused coping possible and the outcome.

There are a variety of possible solutions to this problem, but the choice of solution depends on what investigators feel is most important to study, what compromises they are willing to make, and which issues they feel are most easily resolved. One alternative is to calculate coping scores that are based on the proportion of applicable items rather than absolute scores. However, this raises issues concerning the definition of applicability (which is now rather vague) and who determines applicability (subject or researcher?). Another possibility is to identify categories of similar problems and to study coping and outcome only within a single-problem category (e.g., bereavement), thereby making item applicability uniform across problems. However, here problems arise in the determination of the level of specificity for problem categories (how restrictive should categories be?). Rather than restricting problem content, still

---

[1]However, there may have been problems with some subjects and particular items in the interpretation of our applicability question. We know that at least a couple of times, subjects who were atheists said that they could not possibly have prayed, although certainly they could have—they just chose not to do so.

another way to address this issue is to restrict the type of coping studied. Items representing coping strategies that are cross-situationally applicable could be identified. Examples of this approach include studies on emotional expression (e.g., Notarius & Levenson, 1979) and social support (e.g., Cohen & Wills, 1985). A potential disadvantage of this approach is that it is unknown whether these basic coping strategies are the most important or efficacious ones.

Meaning of the Response Key

There are also scale-interpretation issues pertaining to how coping is quantified. Some situation-oriented coping measures, drawing from the attitude-assessment tradition (described earlier), ask subjects to rate the extent to which they used each strategy. However, unlike attitude-assessment items, coping items refer to specific thoughts and behaviors. What does it mean when subjects say they used a particular strategy "somewhat" or "quite a bit?" Neither the dimension nor the standard of comparison is specified in these extent ratings.

In an effort to understand the extent response key, we again consulted the sample of undergraduates (Stone et al., 1991). Ten WOC items that subjects said they had used to cope with problems were selected, and subjects were asked to explain what they meant by their responses. For example, when they said they had used a particular item "a great deal," we asked if they were referring to the number of times that they did it (frequency), the amount of time that they spent doing it (duration), the effort it took to do it, or how helpful that strategy was (usefulness). There was considerable variability in the meaning of the extent key both within subjects and across subjects. Across all items and all subjects, 33% of responses defined extent as frequency. Looking at within-subject variability, only 37% of the subjects used a single definition for at least half or more of their responses, whereas 68% used all four dimensions. Furthermore, certain items tended to elicit particular meanings of the extent key, but the majority of items (57 out of 66) had different extent meanings for different subjects (i.e., they differed significantly from the expected pattern of at least 85% of extent rating yielding a single dimension).

These results call into question the meaning of the extent response key. Its meaning varies depending on who is using it and which item is being rated, which is a serious problem if the goal is to measure specific coping thoughts and behaviors. Furthermore, although these scales were intended to be used to measure coping efforts and outcomes independently, the fact that on 27% of the items subjects indicated that they were rating usefulness suggests that subjects are incorporating efficacy judgments into their responses, thereby confounding effort and outcome.

One possible solution to this problem is to instruct subjects to rate items on a clearly defined dimension. However, it is not clear which dimension to choose. Frequency and duration are difficult to rate accurately for cognitions (see Stone, Kessler, & Haythornthwaite, in press). Effort is a rather amorphous dimension and is probably confounded by motivation and ability, and usefulness is not independent of efficacy. Another alternative is to use a dichotomous response key, as the original WOC did, so that subjects report whether or not they used a particular item. Scale scores that are based on this metric characterize diversity in coping efforts, but not amount (i.e., frequency of duration) of coping. However, it is probably better to measure one dimension accurately than several dimensions ambiguously.

Still another possibility is to use the existing response key, but to think about it somewhat differently. Subjects may be using the response key in a way that is more descriptive than quantitative. That is, perhaps coping-extent ratings are being made in a manner similar to the ratings of attitude scales. In other words, the extent rating of "a great deal" could mean that "this item is very true of me" or "this item is very descriptive of how I believe I coped" rather than indicating the amount of the strategy used. This interpretation of subjects' responses is highly speculative. More research is needed to establish how subjects interpret the extent-response key and how much between-subject variability there is in this interpretation. Furthermore, coping researchers need to think carefully about what it is they want the response key to measure and how best to do this uniformly and unambiguously.

Conclusion

Our goal in writing this chapter was to stimulate thinking and provoke discussion about the construct of situational coping and the way it is measured. The fundamental assessment questions of "What are we measuring?" and "What do we want to measure?" must be explicitly considered if we are to have confidence in the validity of our findings.

There will undoubtedly be a wide range of opinion about the importance of the issues we have raised and the best ways to resolve them. Some of the issues, such as coping stages, are fairly easy to remedy, and we hope that they will be addressed immediately. For other issues, we were not able to suggest any simple solutions, but only hard choices. We hope that future researchers will consider and address these issues and that progress in the assessment of self-report, situation-specific coping will continue.

References

Billings, A. G., & Moos, R. H. (1981). The role of coping responses in attenuating the stress of life events. *Journal of Behavioral Medicine, 4,* 139–157.

Brown, G. W., & Harris, T. (1976). *Social origins of depression.* New York: Free Press.

Carver, C. S., Scheier, M. F., & Weintraub, J. K. (1989). Assessing coping strategies: A theoretically based approach. *Journal of Personality and Social Psychology, 56,* 267–283.

Cohen, S., & Wills, T. A. (1985). Stress, social support, and the buffering hypothesis. *Psychological Bulletin, 98,* 310–357.

Folkman, S., & Lazarus, R. S. (1980). An analysis of coping in a middle-aged community sample. *Journal of Health and Social Behavior, 21,* 219–239.

Folkman, S., & Lazarus, R. S. (1985). If it changes it must be a process: A study of emotion and coping during three stages of a college examination. *Journal of Personality and Social Psychology, 48,* 150–170.

Folkman, S., Lazarus, R. S., Dunkel-Schetter, C., DeLongis, A., & Gruen, R. R. (1986). Dynamics of a stressful encounter: Cognitive appraisal, coping, and encounter outcomes. *Journal of Personality and Social Psychology, 50* 992–1003.

Lazarus, R. S., & Folkman, S. (1984). *Stress, appraisal, and coping.* New York: Springer.

Martelli, M. F., Auerbach, S. M., Alexander, J., & Mercuri, L. G. (1987). Stress management in the health care setting: Matching interventions with patient coping styles. *Journal of Consulting and Clinical Psychology, 55,* 201–207.

Notarius, C. I., & Levenson, R. W. (1979). Expressive tendencies and physiological response to stress. *Journal of Personality and Social Psychology, 37,* 1204–1210.

Pearlin, L. I., & Schooler, C. (1978). The structure of coping. *Journal of Health and Social Behavior, 19,* 2–21.

Stone, A. A., Greenberg, M. A., Kennedy-Moore, E., & Newman, M. G. (1991). *Self-reported, situation-specific coping questionnaires: What are they measuring?* Manuscript submitted for publication.

Stone, A. A., Helder, L., & Schneider, M. S. (1988). Coping with stressful events: Coping dimensions and issues. In L. H.Cohen (Ed.), *Life events and psychological functioning: Theoretical and methodological issues.* Newbury Park, CA: Sage Publications.

Stone, A. A., Kennedy-Moore, E., Newman, M. G., Greenberg, M. A., & Neale, J. M. (in press). Conceptual and methodological issues in current coping assessments. In B. N. Carpenter (Ed.), *Personal coping theory, research, and application.* New York: Praeger.

Stone, A. A., Kessler, R. C., & Haythornthwaite, J. (in press). Measuring daily events and experiences: Methodological considerations. *Journal of Personality.*

Stone, A. A., & Neale, J. M. (1984). A new measure of daily coping: Development and preliminary results. *Journal of Personality and Social Psychology, 46*, 892–906.

Vitaliano, P. P., Russo, J., Carr, J. E., Maiuro, R. D., & Becker, J. (1985). The ways of coping checklist: Revision and psychometric properties. *Multivariate Behavioral Research, 20*, 3–26.

Commentary to Part Three: Improving Coping Assessment: Reply to Stone and Kennedy-Moore

Susan Folkman

O ver the last 20 years, coping has been studied from psychiatric (e.g, Vaillant, 1977), psychological (e.g., Billings & Moos, 1981; Folkman & Lazarus, 1980; Scheier & Carver, 1985; Stone & Neale, 1984), and sociological (e.g., Pearlin & Schooler, 1978) perspectives. Despite their differences, there seems to be agreement about three basic features of coping. First, coping is a complex, multidimensional phenomenon that includes both problem-solving and emotion-regulating activity. Second, coping is variable because of variability in the context in which coping occurs. A given individual, for example, in the course of a week, may have to cope with transitory, resolvable situations as well as chronic, unremitting conditions. Third, coping is variable because of variability in personal characteristics, such as beliefs about the world, goals, coping resources, and skills.

Coping has been assessed with in-depth, idiographic case studies (Vaillant, 1977; Weiss, 1990), structured interviews (e.g., Cohen, Reese, Kaplan, & Riggio, 1986; Pearlin & Schooler, 1978; Stone & Neale, 1984), and paper-and-pencil measures (e.g. Folkman & Lazarus, 1980, 1985; Billings & Moos, 1981; Scheier & Carver, 1985). I am drawn to case studies, such as those of Vaillant (1977) and Weiss (1990), because they provide such rich descriptions of how individuals manage the events of living. However, in this discussion, I am limiting myself to comments about paper-and-pencil coping assessments because of the need in the field for a convenient questionnaire that can be administered easily in a wide variety of settings.

The irony is that a practical, easy-to-administer coping questionnaire may be the most difficult kind of coping assessment to develop. The challenge is to achieve precision in assessment while capturing the multidimensionality and variability of the coping process, or in other words, to achieve reliability without sacrificing validity.

Reliability

Each of the three traditional tests of reliability—test–retest, alternate forms, and internal consistency—is limited in its applicability to coping assessment. Test–retest is appropriate for relatively stable phenomena, such as personality dispositions or intelligence, but it is inappropriate for phenomena that are inherently variable, such as coping processes. The alternate-forms method of assessing reliability is inappropriate because items that describe particular types of coping are not equivalent. Two coping strategies that Stone and Kennedy-Moore selected as examples of the problem-solving type of coping, "I came up with a couple of different solutions to the problem" and "I changed something so things would turn out right," illustrate the problem. Both strategies may be related to problem solving, but they are not equivalent; they describe different aspects, or more specifically, different phases, of the same type of coping. In this sense, Stone and Kennedy-Moore are correct in their description of coping as conceptually more similar to behavioral observation than to measurement of attitudes or traits.

The third traditional test of reliability, internal consistency, is the most appropriate of the three, but the traditional standards of acceptable internal consistency need to be judiciously modified for application to coping assessment. The traditional standards for internal consistency that are applied to attitudinal measures are not appropriate for coping measures for the reason that Stone and Kennedy-Moore highlighted in their discussion: If an individual achieves a desired goal with a given coping strategy of a particular type, there is no reason for that individual to turn to another strategy of the same type. As Stone and Kennedy-Moore and others (e.g., Billings & Moos, 1981) pointed out, this characteristic of coping means that the assumption of item–item covariation, which underlies the internal-consistency approach, is not as supportable as it is in attitudinal measures, and therefore, we cannot expect the same high levels of internal consistency that can reasonably be expected in attitudinal measures. In setting standards for internal consistency in coping assessment, we need to make accommodations to the special characteristics of the phenomenon we are assessing. Thus, rather than using a Cronbach alpha coefficient of .90 as the standard, which is appropriate for measures of attitudes or intelligence, we might consider setting the standard for coping measures at alpha $= .70$.

Reliability is also influenced by measurement error. Given the characteristics of coping that limit the internal consistency of coping assessments, we must be especially vigilant in controlling this additional source of unreliability. Stone and Kennedy-Moore highlighted an excellent example of a source of measurement error—the meaning of the response key. Their studies show that response keys that ask about the extent to which an individual uses a given item pull for responses that refer to frequency, duration, and usefulness. Stone and Kennedy-Moore mentioned and rejected several approaches to this problem, including using effort or usefulness as a response key or using a dichotomous key. I agree with their recommendations that these approaches should not be used. However, I am not at all sure that the approach recommended by Stone and Kennedy-Moore in which they ask subjects to describe the extent to which an item was *true* of them is going to improve matters. More studies about the response key are needed. It is important that such studies be conducted with diverse community samples and not just with students who are likely to find our terminology comfortable because of their exposure to psychological thought and Likert scales of all sorts.

We also need to review items for conventional sources of measurement error, including clarity of meaning, wording, and phrasing. Special care needs to be taken to ensure that items convey comparable meaning and that words and phrases are familiar and comfortable in diverse ethnic groups. Careful evaluation of measurement error in coping assessments should lead to more reliable assessments and increased interitem covariation.

Internal Validity

A second set of issues deal with the internal validity of coping measures. Stone and Kennedy-Moore's discussion of the conceptual categories for coping items concerns the validity of these categories and, in particular, the use of factor analysis to define these categories. They pointed out that factor analysis leads to the elimination of items that do not load distinctly on a single factor, yet such items may be important in coping.

Stone and Kennedy-Moore suggested several approaches as possible solutions using open-ended inquiries about broad categories of coping strategies or using sorting techniques whereby subjects identify the category in which a strategy they have used most clearly belongs. To be useful in applied settings with large samples, which is where much coping research takes place, coping assessments have to be cost-effective. Thus, I would not endorse Stone and Kennedy-Moore's suggestion that we use open-ended inquiries about broad categories of coping strategies because of the labor involved in coding responses reliably.

The sorting mechanism that Stone and Kennedy-Moore suggested can minimize these problems. However, the success of the sorting system depends on the taxonomy of categories that is provided for the subject. But how are these categories to be defined so that they describe a full range of coping? It seems to me that we must fall back on categories that have been derived from theory or from empirical methods such as factor analysis. This process would seem to be essentially circular in that the methods that are used to define open-ended categories are the same methods for which the open-ended approach is supposed to provide an alternative.

I am more sanguine about the use of the factor-analytic approach to identifying categories of coping than are Stone and Kennedy-Moore. It is true that items that do not load distinctly on one factor may be eliminated, thereby reducing the comprehensiveness of the coping measure as a whole. However, this cost is outweighed by the benefits of producing clusters of items that have conceptual as well as empirical integrity, albeit to a lesser degree than items that describe constructs such as attitudes, beliefs, and intelligence. Furthermore, a number of factors appear to be stable across situations and populations (Marshall & Dunkel-Schetter, 1987; Tennen & Herzberger, 1985), and these factors are useful because they help explain diverse outcomes. This pattern suggests that the factor-analytic procedure can reliably produce coping categories that are useful in research.

The factor-analytic approach to the description of coping may have some weaknesses, such as those suggested by Stone and Kennedy-Moore, but it would be imprudent to abandon the approach because of these weaknesses. Factor analysis should be viewed as a tool to help clarify coping concepts. To get the most out of this tool, items that are used in factor analysis should be generated from a theoretical framework. A theoretical framework provides a structure for carefully and systemically evaluating the extent to which the items sample conceptually meaningful domains of coping. A theoretical framework also provides a basis for evaluating the conceptual relevance of empirically derived coping factors. When anchored to theory, factor analysis can be an effective technique to assist developers of coping assessments. If factor analysis is used without a theoretical anchor, it is likely to confuse issues rather than clarify them.

Assessing the Context

Stone and Kennedy-Moore argued that a weakness of most situation-specific coping assessments is that many of the strategies are not relevant in all situations. I would argue that the problem is not with the items, but rather with our failure to assess the context in which coping takes place. Let us not forget that we are using situation-oriented measures of coping. Advances in the assessment of coping must be accompanied by advances in our ability to assess meaningfully the context in which coping occurs.

Sometimes the context is prescribed to a certain extent by the research, such as in studies of breast cancer (Taylor & Lobel, 1990), leukemia (Felton & Revenson, 1984), residential settings for older people (Moos & Lemke, 1984), and examinations (Folkman & Lazarus, 1985). Other times the subject is asked to identify a stressful situation (e.g., Folkman, Lazarus, Dunkel-Schetter, DeLongis, & Gruen, 1986; Stone & Neale, 1984), and information about the context is obtained by asking what the situation is about, that is, work, family, or health, and the controllability or changeability of the stressful situation.

Sometimes the emphasis is on the physical and social environment (see Stokols, this volume). Moos and his colleagues focused on four sets of environmental factors to describe the context: physical features, structural and policy factors, aggregate characteristics of the people in a setting, and social climate (Moos & Swindle, 1990). Brown and Harris (1986) used intensive, semistructured interviews that cover biographical as well as contextual material to describe the personal significance of events. The Brown and Harris method is impressive, but it is not a simply administered paper-and-pencil approach, which is the method on which I am focusing here.

Richard Lazarus and I and our colleagues on the Berkeley Stress and Coping Project assessed the psychological context in which coping took place. Our goal was to learn about the personal significance of an event in terms of the psychological stakes that an individual had in the stressful event he or she reported. We assessed the personal significance in terms of threats to self-esteem, financial security, the well-being of another, or one's own physical well-being, and the extent to which the situation was changeable. We found that the person's appraisal of the personal significance of the event and the options for coping in that situation explained variability in coping (Folkman & Lazarus, 1980; Folkman, et al., 1986). Although we did the best we could to cover a range of psychological stakes in our assessments, we were never satisfied that the items that we used were the best possible exemplars for the stakes that we were assessing or that the stakes and their items were sufficiently generalizable across populations and contexts. A major effort needs to be made to develop an assessment of psychological stakes that are appropriate across diverse situations and individuals. Attention also needs to be given to the assessment of contextual constraints to coping, such as competing goals or competing demands for social, psychological, or material resources (Lazarus & Folkman, 1984).

Prospective Designs

Stone and Kennedy-Moore made an important observation that the outcome of an encounter may influence the subject's recollection of how he or she coped during the event. I agree with Stone and Kennedy-Moore that prospective designs are highly desirable for avoiding this problem. And as Stone and Kennedy-Moore pointed out, prospective designs are also important for understanding changes in coping as an event unfolds (see also Auerbach, 1991; Folkman & Lazarus, 1985).

However, prospective research is often not an option. Our responsibility is then to make sure that retrospective techniques are designed carefully to allow as much accurate recall as possible and to help subjects recount the temporal ordering of their coping processes. Techniques such as having the subject recall details of the stressful situation— where it took place, who was involved, and what was happening—may assist accurate recall. Accurate recall may also be assisted by asking subjects to remember all their coping efforts, regardless of whether they helped or not.

Eliciting a temporal ordering of coping retrospectively is difficult to do. A number of years ago, my colleagues on the Berkeley Stress and Coping Project and I conducted pilot interviews in which we asked subjects to recount their coping efforts in a temporal sequence. Our subjects found the task extremely difficult. Only in those events where there were clear markers of event stages were temporal accounts even possible. For example, an elderly women told about a recent event in which she slipped on the floor of her bedroom. She recalled what she thought and did while crawling to the phone. Then she recalled what she did after the phone conversation. The fall and the phone conversation were markers that helped her recall what she did first and what she did next. However, the events that most subjects recalled from their day-to-day lives did not have clearly defined markers that could be used to assist recollection, and subjects were frustrated by our requests to remember the order of their coping.

Another problem in eliciting temporally ordered accounts of coping is that some coping processes may persist throughout an encounter, others may be used briefly one time only, and yet others might be used several times at different points. Thus, linear accounts in which subjects recall what they did first, what they did second, and so on may not be possible. An alternative is to ask subjects to provide a summary of what they were doing at various points in their stressful encounter. These and other possibilities should be explored in careful methodological studies. When we do not have the benefit of a prospective design, the understanding of how coping changes as an encounter unfolds is dependent on our ability to address these issues effectively.

Situation-Oriented Coping Assessments and Interventions

Stone, Kennedy-Moore, and I are in agreement that situation-oriented coping measures are valuable for theory testing. I would add that situation-oriented coping measures are also important for those who wish to modify maladaptive coping patterns. For example, situation-oriented measures can provide details about the extent to which individuals use coping thoughts and behaviors that are inappropriate for the situation. Interventions can be used to modify the coping patterns of individuals whose coping strategies do not fit the demands of the situations (cf. Folkman, 1984; Folkman et al., 1991). Furthermore, careful assessment of the context in which coping occurs can highlight particular contexts in which the individual is vulnerable to inappropriate coping. The usefulness of coping assessments in applied settings, however, depends on our willingness and ability to improve the reliability and validity of our measures and to give equal time and effort to the assessment of the context in which coping occurs.

Conclusion

Many of the issues that Stone, Kennedy-Moore, and I discussed are endemic to self-report measures. We can improve the reliability and validity of these measures by conscientiously working on measurement error and scale development, but no matter how much we improve their psychometric properties, these measures remain limited by their reliance on self-report. A major challenge for coping research is to develop behavioral measures of coping to complement self-report measures.

Above all, it is important not to lose conceptual richness in our quest for psychometric purity. A measure that is internally consistent and clear but devoid of conceptual meaning does not move us ahead. Ultimately, we want to have reliable and valid measures to describe a process that is inherently subtle, dynamic, and complex.

References

Auerbach, S. M. (1991). Temporal factors in stress and coping: Intervention implications. In B. N. Carpenter (Ed.), *Personal coping: Theory, research, and application.* Westport, CT: Praeger.

Billings, A. G., & Moos, R. H. (1981). The role of coping responses and social resources in attenuating the impact of stressful life events. *Journal of Behavioral Medicine, 4,* 139–157.

Brown, G. A., & Harris, T. O. (1986). Establishing causal links: The Bedford College studies of depression. In H. Katschnig (Ed.), *Life events and psychiatric disorder* (pp. 107–187). Cambridge, England: Cambridge University Press.

Cohen, F., Reese, L. B., Kaplan, G. A., & Riggio, R. E. (1986). Coping with the stresses of arthritis. In R. W. Moskowitz & M. R. Haug (Eds.), *Arthritis and the elderly* (pp. 47–56). New York: Springer.

Felton, B. J., & Revenson, T. A. (1984). Coping with chronic illness: A study of illness controllability and the influence of coping strategies on psychological adjustment. *Journal of Consulting and Clinical Psychology, 52,* 343–353.

Folkman, S. (1984). Personal control and stress and coping processes: A theoretical analysis. *Journal of Personality and Social Psychology, 46,* 839–852.

Folkman, S., Chesney, M., McKusick, L., Ironson, G., Johnson, D. S., & Coates, T. J. (1991). Translating coping theory into an intervention. In J. Eckendrode (Ed.), *The social context of stress* (pp. 239–260). New York: Plenum.

Folkman, S., & Lazarus, R. S. (1980). An analysis of coping in a middle-aged community sample. *Journal of Health and Social Behavior, 21,* 219–239.

Folkman, S, & Lazarus, R. S. (1985). If it changes it must be a process: Study of emotion and coping during three stages of a college examination. *Journal of Personality and Social Psychology, 48,* 150–170.

Folkman, S., Lazarus, R. S., Dunkel-Schetter, C. DeLongis, A., & Gruen, R. (1986). The dynamics of a stressful encounter: Cognitive appraisal, coping, and encounter outcomes. *Journal of Personality and Social Psychology, 50,* 992–1003.

Lazarus, R. S., & Folkman, S. (1984). *Stress, appraisal, and coping.* New York: Springer.

Marshall, G. N., & Dunkel-Schetter, C. (1987, August). *Conceptual and methodological issues in the study of coping: Dimensionality of coping.* Paper presented at the annual convention of the American Psychological Association, New York.

Moos, R., & Lemke, S. (1984). Supportive residential settings for older people. In I. Altman, M. P. Lawton, & J. Wohlwill (Eds.), *Elderly people and the environment* (pp. 159–190). New York: Plenum.

Moos, R. H., & Swindle, R. W., Jr. (1990). Person–environment transactions and the stressor-appraisal-coping process. *Psychological Inquiry, 1,* 3–13.

Pearlin, L. I., & Schooler, K. (1978). The structure of coping. *Journal of Health and Social Behavior, 19,* 2–21.

Scheier, M. F., & Carver, C. S. (1985). Optimism, coping, and health: Assessment and implications of generalized outcome expectancies. *Health Psychology, 4,* 219–247.

Stone, A. A., & Neale, J. M. (1984). New measure of daily coping. Development and preliminary results. *Journal of Personality and Social Psychology, 46,* 892–906.

Taylor, S. E., & Lobel, M. (1990). Social comparison activity under threat: Downward evaluation and upward contacts. *Psychological Review, 96,* 569–575.

Tennen, H., & Herzberger, S. (1985). Ways of Coping Scale. In D. J. Keyser & R. C. Sweetland (Eds.), *Test critiques: Vol. 3.* Kansas City: Test Corporation of America.

Vaillant, G. E. (1977). *Adaptation to life.* Boston: Little, Brown.

Weiss, R. S. (1990). *Staying the course.* New York: The Free Press.

PART FOUR

Conclusion

Stress, Coping, and Health: Conceptual Issues and Directions for Future Research

Camille B. Wortman, Collette Sheedy, Vicki Gluhoski, and Ron Kessler

D oes exposure to stressful life events put individuals at risk for the development of subsequent health problems? If so, are certain ways of reacting to and handling life stress less damaging than others? As is reflected in this volume, these issues are continuing to capture the attention and the imagination of scholars in a wide variety of disciplines.

In our own work we have focused primarily on understanding the impact of sudden, irrevocable losses—that is, losses that involve permanent change and over which we have little, if any, control. Most of this research has examined bereavement (see Wortman & Silver, 1989; Wortman, Silver, & Kessler, in press, for reviews), although we have studied other types of loss as well, including physical disability (Bulman & Wortman, 1977), life-threatening illness (Dunkel-Schetter & Wortman, 1987; Wortman & Dunkel-Schetter, 1979), and criminal victimization (Coates, Wortman, & Abbey, 1979). Ultimate goals of this work are to explicate the processes through which people try to come to terms with the stressful events in their lives and to clarify the theoretical mechanisms through which such events can have deleterious effects on subsequent mental and physical health (Kessler, Price, & Wortman, 1985).

Prior to collecting empirical data, we attempted to identify a theoretical perspective that could enrich and guide our research. In the area of grief and loss, the most influential theoretical models are those that postulate stages of emotional reaction to loss, such as shock, denial, anger, and depression (see Wortman & Silver, 1987, for a review). Although stage models have much to offer in describing the process through which individuals adjust to losses like bereavement, they fail to clarify one of the most intriguing findings to emerge from our own and others' work on stressful life events: the enormous variability that characterizes individuals' reactions to a particular event.

One theoretical orientation that does provide a means of understanding this variability is an approach generally referred to as the *stress and coping model.* This model, enormously influential at the present time, maintains that the impact of a stressful life event on any one person depends largely on the coping resources available to that person. Coping resources that have generated the most research interest include social support, coping strategies, and personality.

For the most part, our research has focused on distinct populations of individuals who have experienced a particular traumatic event, such as permanent paralysis or the death of a spouse or child (e.g., Downey, Silver, & Wortman, 1990; Lehman, Wortman, & Williams, 1987). We have also studied the stress process by using general population surveys (Wortman et al., in press) and on some occasions, experiments (Silver, Wortman, & Crofton, 1990). Designing these studies has made us face a host of conceptual and methodological problems, including how stressful life events should be conceptualized and measured and which coping resources are the most important to include in a given study.

As our own research data have begun to accumulate, the findings that have emerged do not seem consistent with what would be expected on the basis of stage models or the stress and coping model. These models predict that following a stressful life experience, individuals go through a period of disequilibrium or distress. However, our research, as well as the studies of others, has revealed that even following a major life event, some people do not seem to go through a period of disequilibrium. It is generally assumed that the failure to experience or express distress following a major life event will be associated with subsequent health problems. To the contrary, our work and the work of others (see Wortman & Silver, 1989) suggests that those who appear to be doing well shortly after a major life event are the ones who seem to do best in the long run. It is also assumed that those with more coping resources will cope better with a major stress than those with fewer resources. In our own research, however, we have not found this to be the case. We have found that people with many resources appear to be vulnerable to certain kinds of life events. Finally, it is widely believed that over time, people come to terms with the stressful life experience and are able to continue their normal level of functioning. Our work suggests that this is not always the case. Under certain circumstances, which are delineated below, individuals appear unable to resolve and recover from the stressor despite the passage of considerable amounts of time.

We question the value of the stress and coping model that is so widely applied in current research on the impact of stress. Drawing from our own findings as well as the studies of others, we have begun to develop an alternative theoretical perspective. We believe that individuals' appraisals of and reactions to stressful life events are importantly influenced by their philosophical perspective on life or their view of the world. Events that can be incorporated into a person's view of the world may cause little disequilibrium and resultant distress; those that shatter a person's view of the world may cause intense distress and result in subsequent health problems (see also Antonovsky, 1990; Friedman, 1991).

In this chapter, we first discuss our attempts to apply a stage model to our work on coping with loss. We indicate why we decided to supplement this approach with the stress and coping perspective and delineate the predictions that can be derived from that model. Then, we discuss the two major paradigms that have been used to study the link between stress and health: large-scale population surveys and studies that focus on a group of people who are dealing with a particular event such as bereavement or divorce. In comparing these alternative responses, we raise a number of questions abut how to conceptualize and measure stress as well as the dilemmas one faces in selecting which coping resources to study. In so doing, we will discuss particular issues that have arisen in the course of research, as well as findings from our own research program. We will illustrate how these findings, taken together, suggest that the stress and coping model may not be the most appropriate theoretical perspective for understanding reactions to stress. We suggest a new theoretical approach that focuses on how people's reactions to stress are importantly influenced by their views of the world. Finally, we conclude the chapter with some suggestions for future research.

Initial Theoretical Work

Stage Models of Emotional Response

Because our research focuses primarily on reactions to stressful life events involving loss, we initially looked to the literature on grief and loss for theoretical models that might guide our work. The most influential theoretical models are the stage models of grief. According to such models, individuals go through several stages as they attempt to come to terms with the loss of a loved one. One of the most widely cited stage models of bereavement is that of Bowlby (1961, 1973, 1980), who identified and described four stages or phases of mourning. These include a phase of shock or being stunned; a phase of yearning and searching for the lost loved one, which is typically accompanied by feelings of anger and restlessness; a phase of giving up efforts to reunite with the lost loved one, which is characterized by feelings of depression; and a final phase of reorganization or recovery, in which the person is able to establish new ties to others, and there is a gradual return of former interests (see Wortman & Silver, 1987, for a review).

Surprisingly, only a few studies have assessed feelings of shock, denial, anxiety, anger, and depression longitudinally following a major loss. The available data from these studies provide little support for the stage approach. A close examination of the data suggests that there is considerable variability in the intensity of the emotional response, in the kinds of specific emotions that are experienced, and in their sequence (see Silver & Wortman, 1980, for a review). Moreover, these models are difficult to test or disconfirm, because some theorists have contended that people may experience more than one stage simultaneously, may move back and forth among the stages, and may skip certain stages completely (see, e.g., Kubler-Ross, 1969). Because of the lack of evidence in support of such models, it has been suggested that the models may not be as useful as was previously believed. In fact, an authoritative review of bereavement research published by the Institute of Medicine cautioned against the use of the term *stages* of response. It noted that this term "might lead people to expect the bereaved to proceed from one clearly identifiable reaction to another in a more orderly fashion than usually occurs. It might also result in ... hasty assessments of where individuals are or ought to be in the grieving process" (Osterweis, Solomon, & Green, 1984, p. 48). Nonetheless, there is a pervasive belief among caregivers and helping professionals that such stages exist. Over the past 2 decades, stage models have been taught in thousands of courses in medical schools, hospitals, and schools of social work and have also appeared in numerous textbooks and articles written by and for physicians, nurses, therapists, social workers, and patients and their families. Consequently, these models have become firmly entrenched among health care professionals, and they are often used as a yardstick by which to assess the patient's progress.

In our work on reactions to loss, we have found the work of the major stage theorists, particularly Bowlby (1980) and Horowitz (1976, 1985), to be extremely useful in a descriptive sense. The stage models devote considerable attention to the specific processes through which individuals move from emotional distress to adaptation or recovery. In our view, the major weakness of this theoretical approach is that it proposes no specific mechanisms through which loss may exert an influence on subsequent mental or physical health. For this reason, the stage models have no way of accounting for the diversity of outcomes that occur in response to loss events—no way of explaining, for example, why one person is devastated by a given loss event, whereas another person appears to emerge relatively unscathed.

Stressful Life Events

In order to account for this variability of response, we turned to the literature on life events effects. Since the 1960s, there has been considerable interest in the question of whether exposure to stressful life events, such as the loss of a spouse, can affect subsequent mental or physical health. This literature had its origins in the pioneering work of Cannon (1939) and Selye (1956). According to these theorists, life change creates disequilibrium that imposes a period of readjustment. The readjustment period can leave the person more vulnerable to stress and its consequences. Until the mid 1970s, most research on life events focused on the task of demonstrating through epidemiological evidence that exposure to such events can, in fact, lead to illness (Rabkin & Struening, 1976).

In order to assess the relation between exposure to stress and subsequent mental or physical health problems, it was necessary to have a measure of overall exposure to stress. In the late 1960s, such a scale was developed by Holmes and Rahe (1967). Respondents in such surveys are typically asked to indicate which events on the list they have experienced over a particular time period, such as the past year. They are also asked to complete validated inventories of psychological distress and physical symptoms. From the life events scale, it is possible to derive a score assessing the individual's cumulative exposure to stress. In arriving at a score, some researchers (including Holmes and Rahe) have emphasized the importance of weighting the events so that individuals who experience more serious events (e.g., bereavement) receive a higher score than individuals who experience more minor events (see Thoits, 1983, for a more detailed discussion of the weighting issue). In many early studies, significant associations were found between the amount of life stress experienced and mental and physical health (see Rabkin & Struening, 1976; and Thoits, 1983, for representative reviews). However, the relations that have been documented are extremely small. Rabkin and Struening (1976) estimated that no more than 9% of the variance in health outcomes is explained by life events. Early attempts to account for the disappointingly weak relationship between life events and subsequent health problems focused on methodological shortcomings of the research (Dohrenwend & Dohrenwend, 1981). For example, one problem in interpreting an association between life stress and functioning is that prior emotional difficulties can bring about some events, such as divorce or job loss, thus leading to ambiguity in the casual meaning of associations between events and disorder. Indeed, a substantial percentage of the events in standard life event inventories have been judged by a sample of clinicians to be symptoms of emotional disorder (Dohrenwend, Dohrenwend, Dodson, & Shrout, 1984). Moreover, respondents who are distressed may recall more events than nondistressed individuals in order to explain their current distress (Brown, 1974). In order to avoid these problems, investigators have recognized the importance of collecting data on life events and functioning at two separate points in time (e.g., Turner & Noh, 1982) and of limiting their analysis to events judged unlikely to have resulted from prior psychopathology (e.g., Brown & Harris, 1978).

Several other methodological improvements also have been introduced in the measurement of life events, such as clarifying ambiguously worded items with respect to their desirability, and independently verifying events by a second party in order to ensure accuracy of recall. However, these and other refinements have not substantially increased predictive power. Consequently, researchers have attempted to conduct a more careful analysis of the specific sorts of events that are associated with particular kinds of physical and mental health problems. Some improvement results from considering events in terms of their desirability, controllability, predictability, seriousness, and time clustering (Thoits, 1983). Nonetheless, even with these improvements, the relationship between life changes and physical or health problems is modest. The vast majority of people who experience life events do not become mentally or physically ill. In fact, there is emerging evidence that stressful encounters can sometimes promote coping capacity (see Haan, 1982, for a review).

In attempting to clarify the reasons for this weak association, work on the impact of life events has progressed in two directions, both of which have important implications for research on stress and health. First, investigators have recognized that asking respondents merely to check off or list events is not sufficient; it is important to obtain information about the context in which the event occurred, and hence clarify the meaning of the particular event to the respondent. There is general agreement that contextual information is critical for a full appreciation of life event effects. For example, the loss of a parent may have more impact on one person than another because the parent was also the major child-care provider. Similarly, to one mother, the loss of an infant may represent a shattering of hopes and dreams for the future. To another mother, such a loss may represent a way out of an impossible situation and to a widening of hopes and dreams for the future. There is controversy about the best way to obtain contextual information, however, and this is a topic that we will later explore in more detail.

A second major thrust of current theoretical and empirical work in the stress and coping area involves the identification of variables—so-called *vulnerability* or *resistance factors*—that can account for the variability that exists in response to stress. Several different types of factors have been examined in the literature including various personality predispositions, such as neuroticism (e.g., Depue & Monroe, 1986) and dispositional optimism (e.g., Scheier & Carver, 1985); resources, such as intellectual capacity, cognitive flexibility, and financial assets (Menaghen, 1983); coping strategies, such as reinterpretation of the situation as positive, or denial that a problem exists (e.g., Lazarus & Folkman, 1984); and social support (see Cohen & Wills, 1985).

At present, much of the research on the impact of stress on health is loosely guided by a theoretical approach that might be called the stress and coping approach. This model was originally developed by Barbara Dohrenwend and her colleagues (see e.g., Dohrenwend & Dohrenwend, 1978; Dohrenwend & Dohrenwend, 1981) and has been refined by subsequent investigators. The model focuses attention on the possible mechanisms through which exposure to stress leads to subjective perceptions of distress, to short-term psychological and physiological responses to these perceptions, and to changes in mental or physical health (see Kessler et al., 1985, or Martin, 1989, for a more detailed discussion of the model). This general model has been enormously influential during the past decade. As Martin (1989) noted, it was adopted as a heuristic guide by the Institute of Medicine panel on Stress and Life Events in 1981 (Elliot & Eisdorfer, 1982).

This model generally assumes that once a stressful life event is encountered, the appraisal of that stressor, as well as mental and physical health consequences, will depend on the individual's vulnerability or resistance factors. Thus, unlike the stage models discussed earlier, a major advantage of the stress and coping approach is that it can account for variability in response. An implicit assumption underlying the stage models is that virtually everyone will recover from a stressful life experience. However, according to the stress and coping model, those with more coping resources, such as social support, are likely to recover more quickly and completely than those with fewer resources.

Selection of a Paradigm

Overview

In launching a program of empirical research on the effects of loss, the first question facing us involved the selection of a research paradigm. There are two completely different paradigms that have been used to study life events—large-scale population surveys and studies of specific populations of individuals who have experienced a certain life event (Kessler et al., 1985) The use of large-scale populations surveys is grounded in epidemiology: a representative sample of respondents is asked to identify stressful life events they have experienced, typically during the last 6 months or year. They are also asked questions, either at the same time or during a subsequent interview, about their health. Most scientists interested in the impact of life events on health have used this paradigm.

There is also a long history of research on how people react to specific life crises, such as widowhood, cancer, or rape. For the most part, these studies have been conducted by practitioners who were interested in developing an understanding that could guide clinical practice. In these studies, a group of people who have experienced a particular life crisis is followed longitudinally, typically from shortly after the crisis until 1 to 2 years later. Respondents may be interviewed 2 to 3 times during the course of the study, and a major goal is to identify the predictors of good adjustment at the final interview. Until recently, investigators in this latter tradition have not been primarily interested in the impact of the event in question on health, so few measures of physical health are typically included. Instead, investigators in this tradition have focused heavily on predictors of such mental health outcomes as depression. As in the population survey studies of life events, there has been increasing interest in identifying variables that will help explain why some people show long-term distress whereas others recover more quickly. In recent years, investigators have begun to examine the role of social support, coping strategies, and personality in moderating the impact of particular life events (see Carver, Scheier, & Pozo, this volume, for an excellent example of work of this sort). Interestingly, these research traditions have developed independently of each other. Each has important strengths and weaknesses for the study of the impact of life events, and these are discussed next.

Population Surveys of the Impact of Life Events

A major strength of this paradigm is that, for the most part, investigators using it have recognized the importance of using large, representative samples of community residents.

This is not the case for many studies of individuals with particular life crises. The major weakness of the approach is that respondents are asked to provide retrospective data about a stressor that was experienced several months ago. Not only does this create problems with biases in retrospective recall, but it makes it difficult to explore important links in the stress and coping model, such as what signs of short-term distress the person manifests following the crisis, and whether these are predictive of long-term recovery. Also, because this paradigm involves interviews with respondents who have experienced many different kinds of events, such studies make it difficult to examine the specific processes through which a life event can produce deleterious health outcomes. Because they aggregate over individuals with very different experiences, such studies tell us little about the texture of coping with a major life event.

Among investigators working within this paradigm, there has been considerable debate about the best way to measure stress. It is becoming clear to investigators that simply asking respondents to indicate what life events they have experienced will not elucidate the relationship between stress and health. Most investigators now agree that it is critically important to measure the context in which the event occurs. The effects of job loss, for example, may depend on the financial resources that a person has available. Although there is agreement that contextual information is important, there is considerable debate about the best way to obtain such information. Some investigators have argued that the most important information to obtain is not what happened to a person objectively, but his or her subjective reaction to that event (e.g., Sarason, Johnson, & Siegel, 1978). The problem with this approach is that when such measures are used, it is very difficult to detect the impact of coping resources such as support or coping strategies. Such resources may operate by reducing subjective perceptions of distress. Moreover, studies that rely solely on respondents' subjective ratings of perceived stress provide no opportunity to identify the conditions under which particular events are appraised as stressful, or to study how coping resources like support and coping strategies can affect how a given stressor is appraised.

Other investigators have attempted to elicit context information by using a complex procedure whereby an interviewer presents information about the objective circumstances under which the events occurred to a panel of raters who then score the events on a variety of contextual dimensions such as forewarning (Brown & Harris, 1978). This approach has the advantage of elaborating several different dimensions of the objective context that might be consequential for heath outcomes. However, the procedure is so time-consuming that it is rarely used in life stress research. Moreover, if the researcher relies on information about context provided by the respondent, and hence influenced to some degree by the respondent's vulnerability to stress or coping resources, this approach, like the use of subjective ratings, may make it difficult to detect the impact of coping resources. Investigators are continuing to experiment with ways of eliciting objective information about context in population surveys. At present, the most commonly used procedure is to ask the respondents to provide as much objective information as possible about the circumstances under which the event occurred and then to ask them to rate the event in terms of its suddenness, degree of forewarning, physical danger, controllability, and other factors.

Research on Life Crises

For the most part, studies of reactions to specific life crises, such as the loss of a loved one or the development of a life-threatening illness, have consisted of relatively small, descriptive studies focusing on how people react to the crisis and how their reactions change over time. An advantage of this paradigm is that it enables the investigator to study the process of coping with a particular crisis. Such studies also make it possible to examine various links in the stress and coping model, such as the association between short-term distress and recovery. However, studies within this paradigm have traditionally been plagued by major methodological shortcomings. One of these concerns the use of biased, nonrepresentative samples. In the area of widowhood, one review found that 40% of all studies published on conjugal loss between 1973 and 1983 relied on convenience samples, such as members of support groups (Gentry & Schulman, 1985). Even those studies that have applied more rigorous sampling procedures (e.g., newspaper obituaries) have typically focused on a narrow segment of the population. In the case of widowhood, most studies have focused on urban, middle-class, White women (Osterweis et al., 1984).

Equally troubling are the problems with low response rates and attrition that have characterized many studies of life crises. In most studies on a single life crisis, an effort is made to recruit respondents within the first few weeks or months following the loss. In such studies, any problems with the representativeness of the initial sampling frame are often compounded by the problem of a low response rate (Stroebe & Stroebe, 1989). For example, Parkes and Weiss (1983) reported that they identified an initial sample of 231 widows. They were unable to locate 40 (17%), 76 (33%) refused to participate, and 55 (29%) were lost for other reasons, leaving a sample size at Wave 1, 3 weeks after the loss, of 49 (21%). These response rates are typical for research of this sort. The problem of attrition is critical because there may be substantial differences between those who participate and those who decline. Stroebe and Stroebe (1989) demonstrated that the willingness of bereaved persons to participate in an interview is affected by their level of depression, as well as by other psychological variables. Moreover, such selection effects operate differently for men and women: Women are more likely to participate if they are depressed, whereas men are less likely to participate when depressed. Thus, in widowhood studies published to date, sex differences in selection make it impossible to draw conclusions about sex differences in the impact of the loss.

Another shortcoming of the vast majority of studies of individuals going through particular life crises is the failure to include control respondents. Inclusion of a control group is particularly critical for investigators interested in detecting sex differences in reactions to conjugal loss. Many studies without control groups have concluded that widows adjust more poorly than widowers (e.g., Carey, 1980). However, such conclusions "are misleading because the apparently poorer adjustment of the widows than the widowers may be simply a reflection of the general sex differences in depression and maladjustment" (Stroebe & Stroebe, 1983, p. 285).

An additional important shortcoming of research on specific life events is that, for the most part, they have followed respondents for a relatively short time after the event. In the case of bereavement, the most prevalent belief in many Western cultures is that it requires a calendar year to recover from the loss of a spouse (Rosenblatt, 1988). Perhaps because of these cultural beliefs, most research on the effects of bereavement has focused on the first year or so after the loss. By studying individuals in the first year or two after a life event, we are most likely picking up the disequilibrium and stress caused by initial efforts to absorb and cope with what has happened. However, such a design leaves a very important question unanswered: Are people fundamentally changed by life events in ways that may sustain elevated rates of distress for many years?

In recent years, investigators examining the relationship between stress and illness have become interested in reactions to specific life crises. As a result, more methodologically sophisticated research on the impact of particular events is likely to appear in the literature. There are a number of ways in which the methods developed by life events researchers can be profitably applied to the study of life crises. For example, life crisis researchers have, for the most part, devoted little attention to providing an objective characterization of the stressful experience. If one person who loses a spouse takes years to recover, whereas another bounces back quickly, this is assumed to reflect differences in coping resources or capacity. But clearly, the death of a spouse can vary considerably in the coping challenges it initiates. What exactly does a person lose when he or she loses a spouse? For some people, the death may represent the end of an unsatisfactory relationship or the termination of extremely draining or difficult caregiving responsibilities, whereas for others, the death may represent the loss of a great love. Similarly, the losses that people face as a result of job termination differ substantially from one individual to another and may involve money, social contacts, self-esteem, or all of the above. The failure of researchers studying the effects of particular life crises to concern themselves with this problem is unfortunate, because a focus on contextual factors that elucidate the meaning of the loss to a particular person may help to account for the variability in response to that loss. Unless such factors are explored, it is impossible to know whether differences in distress or functioning following a life crisis reflect differences in the meaning of the stress or differences in coping resources or capacity.

Our Program of Research on Bereavement

Studies of Reactions to Specific Life Crises

In the late 1970s, we initiated a program of research designed to clarify the process of coping with an irrevocable loss. Over the next decade, we completed three studies. The first of these focused on how people cope with permanent paralysis following a sudden, traumatic injury to their spinal cord (Silver, 1982; Wortman & Silver, 1987). In this study, interviews were completed with three groups of spinal-cord-injured persons: quadriplegics, paraplegics, and a control group of neurologically intact individuals who had been in an accident, but who had suffered no permanent damage to their spinal cord. Individuals were interviewed at 1, 3, and 8 weeks following their injury. In the second study, we conducted interviews with parents who lost an infant to the Sudden Infant Death Syndrome (SIDS; Downey, Silver, & Wortman, 1990; Wortman & Silver, 1987). Unlike the spinal cord study, which focused primarily on young White males, the SIDS sample was 50% non-White and included mothers and fathers of varying socioeconomic backgrounds. The SIDS study also encompassed a wider time frame: Respondents were interviewed at 2 to 4 weeks, 3 months, and 18 months following the death of their baby. Our third study focused on people who had lost a spouse or child in a motor vehicle crash that was perpetrated by someone else's negligence. This last study was a case-control investigation designed to clarify the long-term impact of a major traumatic loss. People who experienced such a loss were interviewed 4 to 7 years later, and their responses were compared with matched controls who had not experienced the death of their spouse or child.

In our program of research, an attempt was made to incorporate the strengths of empirical work within the life events tradition (e.g., representative samples and use of valid and reliable scales to assess key variables) as well as the literature on specific life crises (i.e., providing useful descriptive information about the process through which people cope with a major loss). Hence, one feature of our work was that it combined a rigorous assessment of key variables with the collection of rich qualitative data about how people feel their lives have been altered by the loss. Second, like life events researchers, we made a major effort in each of our studies to collect contextual information about the life event—that is, what the loss means to the person who experienced it. In each study, we have included questions designed to clarify precisely what was lost and what specific stressors are associated with the loss for a particular person. We also included questions about what the loss meant to the respondent—whether the person has searched for meaning following the incident, and whether he or she had come up with a meaningful account of what had happened. In developing questions designed to clarify the context in which the loss occurred, we relied on an advisory group of individuals who had experienced the loss in question (cf. Wortman & Dunkel-Schetter, 1979). In each of these studies, the suggestions provided by our advisory council have been invaluable in developing the measures, as well as in designing effective procedures for recruiting respondents and minimizing attrition.

Drawing from the stage models of grief and loss, we felt it important to include an assessment of a full array of different emotions at specific points in time following the loss. Without such information, it is difficult to assess key questions, such as whether the majority of individuals experience intense distress following a major loss. In each study, we also included an assessment of variables thought to moderate the relationship between loss and subsequent mental or physical health problems, including social support, personality, and coping strategies.

Taken together, the early studies pointed our attention to three distinct findings, each of which is inconsistent with prevailing views from theorists and researchers in the field of grief and loss and stress and coping. First, it is clear from our own data (Wortman & Silver, 1987), as well as the data of others (see Wortman & Silver, 1990, for a review), that a substantial percentage of people do not appear to experience intense distress following a major loss. In the SIDS study, 30% of the respondents did not show depression at the first interview, even though this was only 2 to 4 weeks after the loss.

Instead, by as early as 1 month following the loss, there was marked variability in response to the loss. Moreover, initial reactions appear to be highly predictive of long-term adjustment.

This pattern of findings raises numerous questions. Do those individuals who fail to exhibit intense depression also fail to show indications of grief (i.e., yearning for the person who has died or strong feelings of distress when confronted with reminders of the lost loved one)? Is it possible that such individuals have already grieved for their lost loved one? Some people may begin grieving before their spouse has died if they have forewarning (e.g., in those cases where the spouse was terminally ill). Moreover, even in those situations where there is no opportunity to grieve for the loved one before the death (e.g., loss of an infant through SIDS), a substantial minority exhibit low distress shortly after the loss. It will be important to establish whether those who fail to grieve or to show intense distress following the loss will experience a delayed grief reaction and whether their failure to grieve will result in subsequent health problems. Taken together, our studies show that if respondents fail to manifest significant depression at Wave 1, they are unlikely to manifest depression at subsequent waves of the study. But depression is not necessarily synonymous with grief. Because the studies to date have included virtually no questions about feelings of grief at different points in time, they do not really address the question of delayed grief reactions nor do they empirically address whether individuals pass through stages. Moreover, as noted earlier, we are aware of no long-term longitudinal studies of the bereaved that have included hard health outcomes. Hence, at this point, virtually nothing is known about the impact of failure to grieve or to exhibit or express feelings of distress on subsequent health.

Results from the SIDS and motor vehicle studies also suggest that the process of resolution may operate differently than we might have expected. Like most clinicians who work in the area, we initially expected that when faced with a major loss, individuals would attempt to find meaning or come to an understanding of why the loss occurred and what it means in their lives. In our studies, only a small percentage of respondents searched for meaning, found meaning, and put the question of meaning aside. In the spinal cord study, less than half of the respondents ever attempted to make sense of the event. In the SIDS study, a substantial minority also never tried to find meaning. Even after 18 months, 83% could not make any sense of the loss. Similar results were obtained in the motor vehicle study where, 4 to 7 years after the loss, 72% were unable to make any sense out of what happened. Moreover, the SIDS study suggested that if people were going to be able to come up with a meaningful account for why the loss occurred, they did so right away. In subsequent studies, it will be important to test the generality of these results in other samples of bereaved individuals and to determine whether individuals are able to achieve a sense of resolution concerning the loss over a longer time span.

Finally, the results of the motor vehicle study, as well as findings from other investigators who have explored the issue (see Wortman & Silver, 1987, for a review), suggest that it may take far longer than we had previously expected for people to recover from the loss of a spouse or child. Compared with controls, respondents in our motor vehicle study were experiencing symptoms and problems in many areas of their lives. It will be important to replicate these findings on other populations of bereaved, as there may be something particularly difficult about coping with a loss caused by another's negligence. As in the case of resolution, we would also like to determine whether people who experience such losses are able to recover over a time span longer than 4 to 7 years.

The pattern of findings from the early studies is not consistent with the grief and loss approach or with the stress and coping approach. Both of these approaches assume an initial period of intense distress, and both assume that, ultimately, recovery will occur. However, they can be understood in terms of a theoretical perspective that focuses on views of the world as an explanatory mechanism. Some individuals, with some particular types of losses, may be able to incorporate the loss in question into their prevailing view of the world and, hence, may not show initial or subsequent distress. For other individuals, the event may challenge their view of the world, but they may be able to regain equilibrium and restore their worldview over time. For still others, the event may so profoundly shatter their worldview that no integration or resolution is possible. In these latter cases, we might expect a "giving up" on the world and the consequent failure to initiate coping efforts in other areas of life.

Large-Scale Studies of Stressful Live Events, Including Bereavement

It is widely recognized that to account for diverse and highly variable responses to conjugal loss, more progress must be made in explicating theoretical mechanisms through which bereavement may lead to a deterioration in health or functioning, as well as mechanisms through which variables such as social support may ameliorate the impact of the loss. For example, bereavement may lead to deleterious health consequences because the loss is accompanied by numerous role strains exhausting the individual's coping capacity. Some researchers (e.g., Thoits, 1983) suggest that life events have their pernicious effects primarily because they result in increased chronic strains. Alternatively, bereavement may exacerbate or precipitate health-compromising behaviors, such as the use of alcohol. The loss and accompanying grief may also trigger feelings of helplessness, which are conducive to the development of disease.

Similarly, although several studies show a relationship between perceived support and adjustment to bereavement, little is known about the processes through which social support may ameliorate the impact of the crisis. For example, does social support protect people from the stress of widowhood by reducing the amount of role strain experienced, by altering the way the loss and stressors related to it are appraised, by providing specific coping strategies useful in accepting the loss, or by encouraging health maintaining behaviors (cf. Kessler, Price, & Wortman, 1985)?

With the difficulties of past work—our own and others—in mind, we attempted to design a program of large-scale studies that would complement and extend our earlier work. For the past several years, we have been involved in a comprehensive, multidisciplinary study of conjugal bereavement. The study has three distinct parts. First, we developed what we believe is the first large, nationally representative database on conjugal loss. Our widowhood study is part of a large-scale interdisciplinary study of health, stress, and productive activities across the life span known as *Americans' Changing Lives* (ACL). In 1986, personal interviews were conducted with a probability sample of 3,617 adults who were 25 years of age and older. Blacks and persons over 60 were oversampled to permit more detailed analyses by race and age, in addition to maximizing the number of widowed respondents to be included. All sample members who could be recontacted ($n = 2,867$) were reinterviewed in 1989. Our database of widowed respondents includes 804 individuals widowed from 3 months to over 60 months prior to the ACL study, 616 of whom were reinterviewed in 1989. Second, we completed a national prospective study of widowhood, including 92 ACL respondents who lost their spouse between Waves 1 and 2. Information on relevant risk factors was assessed before and after the loss as part of the ACL survey. Third, we have launched a separate prospective study of widowhood designed to focus on older bereaved persons. This study, in which baseline data were collected from 1,532 members of older Detroit area couples, is known as the *Changing Lives of Older Couples* (CLOC) study. State death records are monitored to identify respondents who become bereaved; they are recruited into a 4-wave study in which they are interviewed at 6 to 8 months following the loss and regular intervals thereafter (18 months and 49 months following the death). Matched control respondents are interviewed at comparable time periods. This study includes a separate biomedical component, funded by the MacArthur Foundation, in which data on physical health and cognitive functioning, as well as blood and urine samples, are collected from a subsample of still-married respondents, from those who become widowed, and from matched controls. The CLOC baseline data collection was completed in 1988 and a follow up is well underway, with an 84% response rate in recruiting widows and widowers into the study. We have completed approximately 175 Wave 1 and 80 Wave 2 interviews.

In these studies, an effort was made to minimize methodological problems that have characterized much previous work in the area, including biased samples, failure to include a control group, and failure to include valid and reliable measures of key variables. The design of the ACL study, in which individuals were approached to participate in a general study of stress and productive activity across the life span, helps to minimize problems with selection inherent in designs that approach respondents shortly after the loss of a spouse. The prospective CLOC study also includes a large, representative sample of older adults. Moreover, because we will have CLOC baseline data on both respondents who agree to participate in the widowhood follow-up interviews and those who refuse later interviews, we will be able to determine if the two groups differ on major demographic or psychological indicators. All of the study designs will afford the opportunity to compare bereaved and control respondents. In ACL, we will compare widowed respondents with ever-married controls; in the CLOC study, both widowed and control respondents will be interviewed at various points in time following the loss. Each study includes a wide range of outcome variables, including grief, depression, physical health, cognitive functioning, and involvement in productive activities. In the CLOC study, self-report data are supplemented with objective biomedical indicators (e.g., blood pressure, blood lipids, catecholamines, and peak expiratory flow). In both studies, date of institutionalization is recorded for those who become institutionalized, and mortality is continually monitored through the National Death Index and the state of Michigan death records.

The ACL cross-sectional study will permit us to gain information about the specific conditions under which particular outcomes are likely to emerge. For example, we will be able to identify the determinants of searching for and finding meaning following the loss of a spouse. Preliminary analyses suggest that Blacks and the elderly are less likely to search for meaning following the loss of their spouse than non-Blacks or younger respondents. In analyses ongoing at present, we are attempting to determine whether respondents' religious orientations or views of the world influence the search for meaning, and also whether the tendency to search for meaning is influenced by the circumstances under which the loss occurs.

The CLOC and ACL prospective studies are ideally suited to clarify how coping resources, assessed prior to the crisis, such as respondents' worldviews, influence subsequent reactions to the loss. These designs will also permit us to address the issue of how worldviews, as well as other coping resources like social support or personality are affected by the loss of a spouse. For example, widowed respondents may become less trusting of other people following the loss. In assessing changes occurring as a result of the loss, we will give full consideration to the possibility that widowhood may produce long-term positive changes, such as greater self-confidence, as well as negative ones (cf. Wortman & Silver, 1990).

Findings From the ACL Wave 1 National Cross-Sectional Data

In past research, there was some consensus that widowhood has a greater impact on men than it does on women (Stroebe & Stroebe, 1983, 1989). In particular, it appears that there are sex differences in depression following widowhood, with widowed men showing greater vulnerability. However, past studies have failed to clarify why such sex differences exist. In analyses from the ACL study, we drew from the "unpacking" approach to determine whether widowhood may have a different meaning for men and women. Drawing from the literature on stressful life events and gender differences in marital roles, we hypothesized that widowhood results in different types and amounts of strain for men and women—strains related to the loss of roles previously filled by the survivor's spouse. Our results support this notion. It appears that women's primary source of vulnerability following widowhood arises from an increase in financial strain. In contrast, men's greater vulnerability stems in part from their more limited social relationships and in part from their difficulty in assuming tasks previously handled by their wives. Interestingly, our results show that widowhood is associated with significantly more strained relationships, particularly with children, for men but not for women. Many men have relied on their spouses to maintain relationships with children and may find it difficult to assume this role in widowhood. Previous lack of closeness between fathers and children, combined with male difficulty in expressing the need for support, may underlie the strained relationships with children that we found among our male respondents.

On the surface, past research might appear to suggest a sex difference in vulnerability to the same event—widowhood. On closer examination, however, we find that widowhood is not the same event for the two sexes. Gender differences in the experience of various strains created by widowhood help to explain the differential vulnerability seen at a more highly aggregated level of analysis.

We have also completed some preliminary analyses on the effects of age and race, and the results thus far are intriguing. It was revealed that younger respondents are more affected by the loss of their spouse, but that they recover more quickly. We have also obtained information that Whites are hit harder initially and take longer to recover than do Black respondents. A variety of explanatory mechanisms for these findings are currently being pursued.

Data from the national cross-sectional study also corroborated the findings from our earlier research that the effects of widowhood last much longer than was previously expected (see Wortman, Kessler, Bolger, & House, 1991). Respondents who lost a spouse were compared with nonbereaved controls who were similar on a number of dimensions, but who had not lost a spouse. It took bereaved respondents in our study approximately 1 decade to approach control respondents' scores on life satisfaction and nearly 2 decades to approach their scores on depressed mood. In addition, we asked respondents several questions about their current thoughts and memories regarding their spouse. Painful memories were found to decline over time, although it took several decades for such memories to reach their lowest level. Finally, several questions were included to assess cognitive resolution from the loss, such as whether the respondent had been able to find any meaning in the loss or whether he or she regarded the loss as senseless and unfair. Interestingly, such questions showed no time effects whatsoever. Individuals who lost their spouse more than 6 decades earlier were no more likely to have generated a reason for what happened than individuals who lost their spouse during the past year.

Preliminary Findings From the ACL National Prospective Study

As noted earlier, 92 individuals lost their spouse between Waves 1 and 2 of the ACL survey, and we have completed some preliminary analyses of these data. Compared with controls who were married at Wave 1 and did not experience a loss, the bereaved showed significantly higher depression. Further analyses were conducted to identify respondents most likely to experience depression. One set of analyses focused on characteristics of the marriage. According to clinical lore, people with ambivalent and conflictual marriages are at greatest risk for mental health problems following the death of their spouse. However, people involved in such marriages may have more mental health problems before the loss. In our study, we had data available on respondents' depression, as well as their evaluation of their marriage, before the loss. Our analyses show unequivocally that when we control for depression at Wave 1 and look at changes in depression as a function of marital satisfaction and conflict assessed before the loss, those with troubled marriages actually show less depression after the loss. Those who experienced relatively low levels of conflict and high levels of satisfaction were particularly distressed after the loss, suggesting that those with the best marriages may be the most at risk following bereavement and most in need of intervention efforts.

A second set of analyses focused on the impact of coping resources, including social support, self-esteem, and feelings of mastery on the impact of bereavement. The stress and coping model suggests that those with more resources may be more resilient after the loss. An analysis in terms of the impact of life events on worldviews, however, leads to a different prediction. Those with views of the world as controllable, predictable, and safe may be particularly vulnerable to an uncontrollable life event, such as the death of a spouse. We looked at the impact of social support, of subjective perceptions that one is in control (feelings of self-esteem, mastery, and belief that the world is a safe and secure place), and of objective indications of personal control (intellectual resources and financial resources). Surprisingly, social support as assessed prior to the loss had no effect on changes in depression following the loss. In every case, the other resources we studied were found to have a deleterious impact. Those with the highest self-esteem, the highest feelings of mastery, the greatest intellectual resources, and the most financial resources were hit hardest by the loss of their spouse. Interestingly, it was not their spouse's income at Wave 1, but their own income that predicted deleterious effects. Taken together, these findings suggest that those who experience the world as most controllable may be especially vulnerable to the loss of their spouse.

One implication of these findings is that although coping resources are generally assumed to facilitate adjustment in the stress and coping model, such resources are not always as helpful as might be expected. Regarding social support, Kessler (1990) found that there is little evidence that the actual receipt of supportive behaviors facilitates adjustment to stress, although the perception of support is associated with better adjustment. He maintained that the receipt of support often entails a cost to self-esteem that could offset benefits. He also suggested that many support providers fail to respond in a way that is actually helpful. Consistent with this analysis, Lehman, Ellard, and Wortman (1986) demonstrated that in attempting to assist the bereaved, outsiders frequently make comments that are meant to be supportive (e.g., "you can always have another child," "your child was so precious that he was chosen to be with God," "at least you had a number of years with your husband before he died," and "I know exactly how you feel"), but that are very hurtful to the bereaved. Outsiders often tend to make comments that are judgmental of how the bereaved are handling the situation and that minimize the loss.

Whether those going through life crises will receive support or negative responses from others may depend on how much distress the person communicates. In a laboratory study conducted by Silver, Wortman, and Crofton (1990), college students first listened to a taped interview with an actual cancer patient or nonpatient confederate. Cancer patients described themselves as coping well or poorly in the face of the disease or provided a balanced view in which they exhibited distress, but also stated that they were engaged in active coping efforts to deal with it. Respondents were asked to rate the confederate on a number of dimensions and then were placed in a live interaction with the confederate where their discomfort was measured via nonverbal and unobtrusive behavioral measures taken during the interaction, including how close or far away the subject sat from the confederate.

Results of this study indicate that the respondents conveyed more discomfort and distress toward the cancer patients, regardless of their portrayal of their coping efforts, than they did toward healthy controls. However, how the cancer patients presented themselves as coping with their illness strongly affected the respondents' reactions and behaviors. Subjects sat further away from those who indicated that they were coping poorly, reported more distress following the live encounter, and were less willing to interact with the confederate in the future. Interestingly, respondents showed fewer nonverbal signs of discomfort and greater desire for future contact with cancer patients who portrayed a balanced view of their coping than with those who were positive about how things were going. The results of the study are distressing, because they suggest that those who are most distressed, and in need of support, may be least likely to get it.

Similarly, there may be limitations on the value of certain personality characteristics thought to buffer the impact of stress such as optimism. Scheier and Carver (1985) and their colleagues demonstrated that under certain conditions, optimism can be important. However, reports have begun to appear in the literature identifying some conditions under which optimism may be detrimental. For example, Tennen and Affleck (1987) emphasized that because optimists feel invulnerable to harm, they are less likely to take adequate precautions or comply with safety procedures. In addition, they may not cope well with life events that turn out worse than they expected. Tennen and Affleck reported a study in which they examined optimism in women who had just given birth to babies requiring intensive care. Mothers who had been optimistic about having a healthy baby did worse when the child needed medical attention. Weinstein (1982) maintained that unrealistic optimism may have a detrimental impact on health. His research shows that unrealistic optimism undermined risk reduction by decreasing worry about the problem. Because subjects were not worried about developing the problems, they might not have been taking adequate precautions.

In our results, those who believed that they had control over their lives coped worse with the death of a spouse than those who had less of a sense of control and mastery. Perceived control is generally thought to be a desirable asset, as are those indications of personal control such as how much money you earn and how intelligent you are. In an excellent analysis of this issue, Janoff-Bulman and Brickman (1982) reviewed numerous studies suggesting that when an undesirable outcome occurs, those who had high expectations of success and control may cope less effectively than those who had more realistic expectations. They also suggest that those with a strong sense of personal control may persist at a task that is truly uncontrollable much longer than they should. They emphasize the importance of knowing when to give up when the situation is truly not controllable.

In predicting what personal qualities are likely to serve as a coping resource, past research suggests that we should think expansively. Previous work has found that qualities that seem to be quite negative can often facilitate adaptation to a crisis. For example, Lieberman (1975) reported that those elderly individuals who were most aggressive, irritating, narcissistic, and demanding were those most likely to survive a crisis involving relocation. Those who were liked by the staff—who were not troublemakers and who were easy to relate to—fared less well. Similarly, Lowenthal, Thurnher, and Chiriboga (1975) reported that lifelong social isolation, which is generally considered a major indicator of maladaptation, is not necessarily associated with poor adjustment in later life. Apparently, the lifelong social isolate does not suffer as much from age-linked social losses, because he or she had never had social ties. Similarly, these investigators reported that among the older age groups that they studied, resources such as insight, perspective, and competence do not necessarily contribute to a sense of well-being. Those with many resources were even more unhappy than those with few resources and few deficits. The authors speculate that those who have many resources may become increasingly frustrated in their attempts to realize their maximum potential during old age.

Taken together, these findings suggest that the overarching assumption of those working within the stress and coping model—that coping resources are generally adaptive—needs to be viewed more speculatively. It should also be noted that these findings are not consistent with the stress and coping model. Hopefully, future research will help to clarify the conditions under which such resources are truly helpful and the conditions under which they have no effect or are harmful.

Ongoing Theoretical and Empirical Work

If results obtained from further studies are consistent with the findings reviewed herein, we must acknowledge the possibility that a sizable minority of people may come through a major loss relatively unscathed. What are the theoretical implications of this finding? Such results are incompatible with current theories of grief and loss, which assume latent pathology among those who fail to show intense distress following irrevocable losses. However, by dismissing such a reaction as indicative of pathology, attention appears to have been deflected away from identifying strengths or coping resources that may protect people from distress.

As we detailed earlier, a strength of the stress and coping model is that it emphasizes the importance of coping resources in explaining why some people may take longer than others to recover from the effects of a major loss. However, the stress and coping model is based on the assumption that a major loss or change will cause a state of disequilibrium. Hence, this model has no way of accounting for the fact that for a substantial minority of individuals, major loss events do not seem to bring about such a period of disequilibrium. Moreover, the stress and coping model cannot account for the finding that coping resources often do not protect people from the deleterious effects of stress. Taken together, the findings suggest that some people may have something in place beforehand—perhaps a religious or philosophical orientation or a certain view of the world—that enables them to be less vulnerable to the effects of loss.

At present, our theoretical work is focused on the role that might be played by philosophical perspectives or assumptions about the world in coping with a major loss (Janoff-Bulman & Frieze, 1983; Wortman, 1983). We believe that such events may be particularly likely to result in intense distress and subsequent problems in mental and physical health when they shatter a person's assumptions about the world. As Lilliston (1985) indicated, this can happen when a person experiences a sudden, traumatic injury: "A suddenly disabled person who was the victim of accident or disease is given a horrifying and permanent reminder of the world's injustice. If the person formerly believed in a just world, he [or she] must somehow harmonize the dissonance between what he [or she] expected life to be, and what it now has revealed itself to be" (p. 8).

We would predict that sudden and unexpected losses are more likely to shatter such assumptions than losses that occur at an expected time in the life span or losses for which there is time for psychological preparation (see Wortman & Silver, 1990). With respect to bereavement, Parkes and Weiss (1983) wrote that sudden, unexpected losses are particularly debilitating, largely through their "transformation of the world into a frightening place, a place in which disaster cannot be predicted and accustomed ways of thinking and behaving have proven unreliable and out of keeping with the actual world" (p. 245).

To date, researchers in the stress and coping tradition are focusing much of their attention on such variables as personality and social support. In our view, such variables are unlikely to account for the finding that a substantial minority of individuals fail to become significantly distressed following a major loss. We suspect that certain views of the world may serve a protective function in allowing individuals to incorporate a major tragedy. If so, an analysis of life events in terms of their impact on previously held world views could account for the failure to experience initial depression. For example, a person who holds a firm belief that all things are part of God's larger plan may show less distress following the loss of a spouse than a person who does not hold this view. The belief that one will be reunited with the loved one for all of eternity may also serve a protective function. Similarly, individuals who have the perspective that bad things can happen at any time and that suffering is part of life may find it easier to cope with loss than those individuals who believe that if they work hard and are good people, they will be protected from misfortune (cf. Janoff-Bulman & Frieze, 1983). In our judgment, religious or philosophical orientations that might lead individuals to incorporate loss events into their view of the world and, hence, be protected from distress are in need of considerably more research (cf. Antonovsky, 1990).

We would expect the shattering of worldviews to have profound consequences for mental and physical health and for the initiation of subsequent coping efforts. Those individuals who believe that good behavior and hard work are rewarded may be particularly vulnerable to events in which the fruits of their efforts are unexpectedly destroyed. Such a reaction may be experienced by, for example, a person who loses a spouse or child to a drunk driver who receives no punishment or censure for this crime (Lehman et al., 1987). Following such a loss, individuals may be deeply distressed by their recognition that they cannot control the important things in their lives. They may be reluctant to engage in subsequent coping efforts, because the event has shown them that all of their efforts can be taken away in a matter of seconds.

Once an individual has experienced a loss that shatters the assumptions on which his or her world is based, we are interested in the mechanisms through which some individuals are able to develop a new worldview that eventually allows them to continue a meaningful and rewarding life. In contrast, others may come to see the world as generally uncontrollable, may feel vulnerable to subsequent tragedy, and may view most people as generally untrustworthy. We are also interested in the conditions under which the worldviews developed in response to major losses are adaptive in the face of subsequent losses and the conditions under which they are maladaptive.

We believe that a theoretical account of the process of coping with loss that considers the impact of such losses on one's worldview has a number of advantages over previous formulations. First, as noted earlier, such a model can account for the paradoxical finding that a substantial minority of respondents do not appear to become intensely distressed following a major loss. Second, such a model can account for the striking variability in response that is often seen in response to a single life crisis, such as cancer (see Silver & Wortman, 1980, for a more detailed discussion). A person who viewed illness as preventable through diet and exercise and who went to considerable lengths to eat the right foods and get regular exercise may be far more likely to experience a challenge to his or her worldview than a person who sees the development of disease as a more random and multidetermined process. Third, the model can help to account for the paradoxical finding that sometimes relatively trivial events seem to perpetuate major distress. For example, Brown and Harris (1978) reported that depressive episodes are frequently brought about by relatively small events that challenge one's view of reality, such as learning that a close friend cannot be trusted. Fourth, our analysis suggests a new way of thinking about vulnerability to major losses. In the past, vulnerability has been assumed to be a function of the coping resources that one possesses—for example, one's self-esteem, socioeconomic status, beliefs in the ability to control one's environment, and social support. Our analysis suggests that people who appear to have considerable coping resources—successful, control-oriented people who have a history of accomplishment and who have generally been rewarded for their efforts—may be particularly vulnerable to certain kinds of sudden, undesirable life events. Such people may be more devastated by a loss that challenges the view that efforts are generally rewarded than those who possess considerably fewer coping resources. At present, we are engaged in research designed to test the theoretical ideas delineated here.

Another question that we address in this program of research concerns the impact of prior life events on a person's ability to deal with a major loss. In almost all cases, conjugal bereavement is likely to be experienced against the backdrop of other life stressors. This is especially likely to be the case among elderly couples in the CLOC study, who may have experienced other major losses prior to the loss of their spouse (Rosow, 1973). Some investigators have suggested that experiencing prior losses may bolster a person's ability to cope with later losses. For example, Hamburg and Adams (1967) contended that an individual will develop new coping strategies as a response to life events that are intensely stressful. They maintained that if effective, these strategies become available for use in future crises and may augment the individuals' problem-solving capacity. However, others have suggested that the impact of previous life events may not always be positive, particularly if the prior crisis has not been satisfactorily resolved (Caplan, 1964; Haan, 1977). In fact, Haan (1977) suggested that a crisis may trigger "ominous meaning" or associations for people because of past unresolved conflicts. More research is necessary to determine if experience with prior life crises enhances or diminishes a person's ability to cope with conjugal bereavement and if the effect depends on whether the prior crises also involved loss, as opposed to a different type of stressor. We are particularly interested in the impact of prior stressors, because we suspect that exposure to previous life events may influence respondents' current views of the world.

In summary, we plan to explore the long-term physical and mental health consequences of early failure to experience or express distress. We also plan to determine whether individuals with particular worldviews are especially vulnerable to certain kinds of losses. We will be interested to see whether worldviews and other coping resources are changed as a result of a major loss and if so, how long such resources continue to be diminished. We want to understand more about how previous losses may influence our ability to cope with current losses, and we plan to see whether people who have experienced certain kinds of prior losses differ in current views of the world from people who have not. We hope that this work will result in the elaboration and clarification of our ideas regarding worldviews as an explanatory concept, as well as in the identification of bereaved who are at particular risk for subsequent problems and, hence, in need of intervention.

References

Antonovsky, A. (1990). Personality and health: Testing the sense of coherence model. In H. S. Friedman (Ed.), *Personality and disease* (pp. 155–177). New York: Wiley.

Bowlby, J. (1961). Processes of mourning. *International Journal of Psychoanalysis, 42,* 317–340.

Bowlby, J. (1973). *Attachment and loss: Vol. 2. Separation: Anxiety and anger.* New York: Basic Books.

Bowlby, J. (1980). *Attachment and loss: Vol. 3. Loss: Sadness and depression.* New York: Basic Books.

Brown, G. W. (1974). Meaning, measurement, and stressful life events. In B. S. Dohrenwend & B. P. Dohrenwend (Eds.), *Stressful life events: Their nature and effects.* New York: Wiley.

Brown, G. W., & Harris, I. O. (1978). *Social origins of depression: A Study of psychiatric disorder in women.* New York: Free Press.

Bulman, R. J., & Wortman, C. B. (1977). Attributions of blame and coping in the "real world": Severe accident victims react to their lot. *Journal of Personality and Social Psychology, 35,* 351–363.

Cannon, W. B. (1939). *The wisdom of the body.* New York: Norton and Company, Inc.

Caplan, G. (1964). *Principles of preventative psychiatry.* New York: Basic Books.

Carey, R. G. (1980). Weathering widowhood: Problems and adjustments of the widowed during the first year. *Omega: The Journal of Death and Dying, 10,* 163–174.

Coates, D., Wortman, C. B., & Abbey, A. (1979). Reactions to victims. In I. H. Frieze, D. Bar-Tal, & J. S. Carroll (Eds.), *New approaches to social problems* (pp. 21–52). San Francisco: Jossey-Bass.

Cohen, S., & Wills, T. A. (1985). Stress, social support, and the buffering hypothesis. *Psychological Bulletin, 98,* 310–357.

Depue, R. A., & Monroe, S. M. (1986). Conceptualization and measurement of human disorder in life stress research: The problem of chronic disturbance. *Psychological Bulletin, 99,* 36–51.

Dohrenwend, B. S., & Dohrenwend, B. P. (1978). Some issues in research on stressful life events. *Journal of Nervous & Mental Disease, 166* (1), 7–15.

Dohrenwend, B. S., & Dohrenwend, B. P. (1981). Life stress and illness: Formulation of the issues. In B. S. Dohrenwend & B. P. Dohrenwend (Eds.), *Stressful life events and their contexts* (pp. 1–27). New York: Prodist.

Dohrenwend, B. S., Dohrenwend, B. P., Dodson, M., & Shrout, P. E. (1984). Symptoms, hassles, social supports, and life events: Problem of confounding measures. *Journal of Abnormal Psychology, 93,* 222–230.

Downey, G., Silver, R. C., & Wortman, C. B. (1990). Reconsidering the attribution–adjustment relation following a major negative event: Coping with the loss of a child. *Journal of Personality and Social Psychology, 59,* 925–940.

Dunkel-Schetter, C., & Wortman, C. B. (1987). Conceptual and methodological issues in the study of social support. In A. Baum & J. E. Singer (Eds.), *Handbook of psychology and health: Vol. 5. Stress* (pp. 63–108). Hillsdale, NJ: Erlbaum.

Elliot, G. R., & Eisdorfer, C. (Eds.). (1982). *Stress and human health: Analysis and implications of research: A study by the Institute of Medicine, National Academy of Sciences.* New York: Springer Publishing Company.

Friedman, H. S. (1991). *The self-healing personality: Why some people achieve health and others succumb to illness.* New York: Henry Holt.

Gentry, M., & Shulman, A. D. (1985). Survey of sampling techniques in widowhood research, 1973–1983. *Journal of Gerontology, 40,* 641–643.

Haan, N. (1977). *Coping and defending: Processes of self-environment organization.* New York: Academic Press.

Haan, N. (1982). The assessment of coping, defense and stress. In L. Goldberger & S. Breznitz (Eds.), *Handbook of stress: Theoretical and clinical aspects* (pp. 254–269). New York: Free Press.

Hamburg, D. A., & Adams, J. E. (1967). A perspective on coping behavior: Seeking and utilizing information in major transitions. *Archives of General Psychiatry, 17,* 277–284.

Holmes, F. M., & Rahe, R. H. (1967). The social readjustment rating scale. *Journal of Psychosomatic Medicine, 11,* 213–218.

Horowitz, M. J. (1976). *Stress response syndromes.* New York: Aronson.

Horowitz, M. J. (1985). Disasters and psychological responses to stress. *Psychiatric Annals, 15,* 161–167.

Janoff-Bulman, R., & Brickman, P. (1982). Expectations and what people learn from failure. In N. T. Feather (Ed.), *Expectations and actions.* Hillsdale, NJ: Erlbaum.

Janoff-Bulman, R., & Frieze, I. H. (1983). A theoretical perspective for understanding reaction to victimization. *Journal of Social Issues, 39,* 1–17.

Kessler, R. C. (1990). Perceived support and adjustment to stress: Methodological considerations. In H. O. F. Veil & U. Baumann (Eds.), *The meaning and measurement of social support.* New York: Hemisphere.

Kessler, R. C., Price, R. H., & Wortman, C. B. (1985). Social factors in psychopathology: Stress, social support, and coping processes. *Annual Review of Psychology, 36,* 531–572.

Kubler-Ross, E. (1969). *On death and dying.* New York: Springer.

Lazarus, R. S., & Folkman, S. (1984). *Stress, appraisal & coping.* New York: Springer.

Lehman, D. R., Ellard, J. H., & Wortman, C. B. (1986). Social support for the bereaved: Recipients' and providers' perspectives on what is helpful. *Journal of Consulting and Clinical Psychology, 54,* 438–446.

Lehman, D. R., Wortman, C. B., & Williams, A. F. (1987). Long-term effects of losing a spouse or child in a motor vehicle crash. *Journal of Personality and Social Psychology, 52,* 218–231.

Lieberman, M. A. (1975). Adaptive processes in late life. In N. Datan & L. H. Ginsberg (Eds.), *Life-span developmental psychology: Normative life crises.* New York: Academic Press.

Lilliston, B. A. (1985). Psychosocial responses to traumatic physical disability. *Social Work in Health Care, 10,* 1–13.

Lowenthal, M. F., Thurnher, M., & Chiriboga, D. (1975). *Four stages of life.* San Francisco, CA: Jossey-Bass.

Martin, J. L., Dean, L., Garcia, M., & Hall, W. (1989). The impact of AIDS on a gay community: Changes in sexual behavior, substance abuse, and mental health. *American Journal of Community Psychology, 17,* 269–293.

Menaghen, E. G. (1983). Individual coping efforts: Moderators of the relationship between life stress and mental health outcomes. In H. B. Kaplan (Ed.), *Psychosocial stress: Trends in theory and research,* 157–191.

Osterweis, M., Solomon, F., & Green, M. (1984). *Bereavement: Reactions, consequences and care.* Washington, DC: National Academy Press.

Parkes, C. M., & Weiss, R. S. (1983). *Recovery from bereavement.* New York: Basic Books.

Rabkin, J. G., & Struening, E. L. (1976). Life events, stress and illness. *Science, 194,* 1013–1020.

Rosenblatt, P. C. (1988). Grief: The social context of private feelings. *Journal of Social Issues, 44,* 67–78.

Rosow, I. (1973). The social context of the aging self. *Gerontologist, 13,* 82–87.

Sarason, I. G., Johnson, J. H., & Siegel, J. M. (1978). Assessing the impact of life changes: Development of the life experiences survey. *Journal of Consulting Clinical Psychology, 46,* 932–946.

Scheier, M. F., & Carver, C. S. (1985). Optimism, coping, and health: Assessment and implications of generalized outcome expectancies. *Health Psychology, 4,* 219–247.

Selye, H. (1956). *The stress of life.* New York: McGraw-Hill.

Silver, R. C., Wortman, C. B., & Crofton, C. (1990). The role of coping in support provision: The self-presentational dilemma of victims of life crises. In I. G. Sarason, B. R. Sarason, & G. R. Pierce (Eds.), *Social support: An interactional view* (pp. 397–426). New York: Wiley.

Silver, R. L. (1982). *Coping with an undesirable life event: A study of early reactions to physical disability.* Unpublished doctoral dissertation, Northwestern University, Evanston, IL.

Silver, R. L., & Wortman, C. B. (1980). Coping with undesirable life events. In J. Garber & M. E. P. Seligman (Eds.), *Human helplessness: Theory and applications* (pp. 279–340). New York: Academic Press.

Stroebe, M., & Stroebe, W. (1983). Who suffers more? Sex differences in health risks of the widowed. *Psychological Bulletin, 93,* 297–301.

Stroebe, M., & Stroebe, W. (1989). Who participates in bereavement research? A review and empirical study. *Omega, 2,* 1–29.

Tennen, H., & Affleck, G. (1987). The costs and benefits of optimistic explanations and dispositional optimism. *Journal of Personality, 55,* 377–393.

Thoits, P. A. (1983). Dimensions of life events that influence psychological distress: An evaluation and synthesis of the literature. In H. B. Kaplan (Ed.), *Psychological stress: Trends in theory and research.* New York: Academic Press.

Turner, R. J., & Noh, S. (1982, September). *Social support, life events and psychological distress: A three way panel analysis.* Presented at the annual meeting of the American Sociological Association, San Francisco, CA.

Weinstein, N. D. (1982). Unrealistic optimism about susceptibility to health problems. *Journal of Behavioral Medicine, 5,* 441–460.

Wortman, C. B. (1983). Coping with victimization: Conclusions and implications for future research. *Journal of Social Issues, 39,* 197–223.

Wortman, C. B., & Dunkel-Schetter, C. (1979). Interpersonal relationships and cancer: A theoretical analysis. *Journal of Social Issues, 35,* 120–155.

Wortman, C. B., Kessler, R., Bolger, N., & House, J. (1991). *The time course of adjustment to widowhood: Evidence from a national probability sample.* Manuscript submitted for publication.

Wortman, C. B., & Silver, R. C. (1987). Coping with irrevocable loss. In G. R. VandenBos & B. K. Bryant (Eds.), *Cataclysms, crises, and catastrophes: Psychology in action* (pp. 189–235). American Psychological Association, Washington, DC.

Wortman, C. B., & Silver, R. C. (1989). The myths of coping with loss. *Journal of Consulting and Clinical Psychology, 57,* 349–357.

Wortman, C. B., & Silver, R. C. (1990). Successful mastery of bereavement and widowhood: A life course perspective. In P. B. Baltes & M. M. Baltes (Eds.), *Successful aging: Perspectives from the behavioral sciences* (pp. 225–264). New York: Cambridge University Press.

Wortman, C. B., Silver, R. C., & Kessler, R. C. (in press). The meaning of loss and adjustment to bereavement. In M. S. Stroebe, W. Stroebe, & R. O. Hansson (Eds.), *Handbook of Bereavement.* New York: Cambridge University Press.

Index

About the Editor

H oward S. Friedman is professor of psychology at the University of California, Riverside. A fellow of the American Psychological Association in health psychology, Friedman has been a leader in the development of health psychology, authoring or editing a number of influential articles and books including, most recently, *Health Psychology, Personality and Disease*, and *The Self-Healing Personality*.

A long-time member of the editorial board of the journal *Health Psychology*, his work has been supported by research grants from the National Institute of Mental Health, the American Cancer Society, the American Heart Association, and the National Institute on Aging. Friedman is an honors graduate of Yale University and received his PhD from Harvard University in 1976.